PHILIP'

STRE

Nottingham

First published 2007 by

Philip's, a division of
Octopus Publishing Group Ltd
2–4 Heron Quays
London E14 4JP

First edition 2007
First impression 2007

ISBN-10   0-540-09070-0
ISBN-13   978-0-540-09070-9
© Philip's 2007

Photographic acknowledgements:
VIII (top) and IX Lucy Ingle
VIII (bottom) Travel and Places / Alamy

Printed by Toppan, China

Contents

II **Key to map symbols**

III **Key to map pages**

IV **Route planning**

VIII **Sights of Nottingham**

2 **Street maps** at 4½ inches to 1 mile

106 **Street maps of Nottingham city centre**
at 7 inches to 1 mile

110 **Index**

134 **List of numbered locations**

Katie
O'Brien

Key to map symbols

Roads

(12) Motorway with junction number

A42 Primary route – dual, single carriageway

A42 A road – dual, single carriageway

B1289 B road – dual, single carriageway

Through-route – dual, single carriageway

Minor road – dual, single carriageway

Rural track, private road or narrow road in urban area

Path, bridleway, byway open to all traffic, road used as a public path

Road under construction

Pedestrianised area

Gate or obstruction to traffic restrictions may not apply at all times or to all vehicles

P **P&R** Parking, Park and Ride

Railways

Railway

Miniature railway

Metro station, private railway station

Emergency services

Ambulance station, coastguard station

Fire station, police station

H **+** Hospital, Accident and Emergency entrance to hospital

General features

+ **PO** Place of worship, Post Office

i Information centre (open all year)

Bus or coach station, shopping centre

Important buildings, schools, colleges, universities and hospitals

Woods, built-up area

Tumulus FORT Non-Roman antiquity, Roman antiquity

Leisure facilities

Camping site, caravan site

Golf course, picnic site

Boundaries

• • • • • • • Postcode boundaries

— · — County and unitary authority boundaries

Water features

River Ouse — Tidal water, water name

Non-tidal water – lake, river, canal or stream

Lock, weir

Enlarged mapping only

Railway or bus station building

Place of interest

Parkland

Scales

Blue pages: 4½ inches to 1 mile 1:14 080

0   220 yds   ¼ mile   660 yds   ½ m

0   125m   250m   375m   ½ km

Red pages: 7 inches to 1 mile 1:9 051

0   110 yds   220 yds   330 yds   ¼ mile

0   125m   250m   375m   ½ kr

44 Adjoining page indicators The colour of the arrow and the band indicates the scale of the adjoining page (see above)

Abbreviations

Acad	Academy	Mkt	Market
Allot Gdns	Allotments	Meml	Memorial
Cemy	Cemetery	Mon	Monument
C Ctr	Civic Centre	Mus	Museum
CH	Club House	Obsy	Observatory
Coll	College	Pal	Royal Palace
Crem	Crematorium	PH	Public House
Ent	Enterprise	Recn Gd	Recreation Ground
Ex H	Exhibition Hall	Resr	Reservoir
Ind Est	Industrial Estate	Ret Pk	Retail Park
IRB Sta	Inshore Rescue Boat Station	Sch	School
		Sh Ctr	Shopping Centre
Inst	Institute	TH	Town Hall/House
Ct	Law Court	Trad Est	Trading Estate
L Ctr	Leisure Centre	Univ	University
LC	Level Crossing	Wks	Works
Liby	Library	YH	Youth Hostel

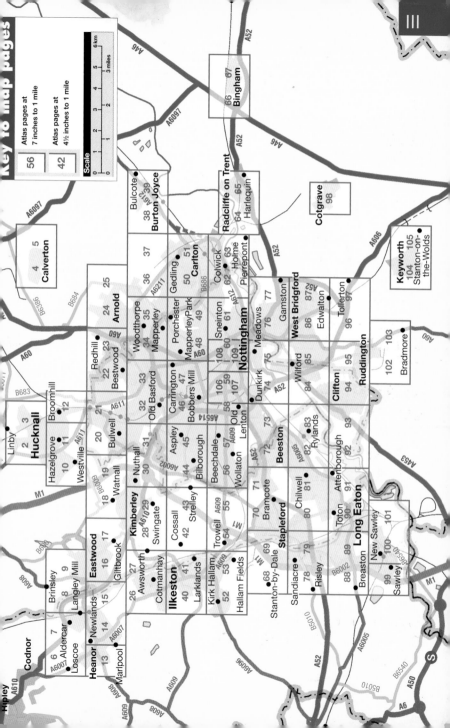

Key to map pages

Atlas pages at
7 inches to 1 mile

56

Atlas pages at
4½ inches to 1 mile

42

Scale

0   1   2   3   4   5   6km

0   1   2   3 miles

Codnor

Ripley

Heanor

Marlpool 13

Loscoe 6

Aldercar 7

Newlands 14

Brinsley 8

Langley Mill 9

Eastwood

15   16   17

Giltbrook

26   27

Ilkeston

Cotmanhay

Awsworth 28

Kimberley

Swingate 29

Cossall 42

Strelley 43

Trowell 54

Stanton-by-Dale 68

Dale 69

Stapleford

Sandiacre 78   79

Risley

Long Eaton

Breaston 88   89

New Sawley 100   101

Sawley 99

Toton 90   91

Attenborough 92   93

Chilwell 80   81

Bramcote 70   71

Beeston

72   73

Wollaton 56   57

Beechdale

Bilborough 44

Aspley 45   46   47

Old Basford 32   33

Bobbers Mill

Carrington

Bulwell 20   21

Hucknall

Hazelgrove 10   11

Westville 12

Broomhill

Watnall 18   19

Nuthall 30   31

Linby 1

2   3

Redhill

Bestwood 22   23

Arnold

24   25

Woodthorpe 34   35

Mapperley

Porchester

Mapperley Park 48   49

Nottingham

Sneinton 60   61

Meadows 75

Dunkirk 58   59

Lenton

Old Lenton

Wilford 84   85

Clifton

94   95

Ruddington

102   103

Bradmore

Gedling 50   51

Carlton

Colwick 62   63

Holme Pierrepont

Radcliffe on Trent

64   65

Harlequin

Bingham 66   67

Cotgrave

98

Gamston

West Bridgford

76   77

Edwalton 86   87

Tollerton 96   97

Keyworth

104   105

Stanton-on-the-Wolds

Calverton

4   5

Old 106   107   108   109

Kirk Hallam 40   41

Larklands

Hallam Fields 52   53

Cossall 42

Route planning

Scale

0   1   2   3   4km

Hills

Sights of Nottingham

Museums and Galleries

Angel Row Gallery *Central Library Building*
Contemporary visual art gallery displaying
work by living artists, with a lively
education programme. ☎0115 915 2869
🖳www.angelrowgallery.com 109 A2

Bonington Art Gallery *Dryden Street,
Nottingham Trent University* Exhibition and
event venue for contemporary arts.
Promotes diverse range of visual and
performing arts. ☎0115 848 6131
🖳www2.ntu.ac.uk/ntsad/bonington
108 A3

Brewhouse Yard Museum *Castle Boulevard*
Social history of Nottingham over 300
years. Explore the Edwardian grocery shop,
Victorian chemists and 1920s recreated
row of shops. ☎0115 915 3600
🖳www.nottinghamcity.gov.uk 109 A1

Calverton Folk Museum *Main Street,
Calverton* Houses period furniture, fossils,
Victorian kitchen, bedroom and the history
of framework knitting. ☎0115 965 2836
🖳www.welcome.to/Calverton 4 C2

City of Caves *Drury Walk* Original Anglo-Saxon
tunnels, water wells, air raid shelter and the
conditions of a Victorian Slum. ☎0115 952
0555 🖳www.cityofcaves.com 109 B2

D H Lawrence Heritage Birthplace Museum
Victoria Street, Eastwood Lawrence's Victorian
family home, containing the Rainbow
Gallery with craft centre. ☎01773 717353
🖳www.broxtowe.gov.uk 16 A4

Galleries of Justice *Shire Hall, High Pavement*
Three centuries of crime and punishment.
Witness a real trial in the original Victorian
Courtroom. View the dock and prison cells.
HM Prison Service National Collection on
permanent display. ☎0115 952 0555
🖳www.galleriesofjustice.org.uk 109 C2

Industrial Museum *Wollaton Park, Courtyard
Stables* Displays of textile, transport and
technology from Nottingham's past.
The Steam Engine House has a fully
operational Steaming Day on the last
Sunday of every month. ☎0115 915 3900
🖳www.nottinghamcity.gov.uk 57 B1

Longdale Craft Centre *Longdale Lane,
Ravenshead* Award winning craft centre,
museum and restaurant. Located in a
recreated Victorian street. Also houses the
exhibition 'The History of Antiques and
Collectables'. ☎01623 794858
🖳www.longdale.co.uk

Natural History Museum *Wollaton Hall,
Wollaton* Array of specimens and minerals.
Various educational exhibitions with creepy
crawlies on show. ☎01623 463088
🖳www.mansfield.gov.uk/museum 57 B1

Patchings Art Centre *Patchings Farm,
Oxton Road, Calverton* Various exhibitions
of art and crafts within numerous
galleries. ☎0115 965 3479
🖳www.patchingsartcentre.co.uk 4 A3

Ruddington Framework Knitters' Museum
Chapel Street, Ruddington A Victorian time-
capsule displaying the lives and works of
knitters. Explore outbuildings, washhouse
and chapel. ☎0115 984 6914
🖳www.rfkm.org 102 C4

Surface Gallery *Mansfield Road* Independent
art gallery showing works from emerging
contemporary artists in Nottingham. ☎0115
934 8435 🖳www.surfacegallery.org 108 B3

William Booth Birthplace Museum *Notintone
Place, Sneinton* An outline of the life of
William Booth and the development of
The Salvation Army. ☎0115 950 3927
🖳www1.salvationarmy.org 60 C2

Yard Gallery *Wollaton Hall, Wollaton* Vibrant
exhibitions exploring art and the environment
with nationally acclaimed artists. ☎0115 915
3900 57 B1 🖳www.nottinghamcity.gov.uk

Historic Sites

Creswell Crags *Creswell* Limestone gorge
with caves. Stone tools and remains of
animals found in the caves illustrate life
during the Ice Age. ☎01909 720378
🖳www.creswell-crags.org.uk

Council House *The Guildhall, Burton Street*
Magnificent Council building designed by
Cecil Howitt with a 200 foot high dome.
On the site of the former Nottingham
exchange. Contains 'The Ballroom', similar
to the Palais de Versailles. ☎0115 915 5555
🖳www.nottinghamcity.gov.uk 108 B3

Nottingham Castle *Friar Lane, Off Maid Marian
Way* A 17th century ducal mansion built
on the site of the original medieval castle.
Museum and art gallery house silver, glass,
armour and paintings . ☎0115 915 3700
🖳www.nottinghamcity.gov.uk 109 A1

Wollaton Hall & Park *Wollaton* Sensational
Elizabethan house, completed in 1588 in
500 acres of historic park. Dramatic
facade. ☎0115 915 3900
🖳www.nottinghamcity.gov.uk 57 B1

▲ *St Peter's Parish Church*

Places of Worship

St Barnabas' RC Cathedral *North Circus Street*
Built between 1841 and 1844, the architect,
Pugin, also designed the interior of the
Houses of Parliament. Full choir. ☎0115 953
9839 🖳www.stbarnabasnottingham.org.uk
109 A2

St Mary the Virgin, Parish Church *High
Pavement, The Lace Market* The oldest church
in Nottingham, mentioned in the Domesday
Book and noted for its uniformity of style.
Choir and bell-ringers. ☎0115 953 9839
🖳www.stmarysnottingham.org 109 C2

St Nicholas Parish Church *Maid Marian Way*
Re-built in 1682, the original was destroyed
in the Civil War in 1643. Holds the grave
of Lawrence Collin. ☎0115 952 4600
🖳www.stnics.org 109 B1

St Peter's Parish Church *St Peter's Square*
A place of worship since the eleventh
century. ☎0115 948 3658
🖳www.stpetersnottingham.org 109 B2

▼ *Council House and market place*

Other Sights

The Albert Hall *North Circus Street, Off Derby Road* Conference and exhibition centre, hosting fashion shows, concerts, grand banquets and award ceremonies.
☏0115 950 0411 108 A2
🖳www.alberthallnottingham.com
Arts Theatre *George Street* A community theatre. ☏0115 947 6096 109 C2
🖳www.artstheatre.org.uk
Great Central Railway *Mere Way, Ruddington* Nottingham's Transport Heritage Centre on 10 miles of ex GCR mainline. Large model railway with a great collection of vehicles.
☏0115 940 5705 🖳www.nthc.co.uk 103 A3
Green's Mill and Science Centre *Windmill Lane, Sneinton* Fully restored and working 19th century tower windmill. ☏0115 915 6878 🖳www.greensmill.org.uk 61 A2
The Lace Market *Carlton Street, Belward Street, Hollowstone* Explore the ancient part of the city centre, transformed from 6th century Saxon settlements. The Lace Market Heritage Point is in the Old Shire Hall and provides information of the Lace Market, past and present. Follow the Lace Market Trail for a self-guided audio tour of Nottingham's architecture.
🖳www.lace-market.com 109 C2
Lace Market Theatre *Halifax Place* An independent vibrant amateur theatre. Shows traditional and modern drama, comedy and musicals. ☏0115 950 7201
🖳www.lacemarkettheatre.co.uk 109 B2
Lakeside Arts Centre *Wellington Circus* Multi-arts centre. Music, theatre, dance, comedy, exhibitions and literature performances. ☏0115 846 7777 🖳www.lakesidearts.org.uk 73 C3
Nottingham Playhouse *University Park* A community theatre. ☏0115 941 9419 109 A2
🖳www.nottinghamplayhouse.co.uk
Papplewick Pumping Station *Longdale Lane, Ravenshead* Victorian Water Works with two James Watt & Co beam pumping machines. ☏0115 915 6878
🖳www.papplewickpumpingstation.co.uk
Tales of Robin Hood *George Street* Medieval adventure with banquets and quests.
☏0115 948 3284 🖳www.robinhood.uk.com 109 B2
The Royal Centre *Theatre Square* Musicals, drama, dance, comedy, opera and classical/contemporary music. Incorporating Theatre Royal and Royal Concert Hall.
☏0115 989 5555 108 B3
🖳www.royalcentre-nottingham.co.uk
Ye Olde Trip to Jerusalem *Brewhouse Yard* From the 12th century, this is England's oldest inn, with tours and tales of its haunted past. ☏0115 947 3171
🖳www.triptojerusalem.com 109 A1

Green Spaces

Bestwood Country Park *Northern Drive, Bestwood Village* A 650 acre park with many varieties of wildlife habitats. Miles of foot-

paths. Good for bird watching. ☏0115 927 3674 🖳www.nottinghamshire.gov.uk 22 B4
Burntstump Country Park *Burntstump Hill* 22 acres of woodland. Long walks and picnic areas. ☏0115 901 3603
🖳www.enjoyengland.com
Colwick Country Park *Racecourse Road* Offers fishing on the Trent, the marina, West Lake and the Loop. Caters for horse riders on the bridle paths. ☏0870 755 7756
🖳www.colwick-hall.co.uk 62 A1
Holme Pierrepont Country Park *Adbolton Lane* 270 acres of park and the home of the National Water Sports Centre. Events held most weekends. ☏0115 982 1212
Naturescape Wild Flower Farm *Maple Farm, Coach Gap Lane, Langar* Numerous species of wildflowers, grasses, lawns, bulbs and wild rose plants. ☏01949 860592
🖳www.naturescape.co.uk
Sherwood Forest Country Park *Edwinstowe, Mansfield* Heritage site of international significance with over 1000 ancient oaks. There is 37 acres reserved for public access. ☏0845 330 4212
🖳www.nottinghamshire.gov.uk

Activities

American Adventure *Ilkeston* Large theme park, for the whole family. Water rides, roller coasters, simulators and railroad. Open all year round. ☏0845 330 2929
🖳www.americanadventure.co.uk 26 A3
The Cornerhouse *Forman Street* Large entertainment complex with shops, restaurants, bars, cinema and health and fitness centre.
☏0115 950 5168 🖳www.cornerhouse.tv 108 B3
Flying Horse Shopping Centre *Flying Horse Walk, The Poultry* Elite shopping centre. ☏0115 948 4926 🖳www.aboutbritain.com 109 B2
The Goose Fair *Forest Recreation Ground, off Mansfield Road* Travelling fair dating back 700 years. Numerous market stalls and over 500 attractions for children and families. ☏0115 948 3284 47 B1
🖳www.nottinghamgoosefair.co.uk
National Water Sports Centre *Holme Pierrepont* Purpose built water sport facilities in 270 acres of country park. Hosts national and international competitions. ☏0115 982 4721
🖳www.nationalwatersportsevents.co.uk
Notts County FC *Meadow Lane* The oldest professional football club in the world.
☏0115 952 9000 🖳www.nottscountyfc.premiumtv.co.uk 76 A4
Nottingham Forest FC *City Ground, Nottingham* The city rival to Notts County. Two times European Champion Cup Winners.
☏0871 226 1980 🖳www.nottinghamforest.premiumtv.co.uk 76 A3
Nottingham Panthers *National Ice Centre, Bolero Square, The Lace Market* Ice Hockey venue for the well supported Panthers. The club is a member of the Elite Ice Hockey League. ☏0115 853 3000
🖳www.panthers.co.uk 109 C2

▲ *Robin Hood statue, Nottingham Castle*

Nottingham Racecourse *Colwick Park* Set in 280 acres of park, this old course plays host to numerous meetings throughout the year. ☏0115 958 0620 61 C1
🖳www.nottinghamracecourse.co.uk
Nottingham Rugby Football Club *The Bay, Holme Road* Venue for Nottingham's premier rugby team. ☏0115 907 0070
🖳www.nottinghamrfc.co.uk 76 B3
Nottingham Tram See the sights of Nottingham via tram, from Hucknall to Station Street, via Hyson Green Market and the Royal Centre. ☏0115 942 7777
🖳www.thetram.net
Nottinghamshire County Cricket Club *Trent Bridge* Attractive test venue, home to the Nottinghamshire Outlaws. ☏0115 982 3000 🖳www.trentbridge.co.uk 76 A3
Rock City *Talbot Street* Popular rock concert venue. ☏0871 3100 000
🖳www.rock-city.co.uk 108 A3
Victoria Shopping Centre *Glasshouse Street and Milton Street* Nottingham's largest covered shopping centre with 120 shops, restaurants, cafes and car park. ☏0115 912 1111 🖳www.victoria-centre-nottingham.co.uk 108 B3
White Post Farm *Farnsfield* Indoor and outdoor play areas, warm reptile house, animal holding and tea rooms. ☏01623 882977
🖳www.whitepostfarmcentre.co.uk

Information

Tourist Information
🛈*Nottingham: 1-4 Smithy Row* ☏0115 915 5330 109 B2
Nottingham City Council
The Guildhall, Burton Street ☏0115 915 5555
🖳www.nottinghamcity.gov.uk 108 B3
Car Parking City Council ☏0115 915 6655
🖳www.nottinghamcity.gov.uk
Car Parking NCP
☏0870 606 7050 🖳www.ncp.co.uk
National Rail Enquiries
☏0845 748 4950 🖳www.nationalrail.co.uk
Local Bus and Rail
☏0870 608 2608 🖳www.traveline.org.uk

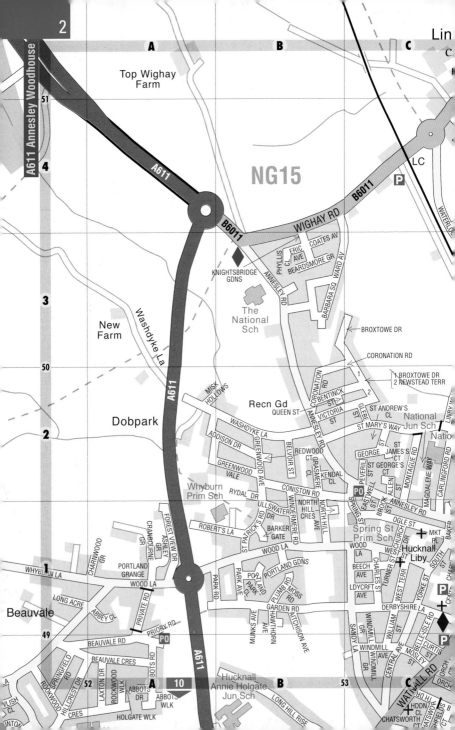

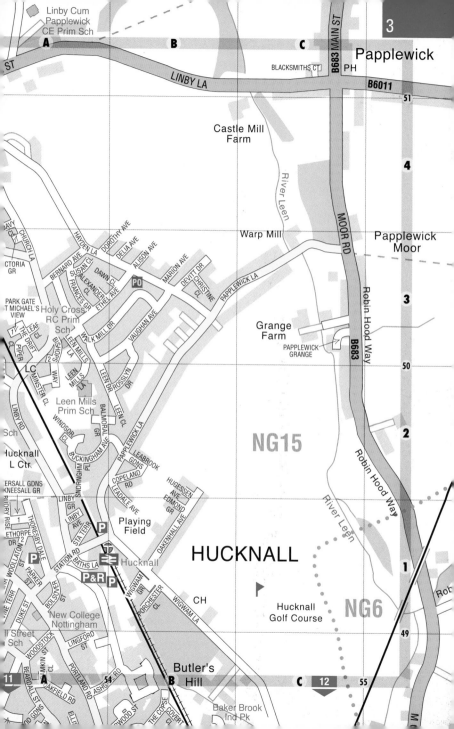

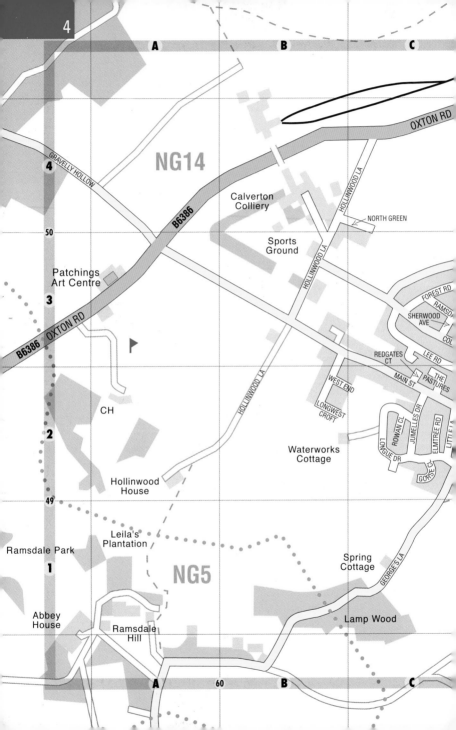

4

A B C

NG14

GRAVELLY HOLLOW

4

OXTON RD

Calverton Colliery

HOLLINWOOD LA

NORTH GREEN

B6386

50

Sports Ground

HOLLINWOOD LA

Patchings Art Centre

FOREST RD

RAMSDA

SHERWOOD AVE

COL

3

OXTON RD

B6386

REDGATES CT

LEE RD

THE PASTURES

MAIN ST

WEST END

LONGWEST CROFT

CH

ROWAN CL

JUMELLES DR

ELMTREE RD

LONGUE DR

LITTLE LA

2

Waterworks Cottage

GORSE CT

Hollinwood House

49

Leila's Plantation

NG5

Spring Cottage

GEORGE'S LA

Ramsdale Park

1

Abbey House

Ramsdale Hill

Lamp Wood

A **60** B C

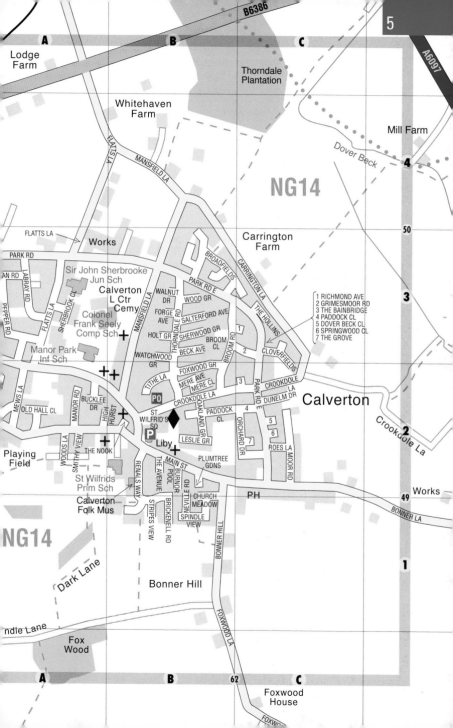

A | B | C

Wood Farm

HUNT'S HILL

Oaks Farm

B600

Moorgreen Reservoir

49

4

Lamb Close

The Dumbles

Beauvale Lodge

Coneygrey Plantation

Coneygrey Farm

3

48

P

Nature Reserve

NG16

LAMB CLOSE DR

BEGGARLEE PK

ENGINE LA

COOMBE RD

DUNSIL RD

2

PARK CRES

THORN TREE GDNS

THORPE RD

NETHER CL

COACH DR

BRYAR RD

ROBEY DR

MEADOW CL

EASTWOOD

LOWER BEAUVALE

LINDLEY ST

DICKENS CT

BRUNEL AVE

HACKWORTH DR

BOSWORTH DR

Manor House

1

DICKS L

BROOKSIDE

GREENHILLS RD

MOORFIELDS AVE

OWLSTON CL

ESTWIC

GARDEN RD

GREENHILLS AVE

GREENHILLS RD

GARDEN RD

DOROTHY AVE

SERLBY RD

KIRBY RD

SMITH RD

METCALF RD

TELFORD DR

MILL RD

ban use tage ntre

ATHERFIELD GDNS

GRANGE VIEW

HOLLIES

KIRBY CL

Lynncroft Prim Sch

LYNNCROFT

Beauvale

PH

47

RINCESS ST

HOPKINS CT

WELLINGTON ST

KING ST

East Wood & Kimberley Coll

P P

Greasley Beauvale DH Lawrence Inf Sch

BEAUVALE

B6010

ALBERT ST

ALEXANDER

GROSVENOR RD

NOTTINGHAM RD

WELLINGTON ST

WALKER ST

BEAUVALE RISE

NORMAN DR

MISK VIEW RD

ABBEY RD

VALE CL

NORTH AVE

INSHIRE

PO

ESSEX ST

PERCY ST

THE CRESCENT

THE SERIES

Greasley Beauvale Jun Sch

48

Liby

47

THREE TUNS RD

16

DOVECOTE

GREASLEY AVE

QUEENS RD N

OXFORD ST

MITRE WAY

NOTTINGHAM

EDWARD RD

SPRINGFIELD

BARBER

DEVON CL

WOOD CL

CLIFFE ST

BISHOP

QUEENS RD

SUTTON RD

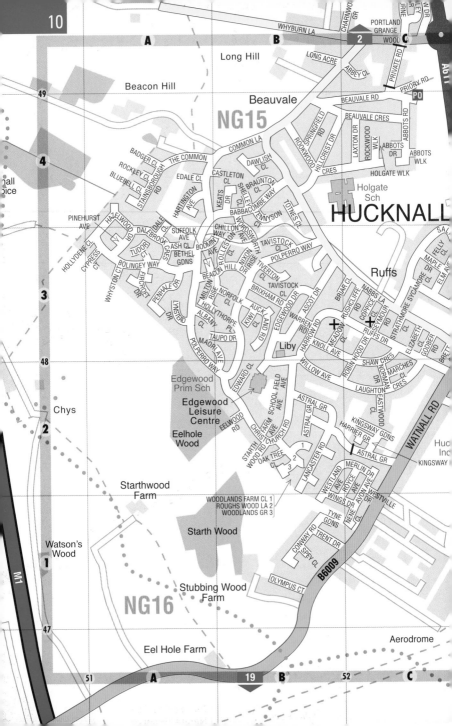

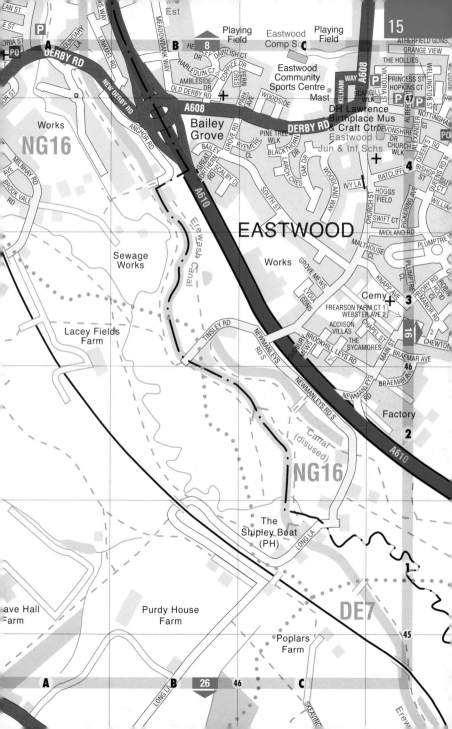

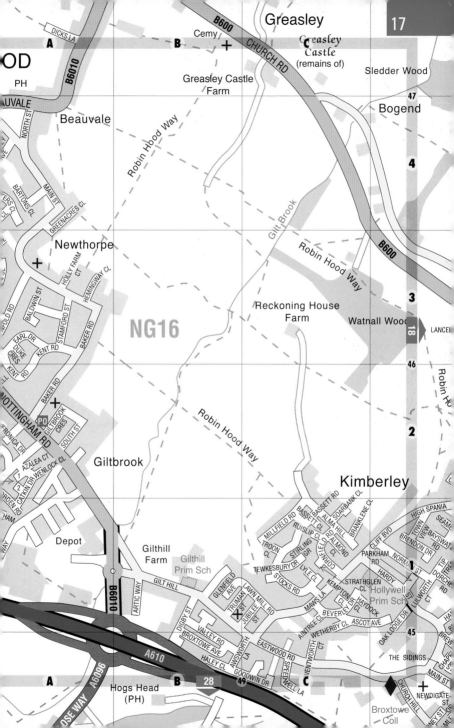

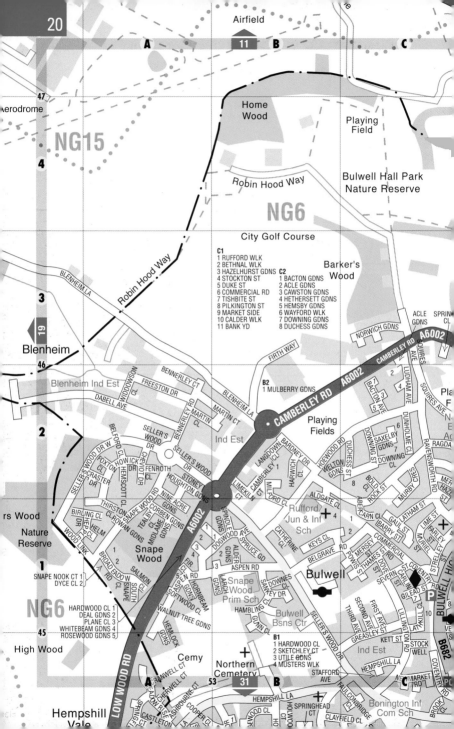

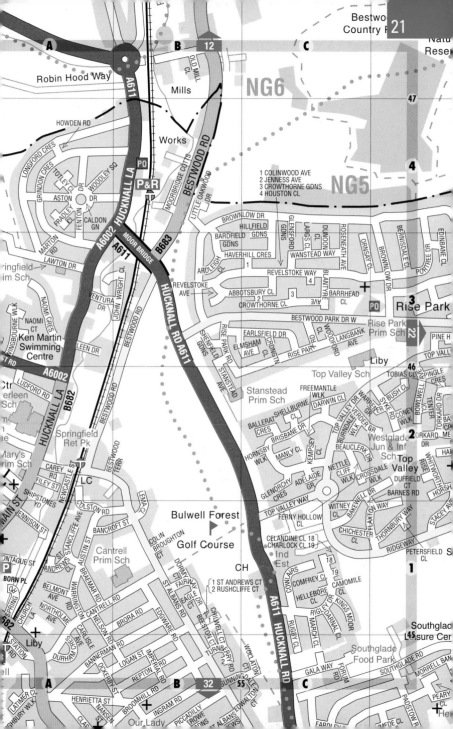

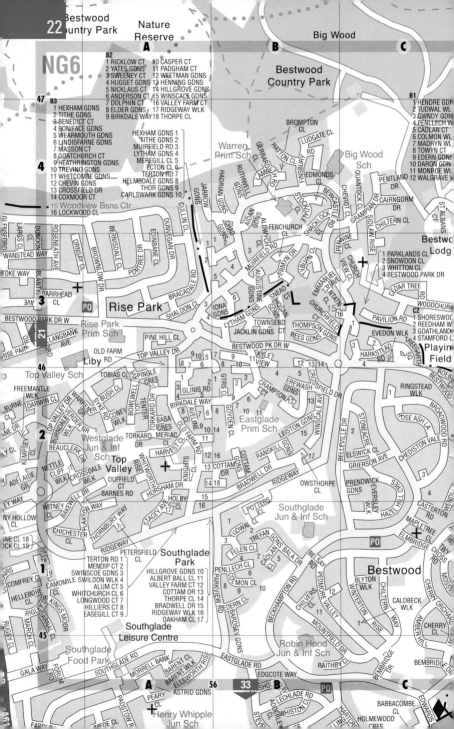

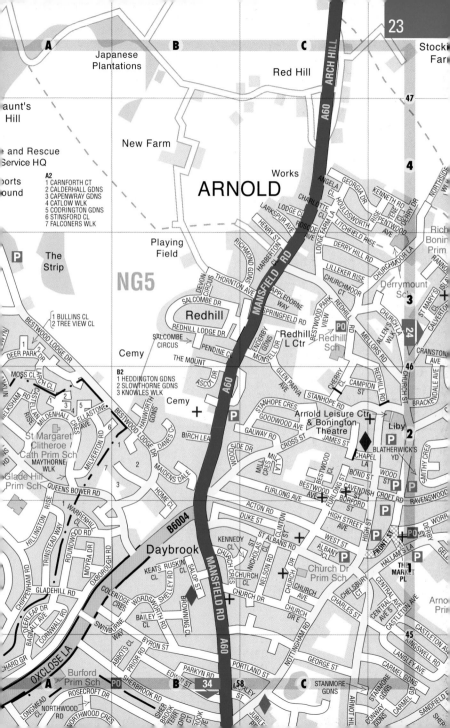

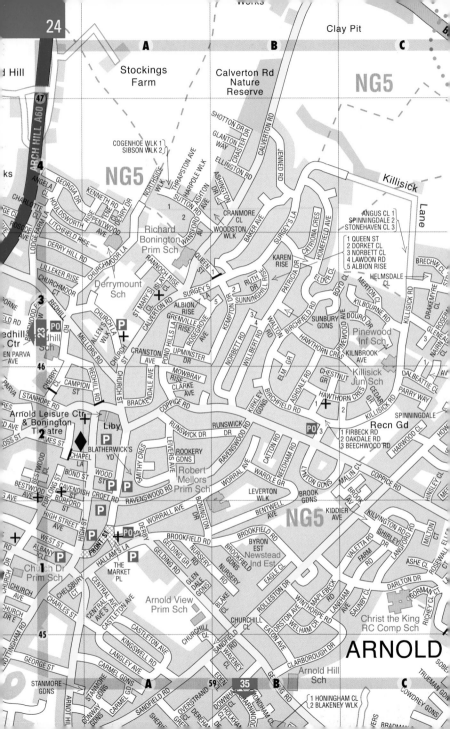

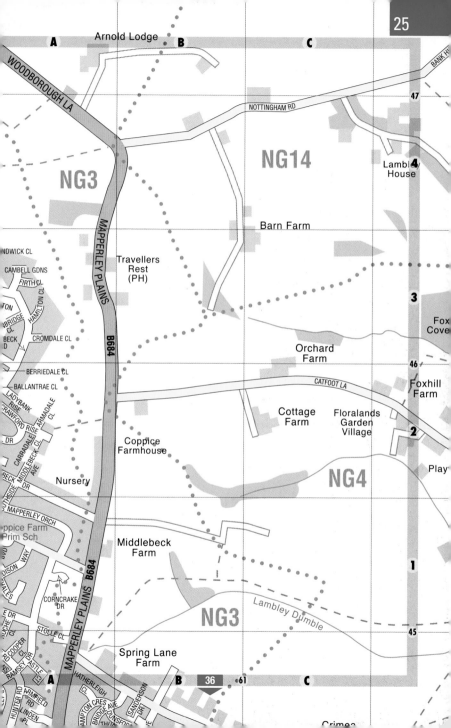

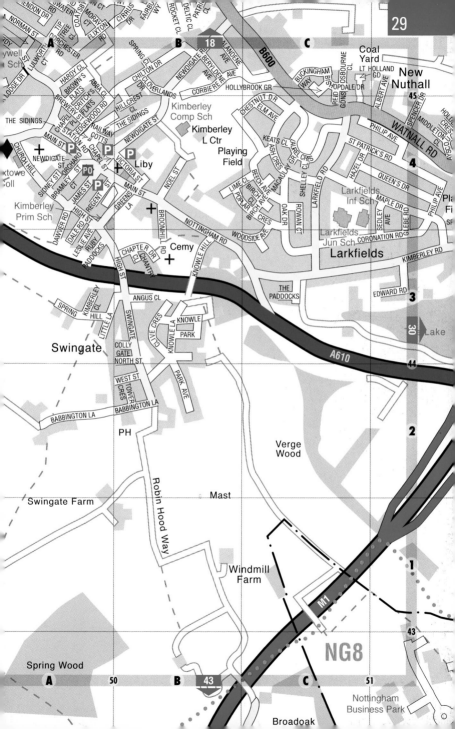

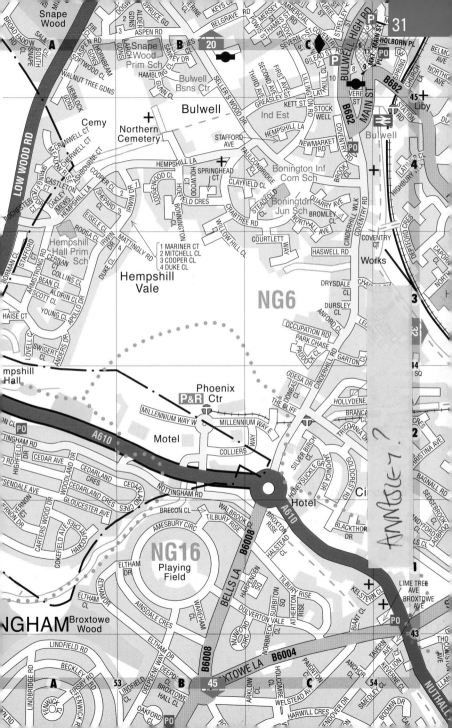

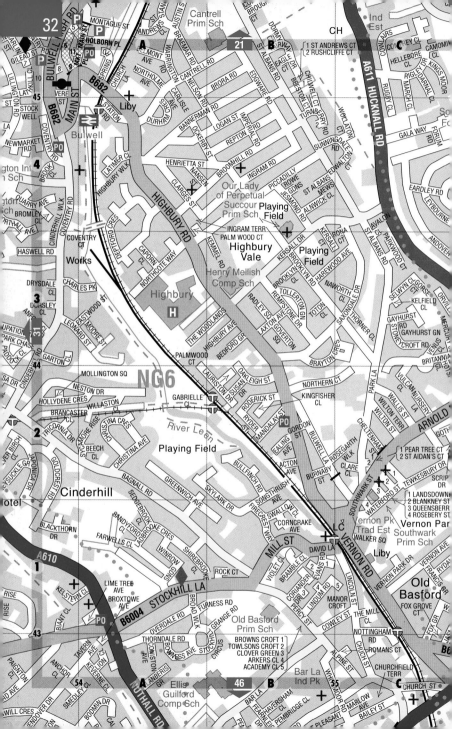

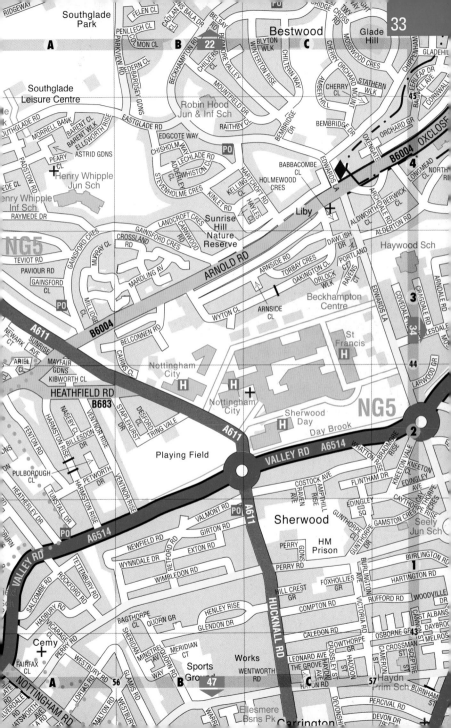

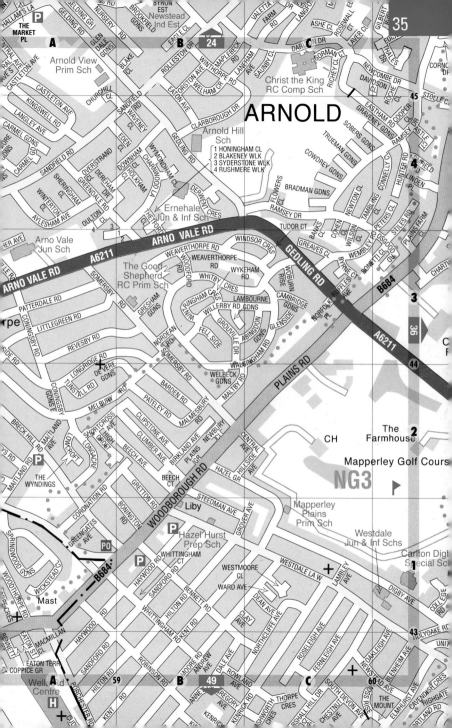

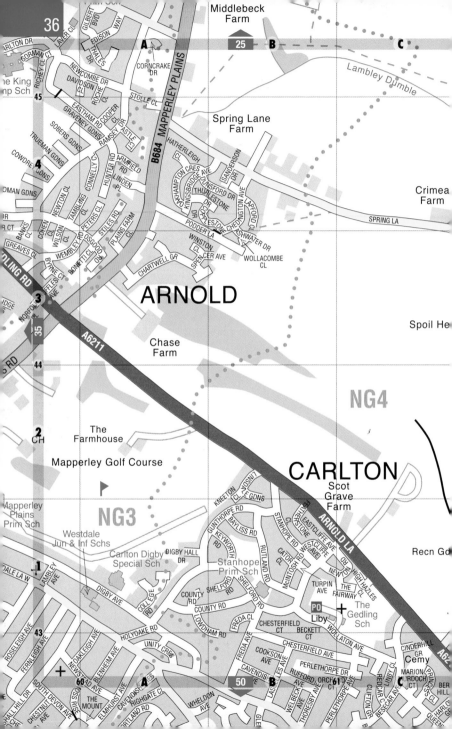

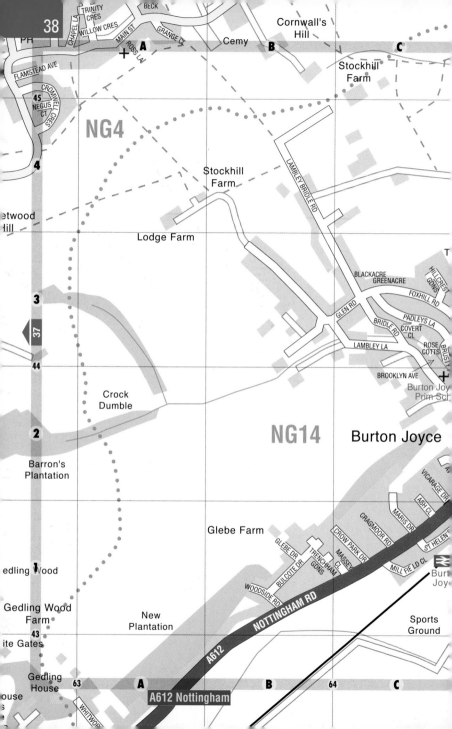

TRINITY
CRES

BECK

CHAPEL LA

WILLOW CRES

MAIN ST

GRANGE CT

ROSS LA

Cornwall's
Hill

Cemy

A **B** **C**

PH

FLAMSTEAD AVE

CROMWELL CRES

45
NEGUS
CT

Stockhill
Farm

NG4

4

Stockhill
Farm

etwood
Hill

LAMBLEY BRIDLE RD

Lodge Farm

T

BLACKACRE
GREENACRE

HILLCREST
GDNS

FOXHILL RD

3

GLEN RD

BRIDLE RD

PADLEYS LA

COVERT
CL

37

LAMBLEY LA

ROSE
COTTS

BRUSTY

44

BROOKLYN AVE

Burton Joy
Prim Sch

Crock
Dumble

NG14

Burton Joyce

2

Barron's
Plantation

VICARAGE DR

ASH CL

CRAGMOOR RD

MARIS DR

ST HELEN

Glebe Farm

GLEBE DR

CROW PARK DR

MASSEY
CL

MILL FIELD CL

dling Wood

1

TRENCHAM
GDNS

BULCOTE DR

WOODSIDE RD

Burt
Joy

Gedling Wood
Farm

43

New
Plantation

NOTTINGHAM RD

Sports
Ground

ite Gates

Gedling
House

63

A

A612

B

64

C

ouse

WHITWOR

A612 Nottingham

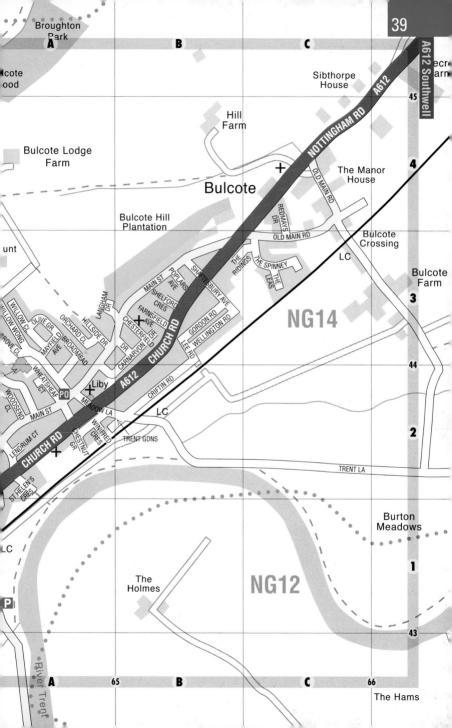

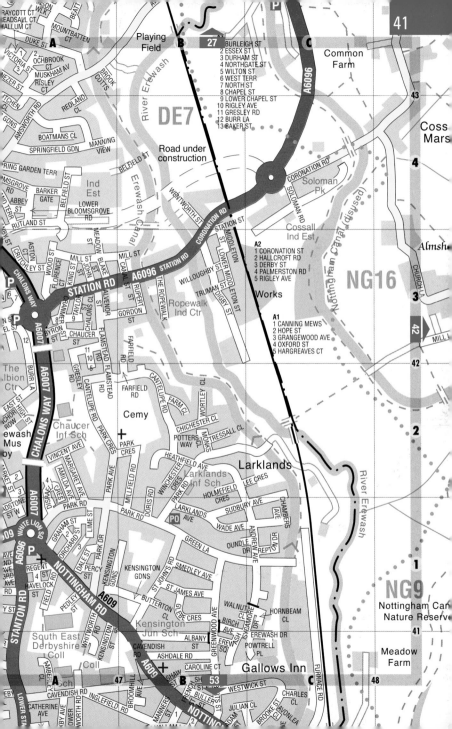

41

Street Index

27 (grid reference BURLEIGH ST area)
1 BURLEIGH ST
2 ESSEX ST
3 DURHAM ST
4 NORTHGATE ST
5 WILTON ST
6 WEST TERR
7 NORTH ST
8 CHAPEL ST
9 LOWER CHAPEL ST
10 RIGLEY AVE
11 GRESLEY RD
12 BURR LA
13 BAKER ST

Playing Field

Common Farm

River Erewash

DE7

Coss Mars

Road under construction

Ind Est

Springfield Gdn

Manning View

Boatmans Cl

Belfield St

Erewash Canal

Coronation Rd

Soloman Pk

Soloman Rd

Cossall Ind Est

Lower Bloomsgrove Rd

Wentworth St

Station St

Mill St

Coronation Rd

Middleton St

Lower Middleton St

A2
1 CORONATION ST
2 HALLCROFT RD
3 DERBY ST
4 PALMERSTON RD
5 RIGLEY AVE

NG16

Almsh

Church La

STATION RD

A6096 STATION RD

Willoughby St

The Ropewalk

Truman

Digby St

Works

Ropewalk Ind Ctr

A1
1 CANNING MEWS
2 HOPE ST
3 GRANGEWOOD AVE
4 OXFORD ST
5 HARGREAVES CT

Nottingham Canal (disused)

MILL

42

The Albion Ctr

Chaucer Inf Sch

Farfield Rd

Canteloupe Rd

Flamstead Rd

Wortley Cl

Farm Cl

Chichester Cl

Tressall Cl

Cemy

River Erewash

Potters Way

ewash Mus by

Vincent Ave

Park Cres

Heathfield Ave

Winchester Cres

Larklands Inf Sch

Larklands

Lee Cres

Holmefield Cres

Sudbury Ave

Chambers Ave

Andrew Ave

Oundle Dr

Repton

NG9

Nottingham Canal Nature Reserve

Margaret Ave

Amilda Ave

Disraeli Cres

Park Ave

Millfield Rd

Doris Rd

Park Rd

Larklands Ave

PO

Wade Ave

Green La

Meadow Farm

Graham St

Orchard St

Dale St

Percy St

Kensington Gdns

St Johns Rd

Smedley Ave

St James Ave

Butterton Cl

Glebe Cres

Greenwood Ave

Walnut Cl

Birch Ave

Hornbeam Cl

Erewash Dr

Powtrell Pl

Pedley St

Whitworth St

Kensington Jun Sch

Kensington

Albany St

Erewsh Sq

Havelock St

Regent St

Field St

South East Derbyshire Coll

Cavendish Rd

Ashdale Rd

Caroline Ct

Gallows Inn

Stanton Rd

Nottingham Rd

A609

Shaw

Broomhill Rd

Manners St

French St

Bullers St

Westwick St

Charles St

Cavendish Rd

Inglefield Rd

Julian La

Brooke St

Lavonlea

Catherine Ave

Lower St

A6096

A6007

Chalons Way

White Lion Sq

P

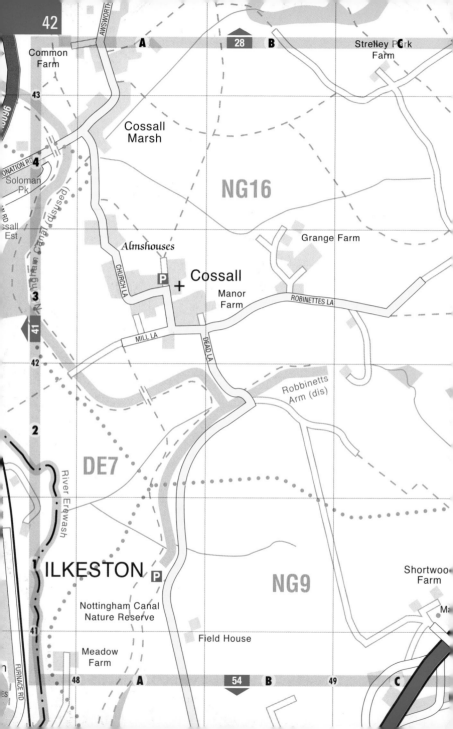

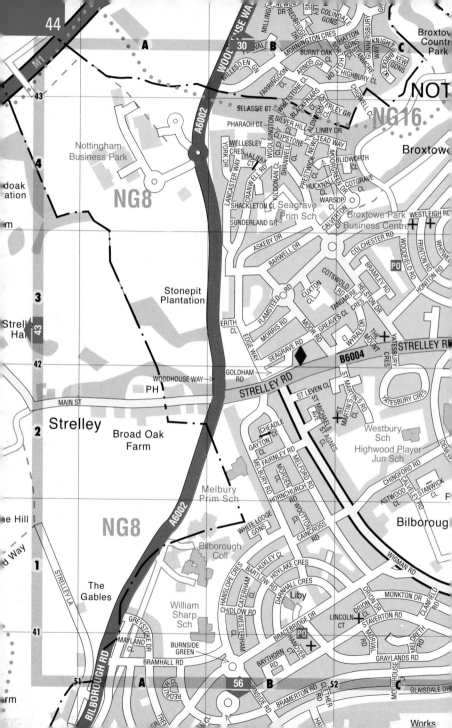

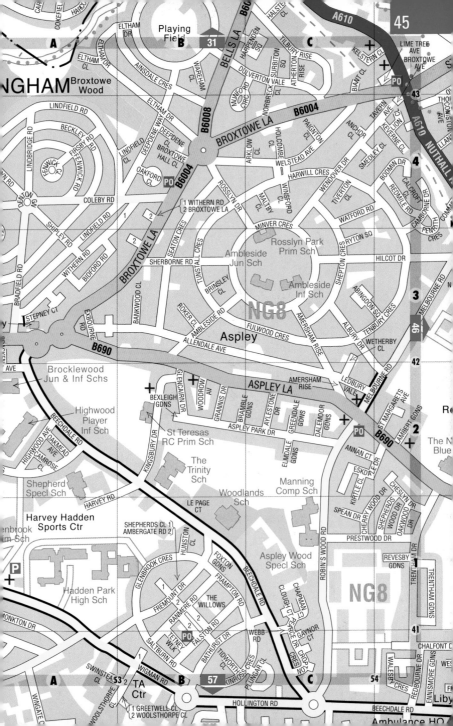

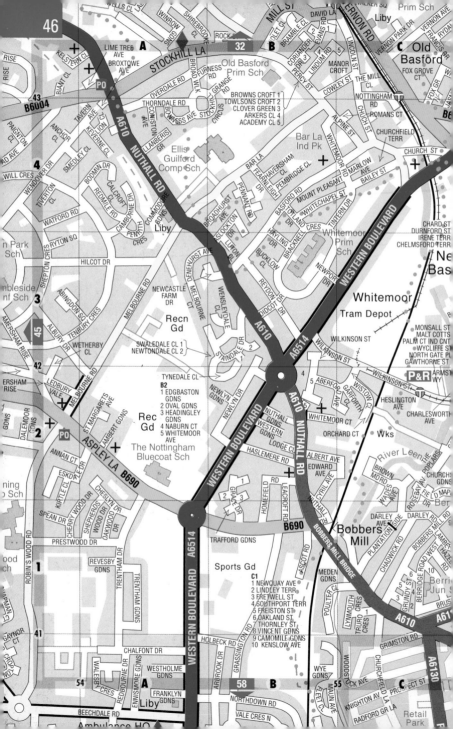

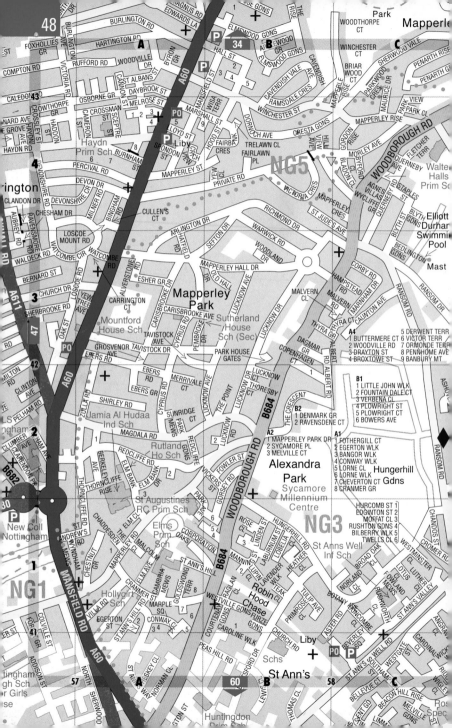

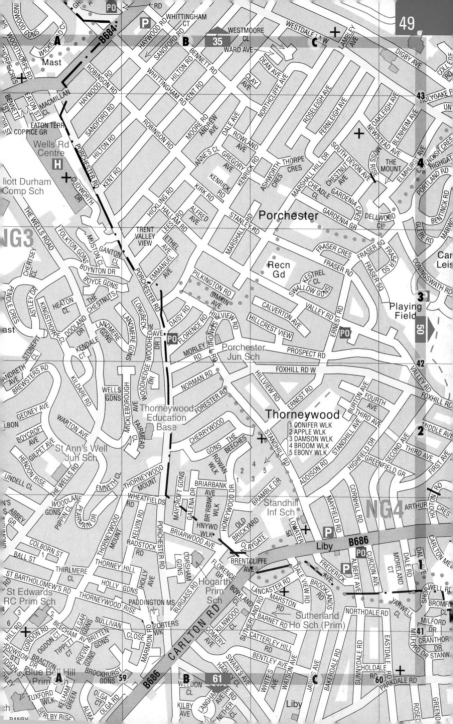

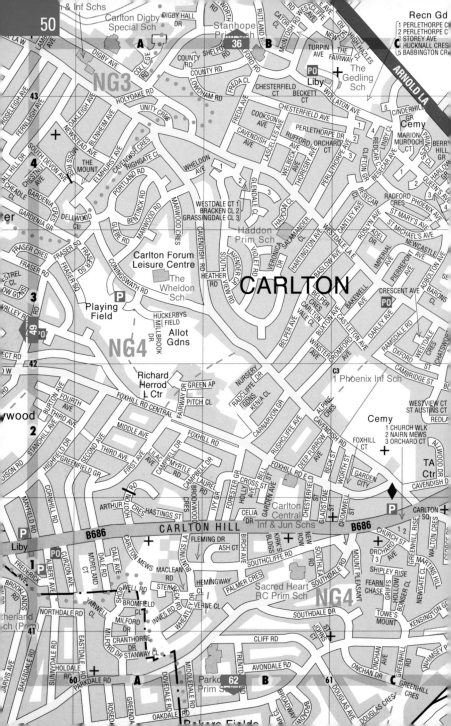

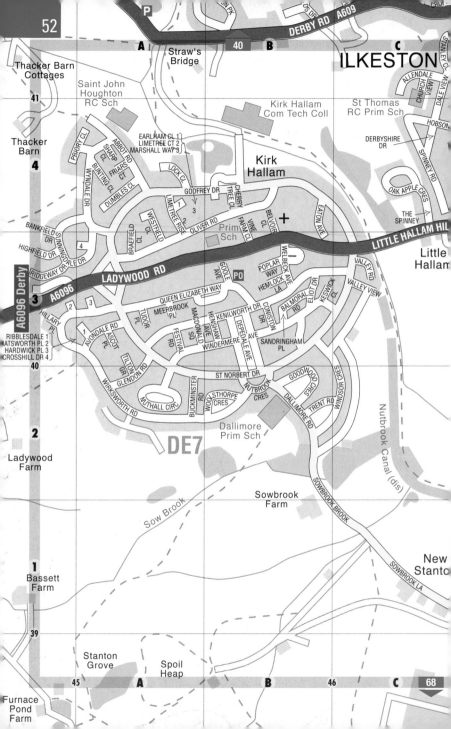

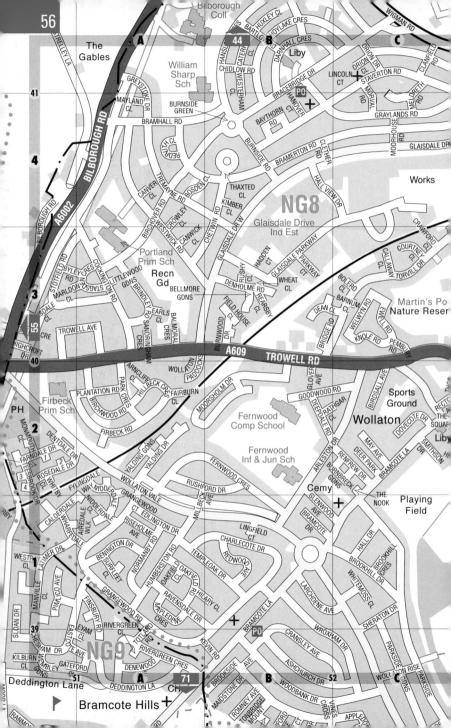

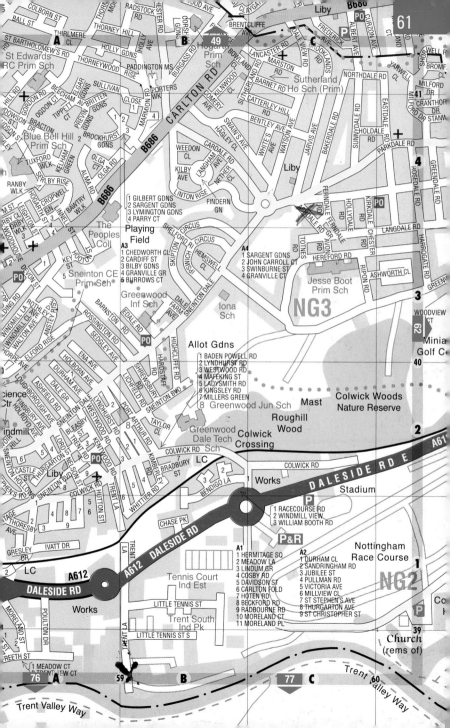

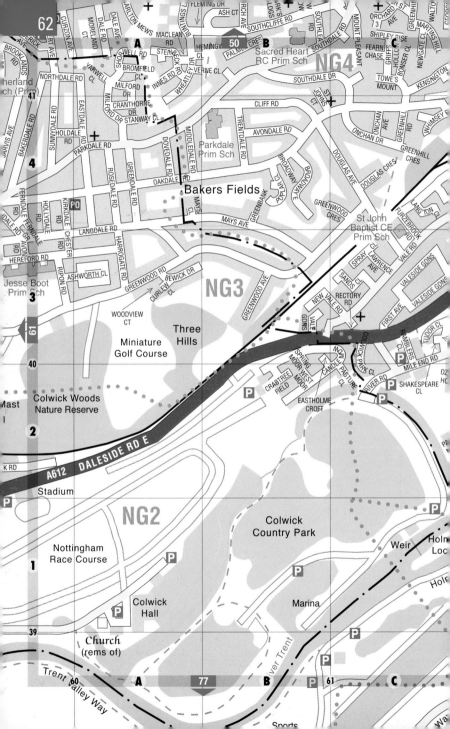

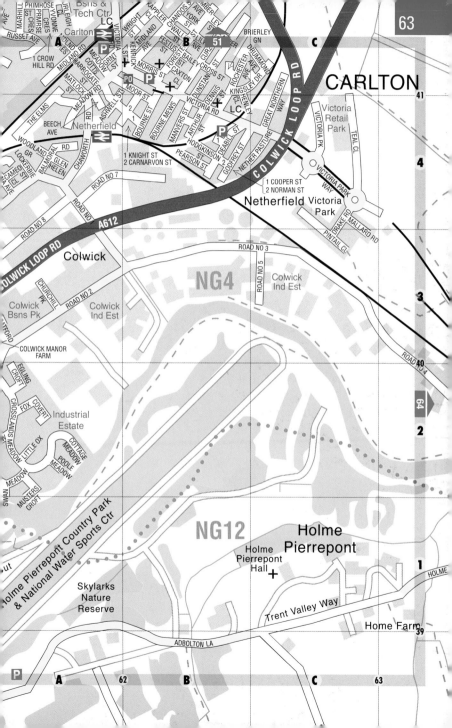

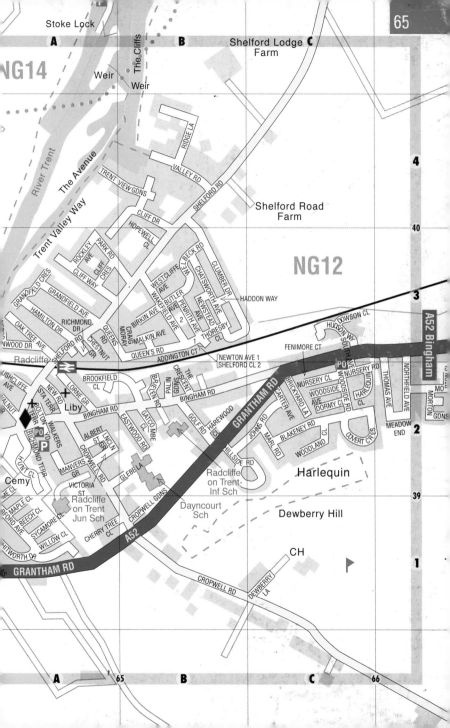

A   B   C

41

A46

4

NEWTON GDNS

Foss Road Farm

NG13

LC 3

CAR

1 STAINMORE GR
2 WINDSOR CT
3 RADNOR GR
4 QUANTOCK GR
5 NEWSTEAD GR
6 RUFFORD GR
7 SHERWOOD GR

WESTERN AVE

HIGHBURY DR

HILL DR

MARGARET PL

BISHOPS RD

40

Lodge
Farm

A46

HIGHBURY RD

COPELAND

BRENDON GR

ARDEN GR

SMITH CT

HARDWICK GR

NEWTON

SHELFORD AVE

QUEEN'S CT

WESTFIELD RD

Saxondale

A6011 Nottingham

MILBURN GR

WYCHWOOD RD

RINGWOOD RD

ROTHBURY GR

NEWTON AVE

CARNARVON PL

GARDEN DR

GRANBY CT

2

A52

A52

GRIZEDALE GR

LANGDALE GR

KIELDER DR

HARRISON CT

BOWLAND

WELBECK GR

FOREST RD

HARVEST CL

ORCHARD AVE

A52 Nottingham (A6011)

BALMORAL

GLENDE GR

ROCKINGHAM GR

CROPWELL RD

THORESBY

ASHDOWN

CHARNWOOD GR

NOTTINGHAM RD

PORCHESTER RD

MUSTERS RD

A46

Newgate
Farm

MALLOW WAY

SORREL DR

CELANDINE GDNS

BETONY CL

CAMPIO N WAY

MEADOWSWEET HILL

PRIMROSE BANK

RUPERT RD

CHAWORTH

SF

1

Foss Farm

THE TEASELS

MALLOW WAY

FOXGLOVES

BLUEBELL BANK

MILL HILL RD

HONEYSUCKLE

Toot Hill

A46 Leicester (A607)

39

NG12

A   69   B   C

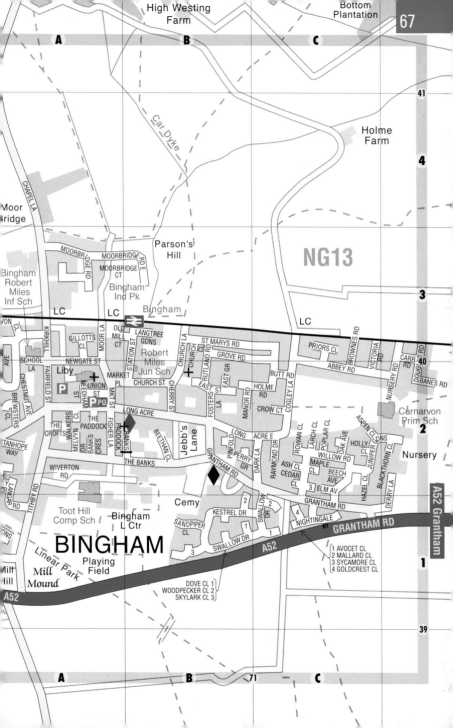

New Stanton

Works

A 52

B

Works **C** 53

Stanton Works

SOWBROOK LA

ILKESTON

LOW'S LA

LC

39

4

LITTLEWELL LA

Works

Stanton-by-Dale

L

hacker Wood

DE7

Stanton-by-Dale

The Manor House

3

CHURCH LA

STANHOPE ST

QUARRY HILL

FLAKE LA

PEPPER LA

PH

38

DALE RD

MAIN ST

THE ORCHARD

QUARRY HILL

QUARRY HILL

BOWLING CL

HALL FARM CT

PO

THE SPINNEY

PARK CL

Manor Farm

2

SCHOOL LA

NO MAN'S LA

1

DE72

The Hewarths

NG10

M1

CHESTNUT GR

SYCAMORE CRES

CORONATION AVE

LINDEN GR

POPLAR AVE

OAS

37

Maywood Farm

The Hewarths Farm

STANTON RD

KILVERSTON RD

STANTON RD

NORBURY WAY

CH

46 **A**

78 **B**

47

C

BARKER AVE N

JACKSON AVE

GOODWIN CL

HILLSIDE

TP

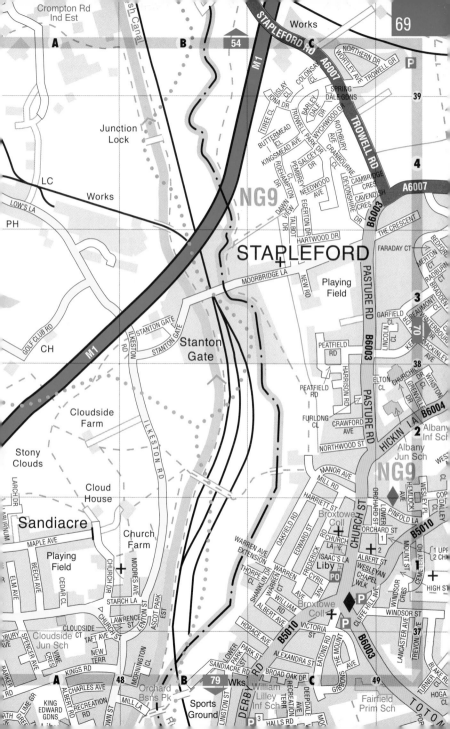

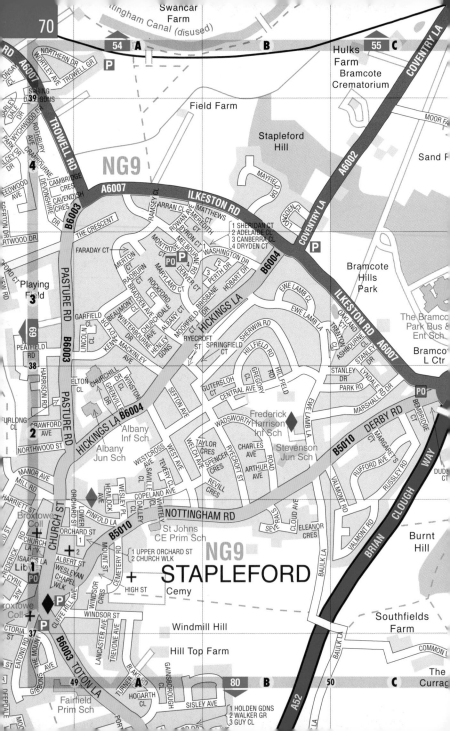

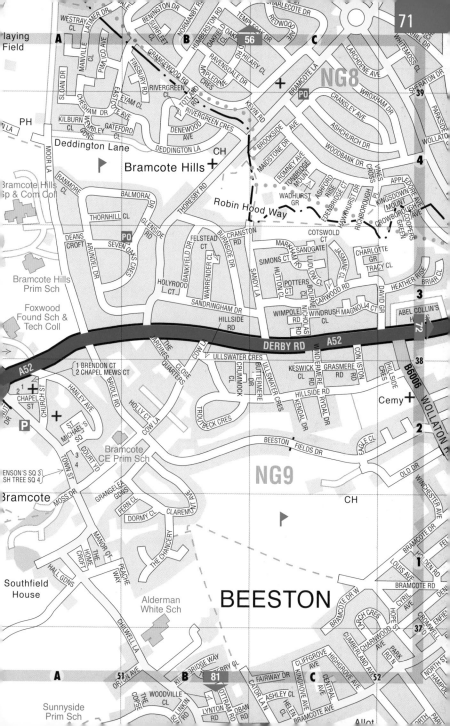

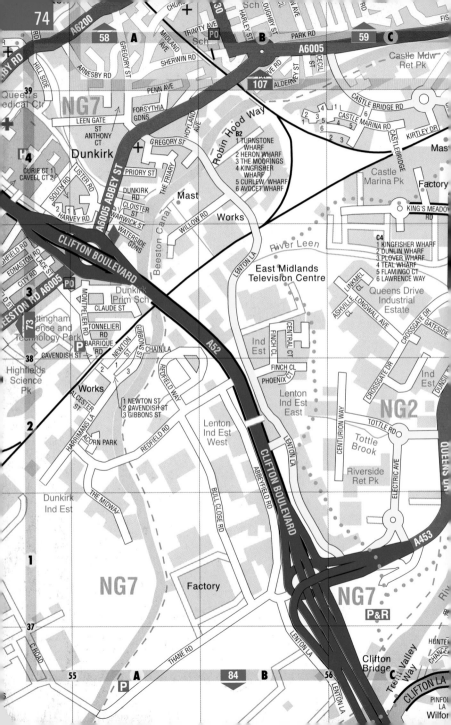

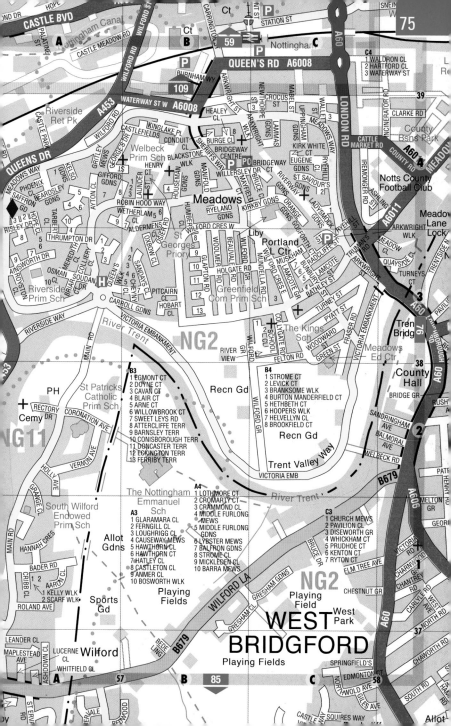

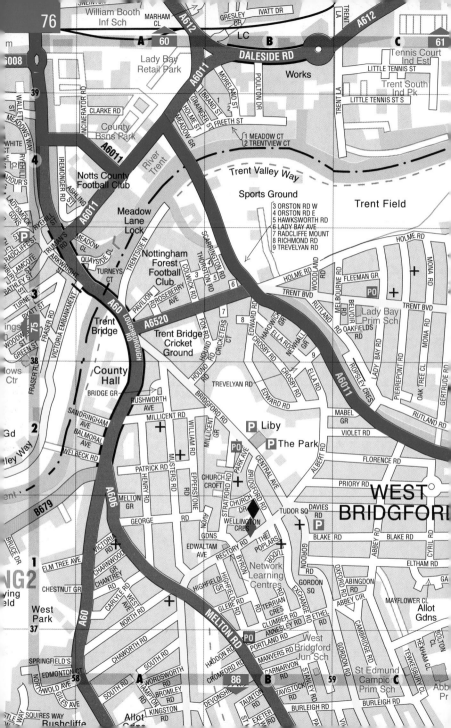

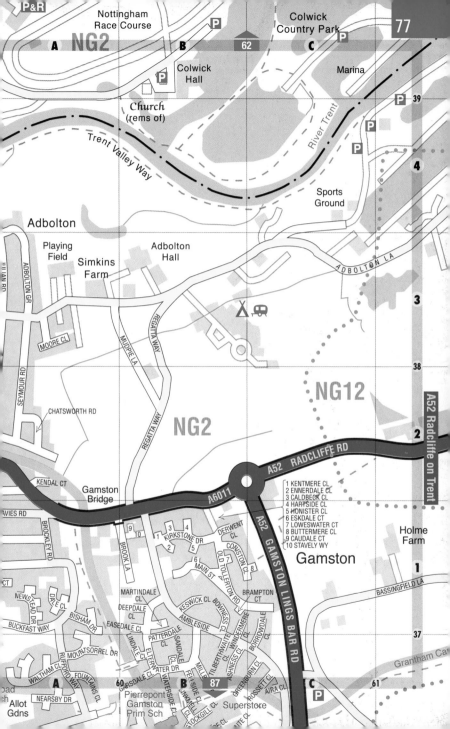

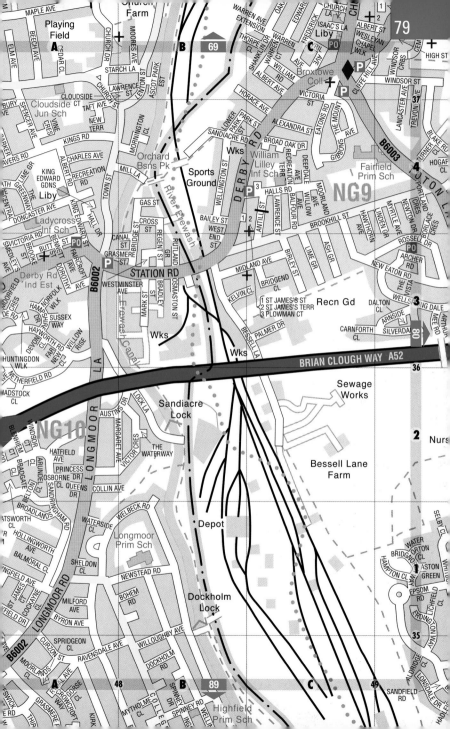

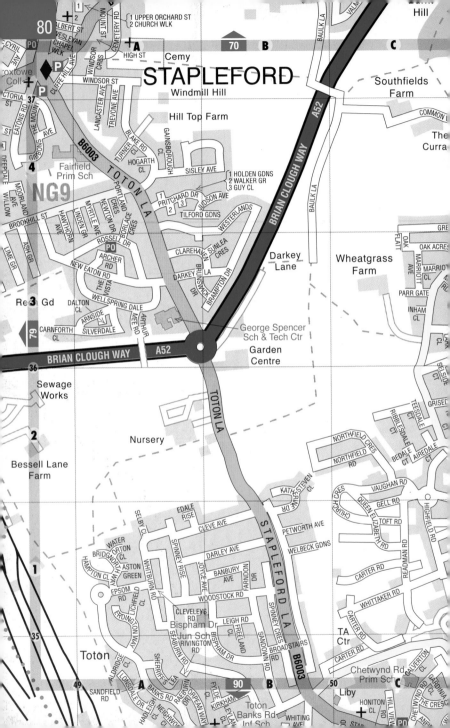

STAPLEFORD

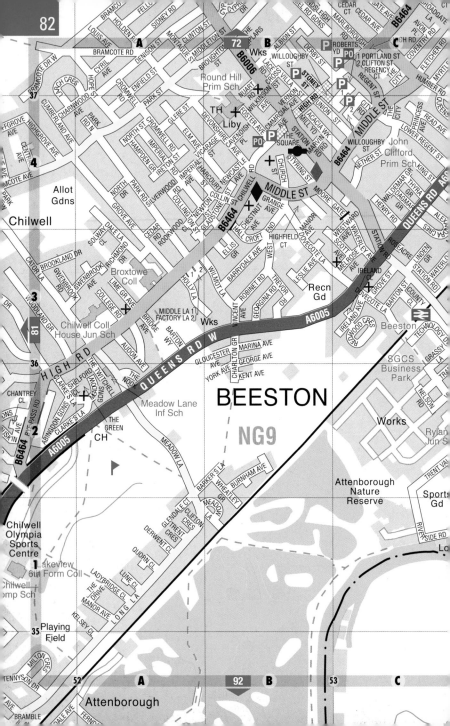

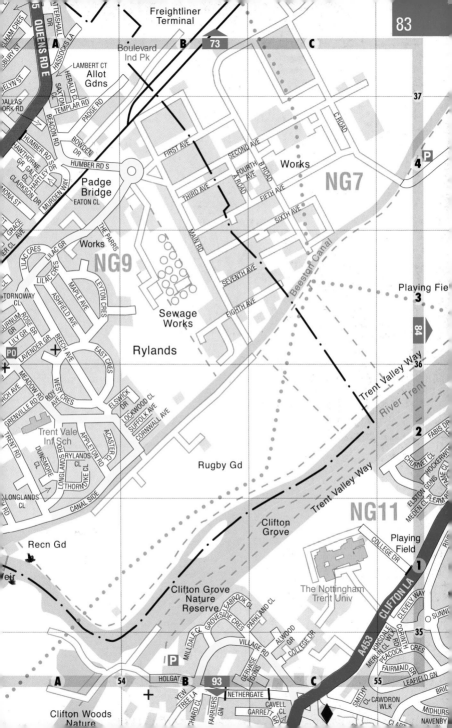

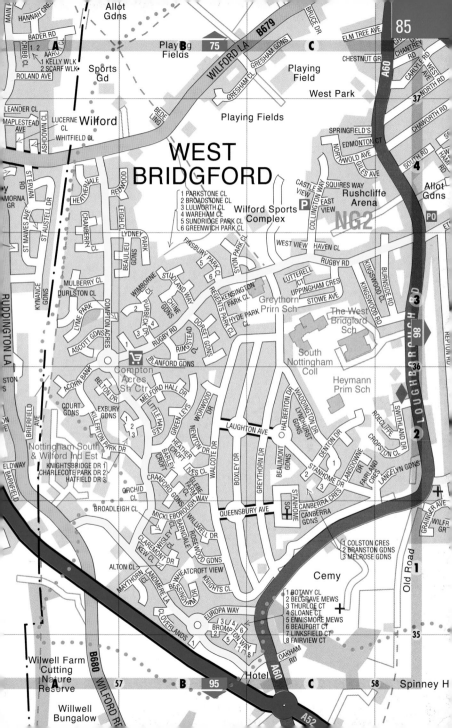

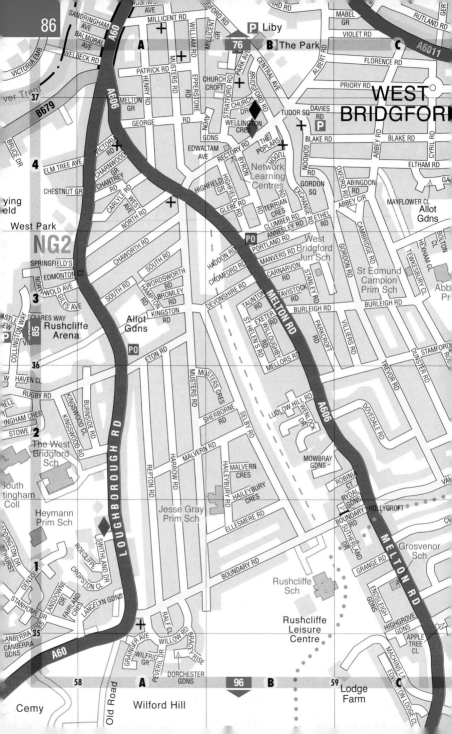

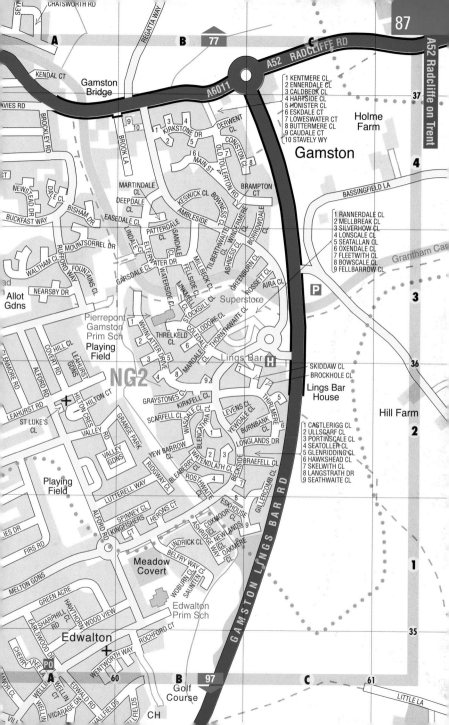

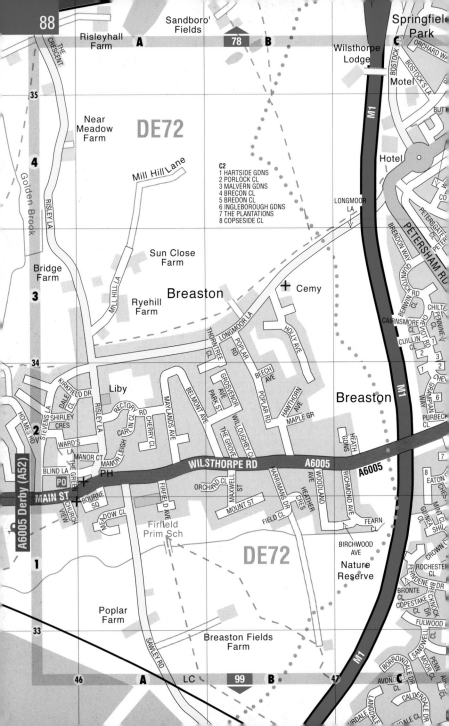

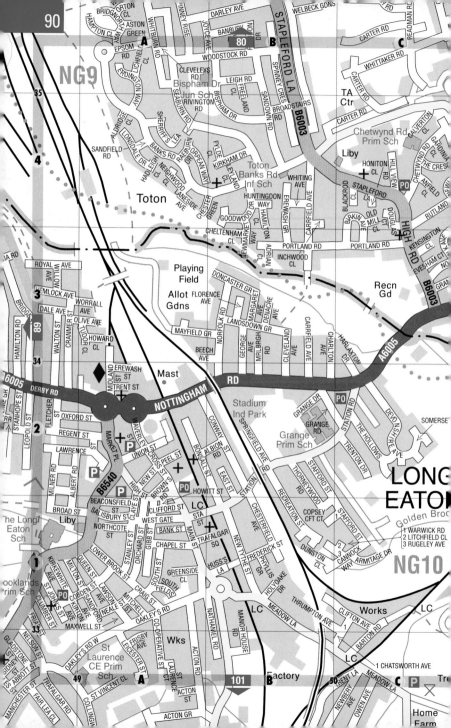

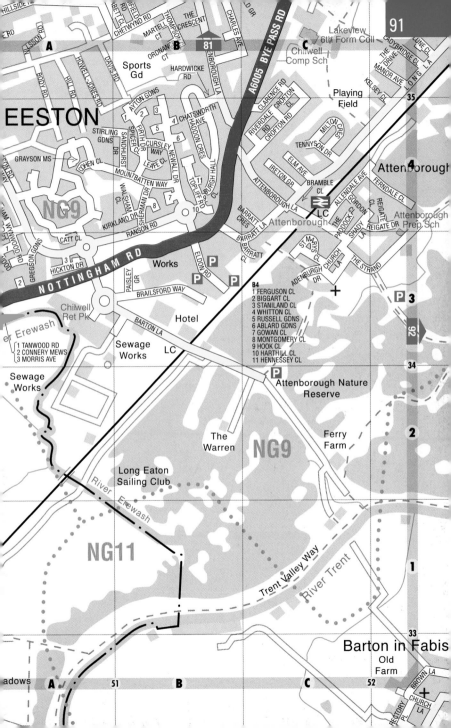

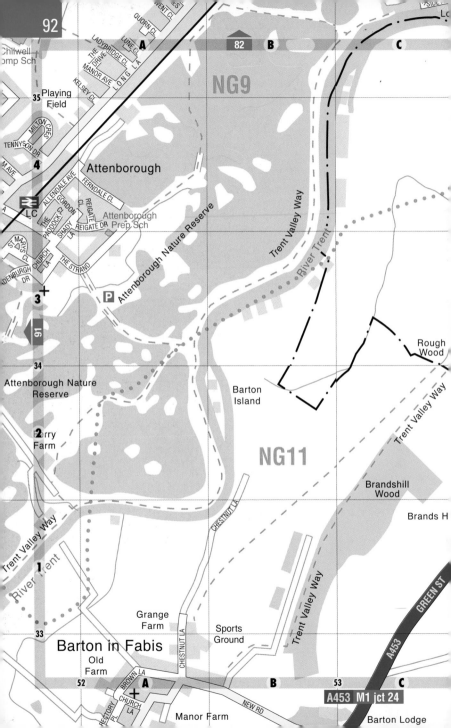

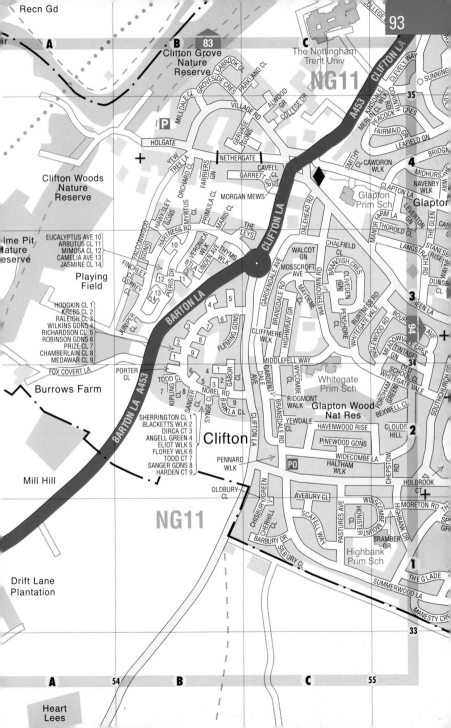

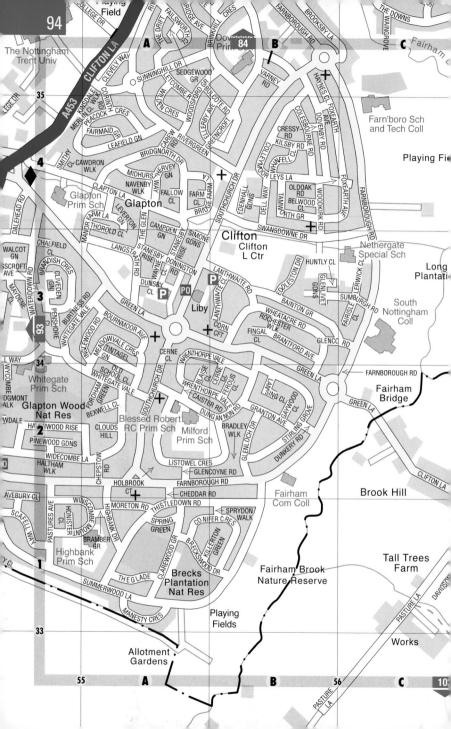

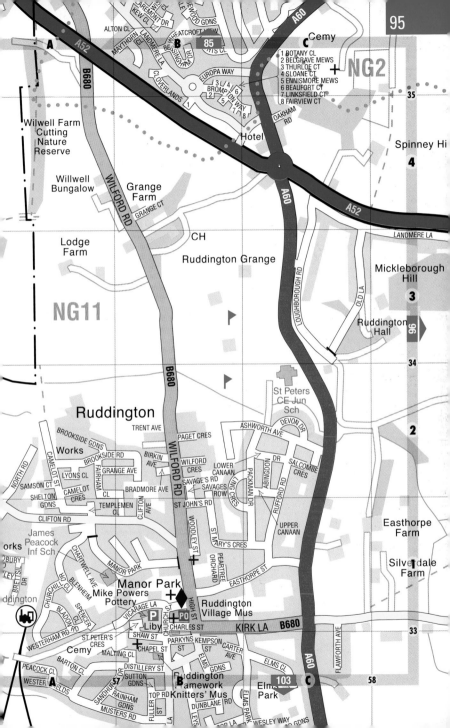

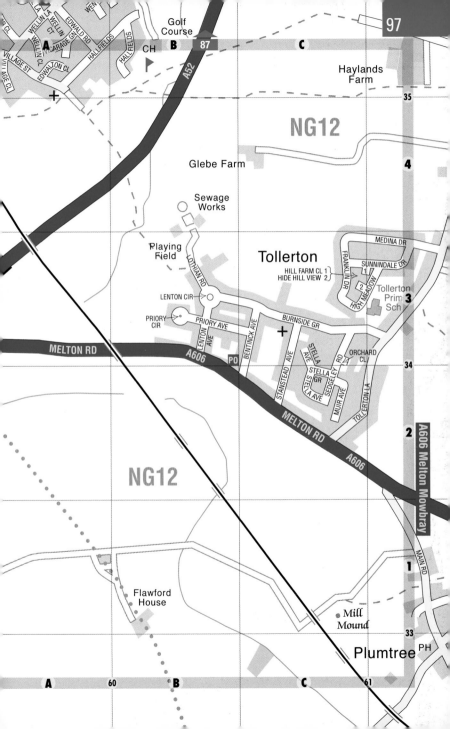

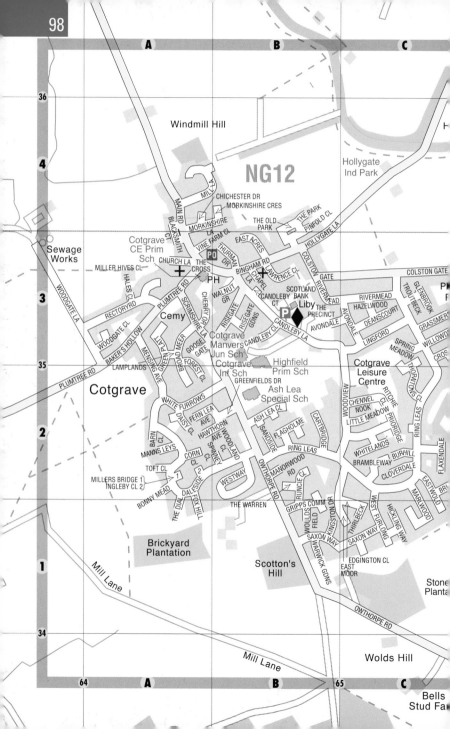

Windmill Hill

NG12

Hollygate Ind Park

Sewage Works

Cotgrave CE Prim Sch

MILLER HIVES CL

CHURCH LA

THE CROSS

PH

Cemy

RECTORY RD

WOODGATE LA

WOODGATE CL

BAKER'S HOLLOW

HALES CL

PLUMTREE RD

PLUMTREE RD

LAMPLANDS

MENSING AVE

GREEN PLATT

BROAD MEER

CHERRY ORCH LA

FOREST CL

GOOSE GATE

RISEGATE

RISEGATE GDNS

Cotgrave Manvers Jun Sch

Cotgrave Inf Sch

Highfield

Cotgrave Prim Sch

GREENFIELDS DR

Ash Lea Special Sch

Cotgrave

WHITE FURROWS

FERN LEA AVE

WHITE DAISY CL

HAWTHORN AVE

BARN CL

MANNS LEYS

CORN CL

TOFT CL

SPINNEY CL

WOODLAND CL

WESTWAY

ASH LEA CL

SANDSIDE

FLAGHOLME

RING LEAS

MILLERS BRIDGE 1
INGLEBY CL 2

BONNY MEAD

THE DIAL

DALESIDE

FOX HILL

THE WARREN

Brickyard Plantation

Scotton's Hill

OWTHORPE RD

GRIPPS COMM

WOULDS FIELD

SAXON WAY

WARWICK GDNS

KINGSTON DR

THIRLBECK

SAXON WAY

EAST MOOR

EDGINGTON CL

WEST FURLONG

HUCKING WAY

MARLWOOD

EASTWOLD

Mill Lane

Mill Lane

Wolds Hill

Bells Stud Fa

Stone Planta

MAIN RD

BLACKSMITH CT

MILL LA

MORKINSHIRE LA

CHICHESTER DR

MORKINSHIRE CRES

VINE FARM CL

THURMAN DR

PO

EAST ACRES

BINGHAM RD

LAWRENCE CL

CHAPEL LA

WALNUT GR

CANDLEBY CT

Liby

SCOTLAND BANK

THE PRECINCT

CANDLEBY LA

CANDLEBY CL

COLSTON GATE

RIVERMEAD

GATE

AVONDALE

AVONDALE

HAZELWOOD

DEANSCOURT

RIVERMEAD

LINGFORD

SPRING MEADOW

THORNTONS CL

RITCHIE

PRIORIDGE

WOODVIEW

CHENNEL NOOK

LITTLE MEADOW

WHITELANDS

BRAMBLEWAY

BURHILL

CLOVERDALE

RING LEAS

Cotgrave Leisure Centre

GLENBROOK

TROUTBECK

GRASSMER

WILLOWD

CROS

RING LEAS

FLAXENDALE

BRI

THE OLD PARK

THE PARK

PINFOLD CL

HOLLYGATE LA

COLSTON GATE

MANORWOOD RD

RUNCIE CL

OWTHORPE RD

CARTBRIDGE

HALES CL

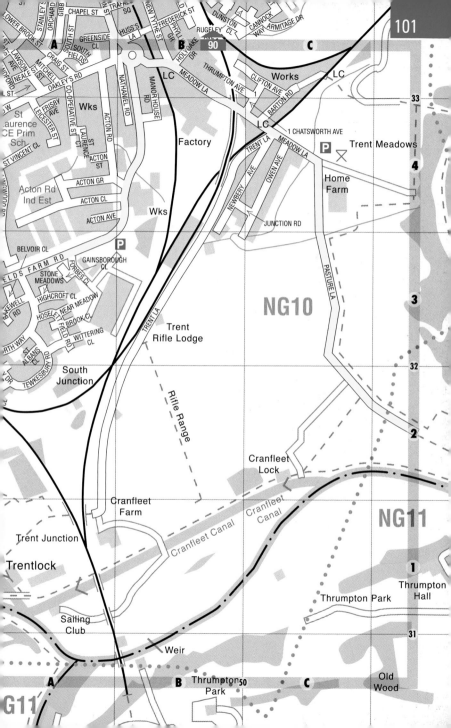

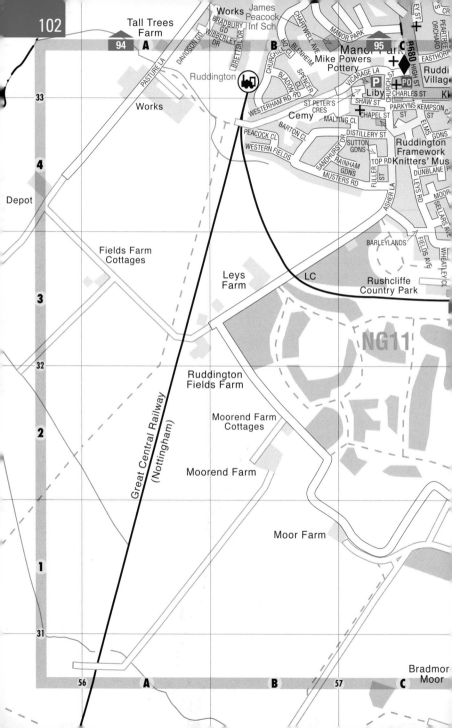

Tall Trees Farm

94 **A**

PASTURE LA

DAVIDSON GD

BRADBURY GD

WIBBERLEY DR

BRETTSLL DR

Works

James Peacock Inf Sch

CHARTWELL AVE

MANOR PARK

CHURCHILL RD

BLENHEIM

SPENCER CL

BLADON RD

B

Manor Park

Mike Powers Pottery

VICARAGE LA

95

HIGH ST

B680

EY ST

CR

PEARTREE ORCHARD

EASTHORP

D

Ruddi Villag

PO

CHARLES ST

Ruddington

Liby

KEMPSON

KI

Ruddington

Works

33

WESTERHAM RD

ST PETER'S CRES

SHAW ST

PARKYNS ST

ELMS GDNS

Cemy

Cemy

CHAPEL ST

MALTING CL

DISTILLERY ST

Ruddington Framework Knitters' Mus

DUNBLANE

4

PEACOCK CL

WESTERN FIELDS

BARTON CL

SANDHURST DR

SUTTON GDNS

RAINHAM GDNS

MUSTERS RD

TOP RD

FULLER ST

ASHER LA

LEYS RD

MOOR

SELLARS AVE

Depot

BARLEYLANDS

FIELDS AVE

WHEATLEY CL

Fields Farm Cottages

Leys Farm

LC

Rushcliffe Country Park

3

NG11

32

Ruddington Fields Farm

Great Central Railway (Nottingham)

2

Moorend Farm Cottages

Moorend Farm

1

Moor Farm

31

Bradmor Moor

56 **A** **B** 57 **C**

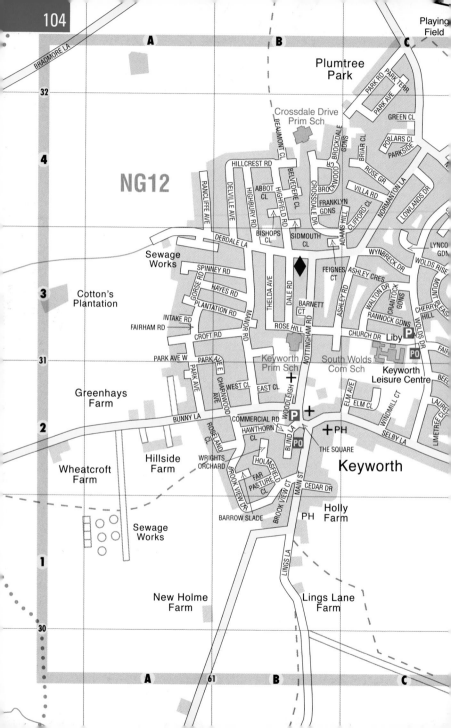

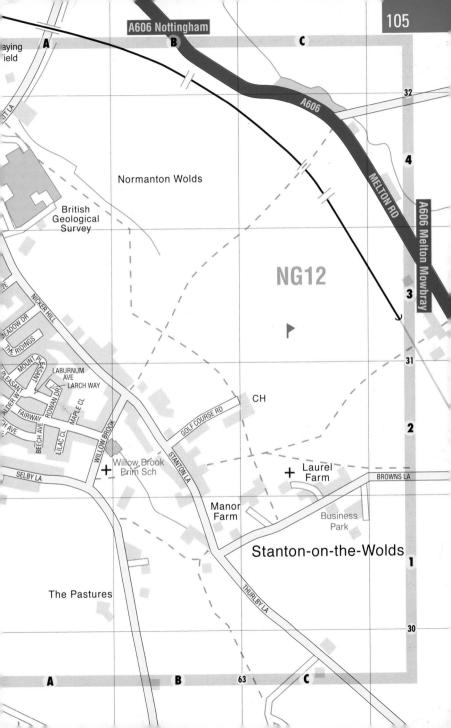

A606 Nottingham

A606

MELTON RD

A606 Melton Mowbray

Normanton Wolds

British
Geological
Survey

NG12

NICKER HILL

MEADOW DR

THE RIDINGS

MOUNT PL

PHEASANT

PLEASANT

LABURNUM
AVE

LARCH WAY

ROWAN DR

MAPLE CL

ALDER W

FAIRWAY

BEECH AVE

LILAC CL

CH AVE

WILLOW BROOK

SELBY LA

Willow Brook
Prim Sch

GOLF COURSE RD

STANTON LA

CH

Laurel
Farm

BROWNS LA

Manor
Farm

Business
Park

Stanton-on-the-Wolds

The Pastures

THURLBY LA

32

4

3

31

2

1

30

A

B

C

63

Scale: 7 inches to 1 mile

0 110 yards 220 yards
0 125 m 250 m

108

405

47

46

405

58

A6130

A610

A609

A610

A609

ILKESTON RD

RADFORD BVD

ALFRETON RD

WOLLATON ST

ST HELEN'S ST

CANNING CIRC

PARK HILL

HERMON ST

WELLINGTON

ARUNDEL ST

SEEL

1 WANSBECK CL
2 GREEK ST
3 WOODGATE CT
4 WELLINGTON TERR
5 WELLINGTON VILLAS
6 ASHBOURNE ST

Cemy

OLIVER ST

CROMWELL ST

PORTLAND RD

IRETON ST

RUNNYMEDE

STONELEIGH ST

RALEIGH ST

FRANCIS ST

ALL SAINTS' TERR

ALL SAINTS' ST

GOODWIN ST

MONTGOMERY ST

WALTER ST

WILDMAN ST

TENNYSON ST

BURNS ST

BURNS AVE

ARTHUR ST

WAVERLEY ST

BRONTE CT

DERWENT CT

GEDLING GR

FOREST RD E

Waverley House PNEU School

MOUNT HOOTON RD

FOREST GR

WATERLOO CRES

WATERLOO PROM

LAWSON ST

HARDY ST

FOREST RD W

LARKDALE ST

Unity Prim Sch

SOPHIE RD

WESTON

THE GROVE

GROVE AVE

ELMORE

GADD ST

DITZEN

LIMPENNY ST

SUNBOURNE

LYLE ST

PEVERIL ST

ASPLEY PL

FOREST RD

THORNTON ST

NEWGATE VILLAS

LENDAL CT

GAMBLE ST

NEWDIGATE ST

RUSSELL ST

HIGHURST ST

MOORGATE ST

MONTFORT

GRAFTON CT

BALDWIN ST

DENMAN ST E

GRANT ST

KYME ST

THACKERAY ST

BODEN ST

CLIFFORD CT

OLD MILL CL

CLIFFORD ST

HIGHCROSS CT

INDEPENDENT ST

RONALD ST

WOLSEY AVE

BLOOMSGROVE ST

HORNBUCKLE CT

GARDEN ST

RADFORD CT

NORTON ST

ARGYLE CT

ARGYLE ST

DENISON ST

ADDINGTON RD

BOVILL

BLOSSOM ST

CREWE CL

NORTON ST

LEROY WALLACE AVE

BEN MAYO CT

HUBERT CT

CAULTON ST

A COURT

BIRKIN AVE

COPE ST

PALM ST

BENTINCK RD

BENTINCK

BURWELL ST

COLLISON ST

THURMAN ST

BECKENHAM RD

LIVINGSTONE RD

Peoples College

Bentinck Prim Sch

HARTLEY CT

NORTON ST

DORKING RD

COLERIDGE ST

HARTLEY RD

BYFIELD CL

Mellers Prim Sch

TRAFALGAR CL

PLAYER ST

BEN ST

WALLAN ST

OSBORNE ST

PROSPECT TERR

WILTON RD

LANDSEER RD

MOZART ST

WARNER ST

GARFIELD RD

DENMAN ST CENTRAL

1 WYVILLE CL
2 BERESFORD ST

NORTON ST

Bloomsgrove Ind Est

BULWER RD

RAYNER

GRAHAM ST

John Carroll L Ctr

FORSTER ST

FORSTER ST

REDOUBT ST

BRAMCOTE WLK

CLEVELAND CL

LISMORE CL

HOPEDALE CL

BASTION ST

GATLING ST

BRAMCOTE ST

DENMAN ST W

CITADEL ST

RIFLE ST

AUCKLAND CL

DULWICH RD

CLAPHAM ST

Radford Prim Sch

TARGET ST

NORWOOD RD

BRIXTON RD

CROYDON RD

LONSDALE RD

LEEN PL

ST PETER'S ST

DEAKINS PL

Radford Works

NEW RD

MAUN AVE

BAKERS CL

MILLERS CT

RADFORD GROVE LANE

KNIGHTON AVENUE

CHURCHFIELD LA

PROSPECT ST

GLENTWORTH RD

WORDSWORTH RD

GRIMSTON RD

KINGSFORD AVE

WOODSTOCK

HARTLEY RD

Castle Retail Park

Radford

109

395

2

1

A6005

Castle Meadow
Retail Park

Castle Marina
Park

C

TENNIS
MEWS

The Park
Tennis Club

TATTERSHALL DR

TUNNEL RD

HOLLES CRES

PARK RAVINE

PARK DR

The Park

CAVENDISH RD E

CLUMBER RD E

SOUTH RD

CLUMBER CRES S

LENTON RD

CLIFTON
TERR

HERMITAGE WLK

FISH POND DR

FOXES
CL

ALBURY SQ

CRES N

NORTH RD

LINCOLN CIR

CLUMBER CRES N

CAVENDISH

1 DUKE
WILLIAM
MOUNT

NEWCASTLE
CIR

YEOMANS
CT

CLUMBER
CT

CAVENDISH CRES S

PARK
HTS

FIENNES
CRES

FRIARS CT

ROCK ST

CASTLE BVD

Robin Hood Way

Nottingham Canal

PELHAM CRES

BARRACK LA

PEVERIL
MEWS

HARDWICK
GR

ALEXANDER RD

MAXTONE RD

CLUMBER RD W

CAVENDISH RD W

HARDWICK RD

LENTON AVE

HARLAXTON DR

PARK RD

ALLEN FIELD
CT

CASTLE BRIDGE RD

CECIL ST

560

CHIPPENDALE
ST

New Lenton

HARLAXTON DR

HARROWBY RD

HARRINGTON DR

GALWAY RD

ROLLESTON DR

ALLINGTON AVE

ALDERMAN MEWS

GROVE RD

CASTLE GDNS

PETERSHAM MEWS

DERBY RD

B

74

AVE

TEVERSAL AVE

BUTE AVE

WELBY AVE

PARK ST

NEWGATE
CT

ABBEY
CT

LENTON
CT

DIGBY
CT

WILLOUGHBY ST

MAXWELL CL

CHURCH
SQ

WILLOUGHBY ST

OSMASTON
ST

PROSPECT
PL

HARLEY
ST

A6005

BROADHOLME STREET

ABBEY BRIDGE

COTTESMORE RD

ASHBURN

Sandfield
Ctr

SANDFIELD RD

ARTHUR
AVE

WILLOUGHBY
AVE

GREGORY
AVE

LOMBARD CL

ROB ROY
AVE

FREDERICK
GR

METHAM
ST

HART ST

CHILWELL
ST

A6130

LENTON BVD

Lenton
Business
Centre

1 HAZELMERE GR
2 PEREGRINE CL

DUNLOP AVE

ELMSTHORPE
AVE

JOHNSON RD

DEVONSHIRE
PROM

HENRY RD

GLOUCESTER
AVE

CHURCH
AVE

TRINITY AVE

ALBERT
RD

LOIS
AVE

Lenton
Prim Sch

CHURCH ST

555

A

SANDPIPER WY

HINCHIN
BROOK

HERON

FALCON CL

CYCLE RD

Playing
Field

Greenholme
Sch

MIDLAND AVE

MIRBERRY
MEWS

SHERWIN RD

WISHFORD
AVE

HUNGERTON
ST

PENN AVE

COLBY AVE

BEDARRA GR

SALISB
SQ

GRINSBROOK

BRADDOCK CL

WICKET
GR

SHELBY CL

KITTIWAKE
MEWS

FARADAY RD

RADMARSH RD

GREGORY ST

LENTON
MANOR

SAXON
GN

GREGORY ST

THE
ALBERT BALL
MEMORIAL
HOMES

War Memorial
GR

SWENSON
AVE

PENN AVENUE

DERWENT
WY

INGHAM
GR

ARNESBY RD

MARTINMASS
CL

TRIUMPH RD

A6200

RATHLINES CL

GREGORY CT

CHURCH STREET

395

58

2

1

Scale: 7 inches to 1 mile

0 110 yards 220 yards
0 125 m 250 m

60
48
47
106
405

C B A

NG3
NG1
NG7

Library
Church Rd
St Ann's
Sycamore Jun & Inf Schs

Wadhurst Gdns
Jedburgh Wlk
Jedburgh Ct
Jenimore Gdns
Thomas Cl
Lewis Cl
Ellis Ct
Curzon Gdns
Curzon Ct
St Ann's Well Rd
Havelock Gdns
Hutchinson
Ginn
Northumberland Cl
Dane Cl
Curzon St
Modele Wlk
Aison
Hadderley Wlk
Comyn Gdns
Truman
Booth Cl

Plantagenet St
Salford Gdns
Campbell Gr
Promenade
Victoria Pk
Bath St Ctr
Victoria L Ctr
Edford St
Lamartine St
Lamartine Ct
Mowbray Ct 1
Foljambe Terr 2
Harborough 3
Scarborough St 4
Robin Hood Terr 5
Campbell St 6
St Mary's Rest Gdn
Cowan St
Beck St
Convent
King Edward St
Kent St
Pelham St
Howard St
St Mary's
Glasshouse St A60
Clare St
Newcastle St
Mkt
Old St
Victoria Shopping Centre

Cecilia Gdns
Peas Hill Rd
Bullivant St
Hartwell St
Abbotsford Dr
Penrhyn Cl
Palmerston Gdns
Shelton St
Grimsby Terr
Great Freeman
Watkins St
Wellington St
Cairns St
Union Rd
Huntingdon St
The Glasshouse Shopping Centre
Curzon Pl
St Mark's St

Saddleworth Ct
Alfred St N
Alfred Ct
Alfred Terr
Woodborough Rd
Huntingdon Prim Sch
Playing Field
Alfred St Central Sch
Haralaxton Wlk
Norman Cl
Hesley Wlk
Welbeck Wlk
Church Ave
St Ann's Way
Sherwin
Sherwin Wlk
York St
Ridding Cl
B684
Vicarage
Pilcher
Major
Milton Street
YMCA

Mansfield Rd
Chatham
North Sherwood St
Birkland Ave
Clipstone Ave
Ossington Cl
Alma Cl
YMCA International Community Cen
North Sherwood St
Bluecoat St
Bluecoat Cl
Clinton Ct
Matlock Ct
Adult Educ Cen
Peachey
Shakespeare St
Trinity Sq
Trinity Wlk
King's Trinity Wlk
N Church St
Burton St
S Sherwood St
Guildhall
The Royal Cornerhouse
Theatre Royal
Forman St

Welbeck
Alfred St N
Blackburn
Newstead Gr
Annesley Gr
Dryden St
Dundas Cl
Shakespeare Villas
Bonnington Art Gal
Nottingham Trent Univ
Bilbie Wlk
Goldsmith St
The Royal Centre
Parliament Terr
Goldsmith St

Tudor Gr
Colville St
Alpha Terr
Mansfield Gr
Addison St
Gill St
Peel St
Canterbury Ct
Hampden St
Liby
Nottingham Trent Univ
Goldsmith St
Chaucer St
High Pavement Sixth Form Coll
Goldsmith Square
Stanley Pl
Russell Pl
Talbot St
Hanley St
Wollaton St

Nottingham High School for Girls
The Arboretum
Balmoral Rd
Nottingham High Jun Sch
Nottingham High School
Arboretum
Clarendon Sixth Form Coll
Waverley Terr
Waverley St
Cromwell St
Portland Rd
Cemy
Clarendon St
St Josephs Council Offices
St Josephs School
Wollaton St

B684
575
570
A60

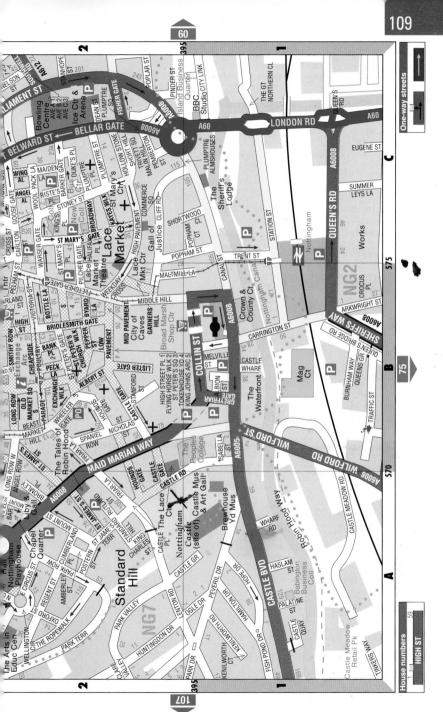

Index

Street names are listed alphabetically and show the locality, the Postcode district, the page number and a reference to the square in which the name falls on the map page

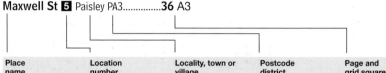

Maxwell St 5 Paisley PA3...............36 A3

Place name	Location number	Locality, town or village	Postcode district	Page and grid square
May be abbreviated on the map	Present when a number indicates the place's position in a crowded area of mapping	Shown when more than one place has the same name	District for the indexed place	Page number and grid reference for the standard mapping

Towns and villages are listed in CAPITAL LETTERS
Public and commercial buildings are highlighted in magenta. **Places of interest** are highlighted in blue with a star*

Abbreviations used in the index

Acad	**Academy**	Ct	**Court**	Hts	**Heights**	Pl	**Place**
App	**Approach**	Ctr	**Centre**	Ind	**Industrial**	Prec	**Precinct**
Arc	**Arcade**	Ctry	**Country**	Inst	**Institute**	Prom	**Promenade**
Ave	**Avenue**	Cty	**County**	Int	**International**	Rd	**Road**
Bglw	**Bungalow**	Dr	**Drive**	Intc	**Interchange**	Recn	**Recreation**
Bldg	**Building**	Dro	**Drove**	Junc	**Junction**	Ret	**Retail**
Bsns, Bus	**Business**	Ed	**Education**	L	**Leisure**	Sh	**Shopping**
Bvd	**Boulevard**	Emb	**Embankment**	La	**Lane**	Sq	**Square**
Cath	**Cathedral**	Est	**Estate**	Liby	**Library**	St	**Street**
Cir	**Circus**	Ex	**Exhibition**	Mdw	**Meadow**	Sta	**Station**
Cl	**Close**	Gd	**Ground**	Meml	**Memorial**	Terr	**Terrace**
Cnr	**Corner**	Gdn	**Garden**	Mkt	**Market**	TH	**Town Hall**
Coll	**College**	Gn	**Green**	Mus	**Museum**	Univ	**University**
Com	**Community**	Gr	**Grove**	Orch	**Orchard**	Wk, Wlk	**Walk**
Comm	**Common**	H	**Hall**	Pal	**Palace**	Wr	**Water**
Cott	**Cottage**	Ho	**House**	Par	**Parade**	Yd	**Yard**
Cres	**Crescent**	Hospl	**Hospital**	Pas	**Passage**		
Cswy	**Causeway**	HQ	**Headquarters**	Pk	**Park**		

Index of towns, villages, streets, hospitals, industrial estates, railway stations, schools, shopping centres, universities and places of interest

1st–Alb

1st Ave Ilkeston DE7 ......41 A1
Nottingham NG7.........47 C2
2nd Ave Ilkeston DE7......41 A1
Nottingham NG7......47 C2
3rd Ave Ilkeston DE7 ......41 A1
Nottingham NG7..........47 C2
4th Ave NG7...............47 C2

A

Aaron Cl NG11...........75 A1
Abba Cl NG16..............18 A1
Abbey Bridge NG7......74 A4
Abbey Cir NG2.............76 C1
Abbey Cl NG15............2 A1
Abbey Ct Beeston NG9 ...72 B2
Nottingham NG7.........107 B2
Abbey Dr NG7............72 B1
Abbeyfield Rd NG7 ....74 B2
Abbey Gr NG3 ....49 A1
Abbey Rd Beeston NG9...72 B1
Bingham NG13 ....67 C2
Eastwood NG16 ....16 C4
West Bridgford NG2....76 C1
Abbey Road Prim Sch
  NG2...................86 C4

Abbey St Ilkeston DE7.....41 A4
Nottingham NG7..........74 A4
Abbot Cl NG12...........104 B4
Abbot Rd DE7 ....52 A4
Abbotsbury Cl NG5 .....21 C3
Abbots Cl NG5...........34 B4
Abbots Dr NG15 ....10 C4
Abbotsford Dr NG3 ....108 C4
Abbotsford Mews DE7...26 B1
Abbots Rd NG15 ....10 C4
Abbot St NG16...........28 A2
Abbots Wlk NG15........10 C4
Abbott St Heanor DE75...13 C3
Long Eaton NG10 ......100 C4
Abbotts Way NG8 ......58 A2
Abel Collin's Homes
  NG8...................72 A3
Abercarn Cl NG6.........20 C1
Aberdeen St 3 NG3 ....60 C3
Aberford Ave NG8 ......46 B2
Abingdon Dr NG11......95 C2
Abingdon Gdns
  Arnold NG5.............35 C3
  Beeston NG9 ....81 C2
Abingdon Rd NG2.......76 C1
Abingdon Sq NG8........45 C3
Ablard Gdns 6 NG9 ....91 B4
Acacia Cl NG15 ....11 C3
Acacia Cres NG4........51 A3

Acacia Gdns NG16 ......18 A2
Acacia Wlk NG9 ....82 B4
Academy NG6............46 B4
Acaster Cl NG9 ....83 A2
Acle Gdns NG16 ....20 C3
Acorn Ave NG16 ....16 C2
Acorn Bank NG2.........85 A2
Acorn Dr NG4 ....51 B4
Acorn Pk NG7 ....74 A2
Acourt St NG7..........106 B4
Acton Ave
  Long Eaton NG10 ......101 A4
  Nottingham NG6........32 B2
Acton Cl NG10...........101 A4
Acton Gr NG10 ....101 A4
Acton Rd Arnold NG5 ....23 C1
  Long Eaton NG10 ......101 A4
Acton Rd Ind Est NG10..101 A4
Acton St NG10...........101 A4
Adams Cl DE75 ....13 B1
Adams Ct DE7 ....26 C1
Adams Hill
  Keyworth NG12 ....104 C3
  Nottingham NG7........73 B4
Adam St DE7 ....53 B4
ADBOLTON 77 A4
Adbolton Ave NG4 ......50 C3
Adbolton Gr NG2 ....77 A3
Adbolton La NG12 ......77 C3

Adderley Cl NG5.........33 B4
Addington Ct NG12 .....65 B3
Addington Rd NG7......106 B4
Addison Dr NG15 ....2 B2
Addison Rd NG4.........49 C2
Addison St NG1.........108 A4
Addison Villas NG16....15 C3
Adel Dr NG4.............50 C3
Adenburgh Dr NG9 .....91 C3
Admiral Cl DE75 ....13 B4
Adrian Cl NG9 ....90 B3
Aeneas Ct 6 NG5.......47 C2
Aerial Way NG15........11 A3
Agnes Villas NG3 ....48 C4
Aidan Gdns NG5 ....22 B4
Ainsdale Cres NG8......31 B1
Ainsley Rd NG8.........58 B4
Ainsworth Dr NG2 .....75 A3
Aintree Cl NG16 ....17 C1
Aira Cl NG2.............87 C4
Airedale Cl NG10 ....99 C4
Airedale Ct NG9 ....80 C2
Aisby Wlk NG8..........56 A1
Aitchison Ave NG15....2 B1
Alandene Ave NG16....18 B1
Albany Cl Arnold NG5...23 C1
  Hucknall NG15 ....10 A3

Albany Ct NG9...........70 A3
Albany Inf Sch NG9......70 A2
Albany Jun Sch NG9.....70 A2
Albany Rd NG7 ....47 B2
Albany St DE7 ....53 B4
Albemarle Rd NG5......34 B2
Alberta Terr NG7........47 B2
Albert Ave Carlton NG4...49 C1
  Nottingham NG8........46 B2
  Nuthall NG16 ....30 A4
  Stapleford NG9.........69 C1
Albert Ball Cl NG5 .....22 A2
Albert Dr NG7 ....106 B3
Albert Hall* NG1.......109 A2
Albert Rd Beeston NG9...73 A1
  Long Eaton NG10 ......89 C2
  Nottingham, Alexander Park
    NG3..................48 B2
  Nottingham NG7.......107 A1
  Sandiacre NG10 ....79 A4
  West Bridgford NG2...76 B2
Albert St Carlton NG4...51 A3
  Eastwood NG16 ....9 A1
  Hucknall NG15 ....3 A1
  Ilkeston DE7...........40 C2
  Nottingham NG1.......109 B2
  Radcliffe on T NG12...65 A2
  Stapleford NG9.........69 C1
Albion Ctr The DE7......41 A4

Albion Rd NG10 . . . . 90 B2
Albion Rise NG5 . . . . . 24 A3
Albion St Beeston NG9 . . . 72 B1
 Ilkeston DE7 . . . . 41 A3
 Nottingham NG1 . . . . 109 B1
Albury Dr NG8 . . . . 45 C3
Albury Sq NG7 . . . . 107 C2
Alcester St NG7 . . . . 74 A2
Aldene Ct NG9 . . . . 81 C3
ALDERCAR 7 B2
Aldercar Com Lang Coll
 NG16 . . . . 7 B2
Aldercar Flash Nature
 Reserve* NG16 . . . . . . 7 C4
Aldercar La NG16 . . . . . . 7 B2
Aldercar La NG16 . . . . . . 7 B4
Alder Gdns NG6 . . . . 20 B1
Alderman Pounder Inf Sch
 NG9 . . . . 81 A3
Alderman White Sch
 NG9 . . . . 71 B1
Aldermens Cl NG2 . . . . 75 B4
Alderney St NG7 . . . . . . 107 B1
Alderton Rd NG5 . . . . . . 34 A4
Alder Way NG12 . . . . . . 105 A2
Aldgate Cl NG6 . . . . 20 B2
Aldred's La DE75 . . . . . 14 C4
Aldridge Cl NG9 . . . . . . 90 A4
Aldrin Cl NG6 . . . . 31 A3
Aldworth Cl NG5 . . . . . . 34 A4
Aldwych Cl
 Nottingham NG5 . . . . 22 B3
 Nuthall NG16 . . . . 44 B4
Alexander Cl NG15 . . . . . 3 A3
Alexander Rd NG7 . . . . . 107 C2
Alexander St NG16 . . . . . 16 A4
Alexandra Cres NG9 . . . 82 C4
Alexandra Rd NG10 . . . . 89 C2
Alexandra St
 Nottingham NG5 . . . . 47 C2
 Stapleford NG9 . . . . 79 C4
Alford Cl NG9 . . . . 83 A3
Alford Rd NG2 . . . . 87 A3
Alfred Ave NG3 . . . . 49 B4
Alfred Cl NG3 . . . . 108 B4
Alfred St Central NG3 . . . 108 B4
Alfred St N NG3 . . . . 108 B4
Alfred St S NG3 . . . . 60 C3
Alfreton Rd NG7 . . . . . . 106 B4
Alison Ave NG15 . . . . 3 B3
Alison Wlk NG3 . . . . 108 C4
Allandale Rd DE75 . . . . . 13 B4
Allendale Ct 40 C1
Allendale Ave
 Beeston NG9 . . . . 91 C4
 Nottingham NG8 . . . . 45 B3
Allen Field Ct NG7 . . . . 107 B1
Allen St NG15 . . . . 2 C2
Allen's Wlk NG5 . . . . . . 24 A4
All Hallows CE Prim Sch [2]
 NG4 . . . . 51 A3
All Hallows Dr NG4 . . . . . 51 A4
Allington Ave NG7 . . . . . 107 B1
Allison Gdns NG9 . . . . . . 81 C2
All Saints' St NG7 . . . . . 106 C4
All Saints'Terr NG7 . . . . 106 C4
Allwood Dr NG4 . . . . 50 C2
Allwood Gdns NG15 . . . . 11 C4
Alma Cl Carlton NG4 . . . . 51 B4
 Nottingham NG1 . . . . . . 108 B4
Alma Hill NG16 . . . . 17 C1
Alma Rd NG3 . . . . 61 A4
Alma St NG7 . . . . 47 B2
Almond Cl Hucknall NG15 . 11 C1
 Kimberley NG16 . . . . 17 C1
Almond Wlk NG4 . . . . . . 51 B4
Alnwick Cl NG6 . . . . 32 B4
Alpha Terr NG1 . . . . 108 A4
Alpine Cres NG4 . . . . . . 50 B2
Alpine St NG6 . . . . 46 C4
Althea Ct [1] NG7 . . . . . . 47 B3
Althorpe St NG7 . . . . . . 106 C3
Alton Ave NG11 . . . . 85 A2
Alton Cl NG11 . . . . 85 B1
Alton Dr NG16 . . . . 16 C2
Alum Ct NG5 . . . . 22 A2
Alvenor St DE7 . . . . 41 A3
Alverstone Rd NG3 . . . . 48 A3
Alwood Gr NG11 . . . . . . 93 C4
Alwyn Rd NG8 . . . . 45 A4
Amber Ct [2] DE75 . . . . . 13 C3

Amber Dr NG16 . . . . 14 C4
Ambergate Rd NG8 . . . . 45 B1
Amber Hill NG5 . . . . 22 C1
Amberley Cl DE7 . . . . . . 53 A4
Amberley St NG1 . . . . . 109 A2
Ambleside NG2 . . . . 77 B1
Ambleside Dr NG16 . . . . . 8 B1
Ambleside Inf Sch NG8 . . 45 C3
Ambleside Jun Sch NG8 . 45 B3
Ambleside Rd NG8 . . . . . 45 B3
Ambleside Way NG4 . . . . 51 C2
Amersham Rise NG8 . . . 45 C3
Amesbury Circ NG8 . . . . 31 B1
Amilda Ave DE7 . . . . 41 A2
Ampthill Rise NG5 . . . . . 33 C2
Ancaster Gdns NG8 . . . . 57 B2
Anchor Cl NG8 . . . . 45 C4
Anchor Rd NG16 . . . . . . 15 B4
Anchor Row DE7 . . . . . . 41 A2
Anders Dr NG6 . . . . 31 A3
Anderson Cres NG9 . . . . 72 A2
Anderson Ct [1] NG5 . . . . 22 B2
Andover Cl [1] NG8 . . . . . 57 C4
Andover Rd NG5 . . . . . . 32 B2
Andrew Ave Ilkeston DE7 . 41 C1
 Nottingham NG3 . . . . 49 B4
Andrews Dr NG16 . . . . . . 7 B1
Anfield Cl NG9 . . . . 90 C4
Anford Cl NG8 . . . . 31 C3
Angela Cl NG5 . . . . 23 C4
Angel Alley NG1 . . . . . . 109 C2
Angell Gn NG11 . . . . 93 B2
Angel Row NG1 . . . . . . 109 B2
Angel Row Gall* NG1 . . 109 A2
Angrave Cl NG3 . . . . 48 C1
Angus Cl Arnold NG5 . . . 24 C3
 Kimberley NG16 . . . . 29 B3
Anmer Cl [9] NG2 . . . . . . 75 A3
Annan Ct NG8 . . . . 45 C2
Anne's Cl NG3 . . . . 49 B4
Annesley Gr NG1 . . . . . 108 A4
Annesley Rd Hucknall NG15 2 B2
 West Bridgford NG2 . . . . . 76 B1
Annie Holgate Inf Sch
 NG15 . . . . 11 A4
Annies Cl NG15 . . . . 11 A3
Anslow Ave NG9 . . . . . . 72 C2
Anson Wlk DE7 . . . . 27 A1
Anstee Rd NG10 . . . . . . 100 B2
Anstey Rise NG3 . . . . . . 61 A3
Antill St NG9 . . . . 79 C4
Apollo Dr NG6 . . . . 31 A3
Appleby Cl DE7 . . . . 53 A4
Appledore Ave NG8 . . . . 71 A2
Appledore Way NG5 . . . . 23 C3
Appleton Rd NG9 . . . . . . 83 A2
Apple Tree Cl NG12 . . . . 86 C2
Apple Tree La NG4 . . . . . 51 A4
Apple Wlk NG4 . . . . 49 B2
Applewood Gr NG5 . . . . 34 B1
Arboretum St NG1 . . . . 108 A4
Arbrook Dr NG8 . . . . 58 B4
Arbutus Cl NG11 . . . . . . 93 B3
Archdale Rd NG5 . . . . . . 34 A4
Archer Cres NG8 . . . . . . 57 A3
Archer Rd NG9 . . . . 80 A3
Archer St DE7 . . . . 26 C1
A Rd NG9 . . . . 83 B4
Arden Cl Beeston NG9 . . . 72 C2
 Hucknall NG15 . . . . 12 A3
Arden Gr NG13 . . . . 66 B3
Ardleigh Cl NG5 . . . . . . 21 B3
Ardmore Cl NG2 . . . . . . 61 A1
Ardsley Cl DE75 . . . . . . 14 B4
Argyle Ct NG7 . . . . 106 B3
Argyle St Langley Mill NG16 8 A2
 Nottingham NG7 . . . . . . 106 B3
Ariel Cl NG6 . . . . 33 A3
Arkers Cl NG6 . . . . 32 B1
Arklow Cl NG8 . . . . 45 C4
Arkwright Wlk NG2 . . . . 75 B4
Arleston Dr NG8 . . . . . . 56 B2
Arlington Cl NG15 . . . . . 11 B2
Arlington Dr NG3 . . . . . . 48 A4
Armadale Cl NG5 . . . . . . 25 A2
Armfield Rd NG5 . . . . . . 36 A4
Armitage Dr NG10 . . . . . 90 C1
Armstrong Rd NG6 . . . . . 31 A3
Arncliff Cl NG8 . . . . 56 A2
Arndale Rd NG5 . . . . . . 34 A3
Arne Ct [5] NG2 . . . . 75 B3

Arnesby Rd NG7 . . . . . . 107 A1
Arno Ave [2] NG7 . . . . . . 47 C2
ARNOLD 24 B1
Arnold Ave NG10 . . . . . . 99 C2
Arnold Cres NG10 . . . . . 99 C2
Arnold Hill Sch NG5 . . . . 35 B4
Arnold La NG3 . . . . 36 B2
Arnold L Ctr NG5 . . . . . . 47 C2
Arnold Rd NG5 . . . . 33 B3
Arnold View Prim Sch
 NG5 . . . . 24 A1
Arnos Gr NG8 . . . . 30 B1
Arnot Hill Rd NG5 . . . . . 34 C4
Arno Vale Gdns NG5 . . . 34 C3
Arno Vale Jun Sch NG5 . . 35 A3
Arno Vale Rd NG5 . . . . . 35 A3
Arnside NG9 . . . . 80 A3
Arnside Cl NG5 . . . . 33 C3
Arnside Rd NG5 . . . . 33 C3
Arran Cl NG9 . . . . 70 A4
Arthur Ave
 Nottingham NG7 . . . . . . 107 B2
 Stapleford NG9 . . . . 70 B2
Arthur Cres NG4 . . . . . . 50 A1
Arthur Mee Rd NG9 . . . . 80 A3
Arthur St Carlton NG4 . . . 63 B4
 Nottingham NG7 . . . . . . 106 C4
Artic Way NG16 . . . . 17 B1
Arundel Cl NG10 . . . . . . 79 A2
Arundel Dr NG9 . . . . 71 A3
Arundel St NG7 . . . . . . 106 C3
Ascot Ave NG16 . . . . 17 C1
Ascot Dr Arnold NG5 . . . . 23 B2
 Hucknall NG15 . . . . 11 A4
Ascot Pk Est NG10 . . . . . 79 A2
Ascot Pl DE7 . . . . 52 A3
Ascot Rd NG8 . . . . 46 B1
Ascott Gdns NG2 . . . . . . 84 C3
Ashbourne Cl NG9 . . . . . 70 C3
Ashbourne Ct NG6 . . . . . 31 A4
Ashbourne St NG7 . . . . 106 C3
Ashburnham Ave NG7 . . 107 B2
Ashchurch Dr NG8 . . . . . 71 C4
Ash Cl Bingham NG13 . . . . 67 C2
 Burton Joyce NG14 . . . . . 38 C2
 Hucknall NG15 . . . . 10 A3
Ash Cres NG16 . . . . 29 C4
Ash Ct NG4 . . . . 50 B1
Ashdale Ave NG15 . . . . . 11 B3
Ashdale Rd Arnold NG5 . . 24 B2
 Ilkeston DE7 . . . . 53 B4
 Nottingham NG3 . . . . 61 C4
Ashdown Cl NG11 . . . . . 85 A4
Ashdown Gr NG13 . . . . . 66 C2
Ashe Cl NG5 . . . . 23 C2
Asher La NG11 . . . . 102 C4
Ashfield Ave NG9 . . . . . . 83 A3
Ashfield Rd NG2 . . . . . . 61 A2
Ashford Pl DE7 . . . . 26 C3
Ashford Rise NG8 . . . . . 71 C4
Ashforth Ave DE75 . . . . 14 B3
Ashforth St NG3 . . . . . . 108 C4
Ashgate Rd NG15 . . . . . 11 C4
Ash Gr Keyworth NG12 . . 105 A2
 Long Eaton NG10 . . . . . 100 B4
 Sandiacre NG10 . . . . 68 C1
 Stapleford NG9 . . . . 79 C3
Ashington Dr NG5 . . . . . 24 B4
Ash Lea Cl NG12 . . . . . . 98 B2
Ash Lea Specl Sch NG12 . 98 B2
Ashley Cl NG9 . . . . 81 C4
Ashley Cres NG12 . . . . . 104 C3
Ashley Gr NG15 . . . . 2 A1
Ashley Rd NG12 . . . . . . 104 B3
Ashley St [7] NG3 . . . . . . 60 C3
Ashling St NG2 . . . . 75 C4
Ash Mount Rd NG16 . . . . 7 C1
Ashness Cl NG2 . . . . . . 87 B4
Ashover Cl NG3 . . . . 48 C2
Ashridge Way NG2 . . . . 87 B2
Ash St DE7 . . . . 26 C2
Ashton Ave NG5 . . . . . . 24 A4
Ash Tree Sq NG9 . . . . . . 71 A2
Ashview Cl NG10 . . . . . . 88 C2
Ash Villas [1] NG7 . . . . . 47 C3
Ashville Cl NG2 . . . . 74 C3
Ashwater Dr NG3 . . . . . . 36 B3
Ashwell Gdns NG7 . . . . . 46 C2
Ashwell St NG4 . . . . 63 A4
Ashwick Cl NG11 . . . . . . 84 C3
Ashworth Ave NG11 . . . . 95 B2

Ashworth Bsns Ctr
 NG1 . . . . 108 C4
Ashworth Cl NG3 . . . . . . 62 A3
Ashworth Cres NG3 . . . . 49 C4
Askeby Dr NG8 . . . . 44 B3
Aslockton Dr NG8 . . . . . 46 B4
Aspen Cl NG13 . . . . 67 C2
Aspen Rd NG6 . . . . 20 A1
Asper St NG4 . . . . 51 B1
Aspinall Ct [2] NG8 . . . . . 58 A3
Aspley La NG8 . . . . 46 A2
Aspley Pk Dr NG8 . . . . . 45 C2
Aspley Pl NG7 . . . . 106 B4
Aspley Wood Specl Sch
 NG8 . . . . 45 C1
Assarts Rd NG16 . . . . . . 30 C1
Astcote Cl DE75 . . . . . . 14 B3
Aster Rd NG3 . . . . 48 C1
Astle Cl NG5 . . . . 36 A4
Astley Dr NG3 . . . . 49 A3
Aston Ave NG9 . . . . 72 C3
Aston Ct DE7 . . . . 41 A3
Aston Dr NG6 . . . . 21 A4
Aston Gn NG9 . . . . 80 A1
Astral Gr NG15 . . . . 10 C2
Astrid Gdns NG5 . . . . . . 33 A4
Astwood Cl NG8 . . . . . . 44 C2
Atherfield Gdns NG16 . . . 9 A1
Atherton Rd DE7 . . . . . . 26 A1
Atherton Rise NG8 . . . . . 31 C1
Athorpe Gr NG6 . . . . 32 C1
ATTENBOROUGH 92 A4
Attenborough La NG9 . . . 81 B1
Attenborough Nature
 Reserve* NG9 . . . . . . 92 A3
Attenborough Prep Sch
 NG9 . . . . 92 A3
Attenborough Sta NG9 . . 91 C4
Attercliffe Terr [8] NG2 . . 75 B3
Attewell Rd NG16 . . . . . 15 C4
Aubrey Ave [15] NG2 . . . 60 C2
Aubrey Rd NG5 . . . . 47 C4
Auckland Cl NG7 . . . . . 106 A3
Auckland Rd NG15 . . . . . 10 B3
Audley Cl DE7 . . . . 26 B1
Audley Dr NG9 . . . . 72 B3
Audon Ave NG9 . . . . 82 A3
Augustine Gdns NG5 . . . 22 B3
Austen Ave
 Long Eaton NG10 . . . . . 100 B3
 Nottingham NG7 . . . . 47 B1
Austins Dr NG10 . . . . . . 79 A2
Austin St NG6 . . . . 21 A1
Austrey Ave NG9 . . . . . . 72 C2
Avalon Cl NG6 . . . . 32 C4
Ave A NG1 . . . . 109 C2
Ave B NG1 . . . . 109 C2
Avebury Cl NG11 . . . . . . 93 C2
Ave C NG1 . . . . 109 C2
Ave D NG1 . . . . 60 C2
Ave E [4] NG1 . . . . 60 C3
Avenue Cl NG5 . . . . 22 A2
Avenue The NG14 . . . . . . 5 B2
Averton Sq NG8 . . . . . . 58 B1
Aviemore Cl NG5 . . . . . . 24 C2
Avis Ave DE75 . . . . 14 A1
Avocet Cl Bingham NG13 . 67 C1
 Hucknall NG15 . . . . 3 A3
Avocet Wharf [4] NG7 . . 74 B4
Avon Ave NG15 . . . . 10 C2
Avonbridge Cl NG5 . . . . 25 A3
Avondale NG12 . . . . 98 C3
Avondale Cl NG10 . . . . . 99 C4
Avondale Rd Carlton NG4 . 62 B4
 Ilkeston DE7 . . . . 52 A3
Avon Gdns NG2 . . . . 76 B1
Avonlea Cl DE7 . . . . 53 C4
Avon Pl NG9 . . . . 72 C1
Avon Rd Carlton NG4 . . . . 51 A4
 Nottingham NG3 . . . . 61 C3
AWSWORTH 28 A2
Awsworth La NG16 . . . . . 28 B4
Awsworth Prim Sch
 NG16 . . . . 28 A2
Awsworth Rd DE7 . . . . . 41 A4
Axford Cl NG4 . . . . 51 A4
Aylesham Ave NG5 . . . . 35 A4
Aylestone Dr NG8 . . . . . 45 C2
Ayr St NG7 . . . . 106 C4
Ayscough Ave NG16 . . . . 9 A1
Ayton Cl NG2 . . . . 75 A4

Ayton Gdns NG9 . . . . . . 91 B4
Azalea Ct NG16 . . . . 17 A2

B

Babbacombe Cl NG5 . . . 33 C4
Babbacombe Way NG15 . 10 B4
Babbington Cres NG4 . . . 50 C4
Babbington La NG16 . . . . 29 A2
Babington Ct NG9 . . . . . 81 B3
Back La Ilkeston DE7 . . . . 40 C4
 Nuthall NG8 . . . . 30 B4
Bacon Cl NG16 . . . . 16 B2
Bacton Ave NG6 . . . . . . 20 C2
Bacton Gdns [1] NG6 . . . 20 C2
Baden Powell Rd NG2 . . 61 B2
Bader NG11 . . . . 75 A1
Badger Cl NG15 . . . . 10 A4
Bagnall Ave NG5 . . . . . . 23 A1
Bagnall Rd NG6 . . . . 32 A2
Bagthorpe Cl NG5 . . . . . 33 B1
Baildon Cl NG8 . . . . 58 A1
Bailey Brook Cres NG16 . . 7 B2
Bailey Brook Dr NG16 . . . 7 B2
Bailey Brook Wlk NG16 . . 7 B1
Bailey Cl NG5 . . . . 23 B1
Bailey Ct NG12 . . . . 64 C1
Bailey Gr Rd NG16 . . . . . 15 B4
Bailey La NG12 . . . . 64 C1
Bailey St Carlton NG4 . . . 51 B1
 Nottingham NG6 . . . . 46 C4
 Stapleford NG9 . . . . 79 B4
Bainbridge The NG14 . . . . 5 C2
Bainton Gr NG7 . . . . 94 B3
Baker Ave Arnold NG5 . . . 24 B4
 Heanor DE75 . . . . 14 A1
Baker Brook Ind Pk
 NG15 . . . . 12 A4
Bakerdale Rd NG3 . . . . . 61 C4
Baker Rd NG16 . . . . 17 A3
Bakers Cl NG7 . . . . 106 A4
BAKERS FIELDS 62 A4
Baker's Hollow NG12 . . . 98 A3
Baker St Hucknall NG15 . . 2 C1
 [13] Ilkeston DE7 . . . . . . 41 A3
 Nottingham NG1 . . . . 47 C1
Bakewell Ave NG4 . . . . . 50 C3
Bakewell Dr NG5 . . . . . . 21 C1
Bakewell Rd NG10 . . . . 101 A3
Bala Dr NG5 . . . . 22 B1
Baldwin Ct NG7 . . . . . . 106 B3
Baldwin St
 Eastwood NG16 . . . . 17 A3
 Nottingham NG7 . . . . . . 106 C3
Balfour Rd
 Nottingham NG7 . . . . . . 106 B3
 Stapleford NG9 . . . . 79 C4
Balfron Gdns [7] NG2 . . . 75 A4
Ballantrae Cl NG5 . . . . . 24 C2
Ballerat Cres NG5 . . . . . 21 C2
Balloon Houses NG9 . . . 55 C2
Balloon Wood Ind Est
 NG8 . . . . 55 B2
Ball St NG3 . . . . 49 A1
Balmoral Ave NG2 . . . . . 76 A2
Balmoral Cl Heanor DE75 . 13 A3
 Sandiacre NG10 . . . . 79 A1
Balmoral Cres NG8 . . . . 56 A3
Balmoral Dr NG9 . . . . . . 71 B4
Balmoral Gr NG15 . . . . . . 3 A2
Balmoral Rd
 Bingham NG13 . . . . 66 B2
 Carlton NG4 . . . . 63 A4
 Ilkeston DE7 . . . . 52 B3
 Nottingham NG1 . . . . . . 108 A4
Bamkin Cl NG15 . . . . . . 11 C4
Banbury Ave NG9 . . . . . 83 A1
Banbury Mount [9] NG5 . 48 A4
Bancroft St NG6 . . . . . . 21 A1
Bangor Wlk [3] NG3 . . . . 48 A1
Bankfield Dr NG9 . . . . . . 71 B3
Bank Pl NG1 . . . . 109 B2
Banksburn Cl DE75 . . . . 13 A3
Banks Cl NG5 . . . . 35 C4
Banks Cres NG13 . . . . . . 67 A2
Banks Paddock NG13 . . . 67 B2
Banks Rd NG9 . . . . 90 A4
Bank St Langley Mill NG16 . 8 A1

Bank St continued
Long Eaton NG10 . . . .**90** A1
Banks The NG13 . . . .**67** B2
Bankwood Cl NG8 . . . .**45** B3
Bank Yd 11 NG6 . . . .**20** C1
Bannerman Rd NG6 . . . .**32** A4
Barbara Sq NG15 . . . .**2** B3
Barber Cl DE7 . . . .**27** A1
Barber St NG16 . . . .**16** C4
Barbrook Cl NG8 . . . .**57** B3
Barbury Dr NG11 . . . .**93** C1
Barclay Ct DE7 . . . .**26** A1
Barden Rd NG3 . . . .**35** B2
Bardfield Gdns NG5 . . . .**21** B3
Bardney Dr NG6 . . . .**20** B2
Bardsey Gdns NG5 . . . .**22** B1
Barent Cl NG5 . . . .**33** A4
Barent Wlk NG5 . . . .**33** A4
Barker Ave E NG10 . . . .**78** C4
Barker Ave N NG10 . . . .**78** C4
Barker Gate Hucknall NG15 . .**2** B1
Ilkeston DE7 . . . .**41** A4
Nottingham NG1 . . . .**109** C2
Barker's La NG9 . . . .**82** A2
Barkla Cl NG11 . . . .**93** B2
Bar La NG6 . . . .**46** B4
Bar La Ind Pk NG6 . . . .**46** B4
Barley Croft NG2 . . . .**85** B2
Barley Dale Dr NG9 . . . .**69** C4
Barleylands NG11 . . . .**102** C4
Barling Dr DE7 . . . .**40** A4
Barlock Rd NG6 . . . .**32** C2
Barlow Cotts La NG16 . . . . . .**27** C3
Barlow Dr N NG16 . . . .**27** C2
Barlow Dr S NG16 . . . .**27** C2
Barnby Wlk NG5 . . . .**34** A2
Barn Cl NG12 . . . .**98** A2
Barn Croft NG9 . . . .**81** A3
Barndale Cl NG2 . . . .**85** B1
Barnes Croft DE75 . . . .**13** A2
Barnes Rd NG5 . . . .**21** C2
Barnet Rd NG3 . . . .**49** C1
Barnett Ct NG12 . . . .**104** B3
Barnfield NG11 . . . .**85** A2
Barnsley Terr 9 NG2 . . . .**75** B3
Barnston Rd NG2 . . . .**61** B3
Barnum Cl NG8 . . . .**56** C3
Barons Cl NG4 . . . .**50** C3
Barrack La NG7 . . . .**107** B2
Barra Mews 10 NG2 . . . .**75** A4
Barratt Cl NG9 . . . .**91** C3
Barratt Cres NG9 . . . .**91** C4
Barratt La NG9 . . . .**91** C3
Barrhead Cl NG5 . . . .**21** C3
Barrington Cl NG12 . . . .**64** C1
Barrique Rd NG7 . . . .**74** A3
Barrow Slade NG12 . . . .**104** B2
Barrydale Ave NG9 . . . .**82** B3
Barry St NG6 . . . .**20** C1
Bartlow Rd NG8 . . . .**44** B1
Barton Cl NG11 . . . .**102** B4
Barton La Beeston NG9 . . . . .**91** B3
Nottingham NG11 . . . .**93** B3
Barton Rd NG10 . . . .**101** C4
Bartons Cl NG16 . . . .**17** A4
Barton St NG9 . . . .**82** C3
Barton Wy NG9 . . . .**82** A3
Barwell Dr NG8 . . . .**44** B3
Basa Cres NG5 . . . .**22** A2
Basford Rd NG6 . . . .**46** B4
Baskin La NG9 . . . .**81** B1
Baslow Ave NG4 . . . .**50** B3
Baslow Cl NG10 . . . .**99** C3
Baslow Dr NG9 . . . .**72** C3
Bassett Cl NG16 . . . .**17** C1
Bassett Rd NG16 . . . .**17** C1
Bassford Ave DE75 . . . .**14** A4
Bastion St NG7 . . . .**106** A3
Bateman Gdns 8 NG7 . . . . .**47** A1
Bathley St NG2 . . . .**73** C3
Baths La NG15 . . . .**3** A1
Bath St Ilkeston DE7 . . . .**40** C3
Nottingham NG1 . . . .**108** C3
Bathurst Dr NG8 . . . .**57** B4
Baulk La NG9 . . . .**80** C4
Bawtry Wlk NG3 . . . .**61** A4
Bayard Ct NG8 . . . .**58** A3
Bayliss Rd NG4 . . . .**36** B1

Bayswater Rd NG16 . . . .**18** A1
Baythorn Rd NG8 . . . .**56** B4
Beacon Hill Dr NG15 . . . .**10** B3
Beacon Hill Rise NG3 . . . . . .**60** C4
Beacon Rd NG9 . . . .**83** A4
Beaconsfield St
Long Eaton NG10 . . . .**90** A1
Nottingham NG7 . . . .**47** A2
Bean Cl NG6 . . . .**31** A3
Beardall St NG15 . . . .**11** C4
Beardall Street Prim Sch
NG15 . . . .**11** C4
Beardsley Gdns NG2 . . . .**75** A4
Beardsmore Gr NG15 . . . .**2** B3
Beast Mkt Hill NG1 . . . .**109** B2
Beatty Wlk DE7 . . . .**27** A1
Beauclerk Dr NG5 . . . .**21** C2
Beaufort Cl NG11 . . . .**85** B1
Beaufort Dr NG9 . . . .**81** B3
Beaulieu Gdns NG5 . . . .**85** B3
Beaumaris Dr
Beeston NG9 . . . .**81** A2
Carlton NG4 . . . .**51** C3
Beaumont Cl
Keyworth NG12 . . . .**104** B4
Stapleford NG9 . . . .**70** A3
Beaumont Gdns NG2 . . . .**85** C2
Beaumont St NG2 . . . .**60** C2
Beauvale NG16 . . . .**17** A4
Beauvale Cres NG15 . . . .**10** C4
Beauvale Dr DE7 . . . .**26** C3
Beauvale Rd
Hucknall NG15 . . . .**10** C4
Nottingham NG2 . . . .**73** B3
Beauvale Rise NG16 . . . .**9** B1
Beck Ave NG14 . . . .**5** B3
Beckenham Rd NG7 . . . . . .**106** B4
Becket Sch The NG11 . . . . . .**84** C3
Beckett Ct NG4 . . . .**36** B1
Beckford Rd 8 NG2 . . . .**61** A1
Beckhampton Ctr NG5 . . . . . .**33** C3
Beckhampton Rd NG5 . . . . . .**22** B1
Beckley Rd NG8 . . . .**45** A4
Beckside NG2 . . . .**87** B3
Beck St Carlton NG4 . . . .**50** C2
Nottingham NG1 . . . .**108** C3
Bedale Ct NG9 . . . .**80** C2
Bedale Rd NG5 . . . .**34** B3
Bedarra Gr NG7 . . . .**107** A2
Bede Ling NG2 . . . .**85** B4
Bedford Ct NG9 . . . .**70** A3
Bedford Gr NG6 . . . .**32** B3
Bedford Row NG1 . . . .**108** C3
Bedlington Gdns NG3 . . . . . .**48** C3
Beecham Ave NG3 . . . .**49** A1
Beech Ave Beeston NG9 . . . . .**83** A3
Bingham NG13 . . . .**67** C2
Breaston DE72 . . . .**88** B2
Carlton NG4 . . . .**63** A4
Hucknall NG15 . . . .**2** C1
Keyworth NG12 . . . .**105** A2
Long Eaton NG10 . . . .**90** B3
Nottingham, Hyson Green
NG7 . . . .**47** B2
Nottingham, Mapperley
NG3 . . . .**35** B2
Nuttall NG16 . . . .**29** C4
Sandiacre NG10 . . . .**69** A1
Beech Cl Nottingham NG6 . . .**32** A2
Radcliffe on T NG12 . . . .**65** A1
West Bridgford NG12 . . . . . .**86** C2
Beech Ct NG3 . . . .**35** B2
BEECHDALE **57** C4
Beechdale Rd NG8 . . . .**45** C1
Beechdale Swimming Ctr
NG8 . . . .**58** A4
Beeches The Carlton NG4 . . . .**49** B2
Heanor DE75 . . . .**13** A2
Beechwood Rd NG5 . . . .**24** B2
BEESTON **80** C4
Beeston Ct NG6 . . . .**32** B4
Beeston Fields Dr NG9 . . . . .**71** C2
Beeston Fields Prim Sch
NG9 . . . .**72** B2
Beeston La NG9 . . . .**73** A2
Beeston Rd NG7 . . . .**73** C3
Beeston Sidings Nature
Reserve★ NG11 . . . .**73** B1
Beeston Sta NG9 . . . .**82** C3
Beethan Cl NG13 . . . .**67** B2
Beggarlee Pk NG16 . . . .**9** C2

Belconnen Rd NG5 . . . .**33** B3
Belfield Ct DE75 . . . .**6** A2
Belford Cl NG6 . . . .**20** A2
Belfry Way NG2 . . . .**87** B2
Belgrave Mews NG11 . . . . . .**85** B1
Belgrave Rd NG6 . . . .**20** A2
Belgrave Sq NG1 . . . .**108** A3
Bella Cl NG16 . . . .**7** C2
Bellar Gate NG1 . . . .**109** C2
Belle-Isle Rd NG15 . . . .**2** C1
Belleville Dr NG5 . . . .**22** C2
Bellevue Ct NG3 . . . .**60** C4
Bell La NG11 . . . .**74** C1
Bellmore Gdns NG8 . . . .**56** B3
Bells La NG8 . . . .**31** B1
Bell St NG4 . . . .**50** B2
Belmont Ave
Breaston DE72 . . . .**88** A2
Nottingham NG6 . . . .**21** A1
Belmont Cl Beeston NG9 . . . .**81** A2
Hucknall NG15 . . . .**11** B2
Belper Ave NG4 . . . .**50** B3
Belper Cres NG4 . . . .**50** B3
Belper Rd NG7 . . . .**47** A1
Belper St DE7 . . . .**41** A1
Belsay Rd NG5 . . . .**22** B1
Belsford Ct NG16 . . . .**18** B2
Belton Cl NG10 . . . .**79** A2
Belton Dr NG2 . . . .**85** A2
Belton St NG7 . . . .**47** A2
Belvedere Ave 9 NG7 . . . . . .**47** A1
Belvoir Cl Ilkeston DE7 . . . . . .**52** B4
Long Eaton NG10 . . . .**101** A3
Belvoir Hill NG2 . . . .**61** A2
Belvoir Rd Carlton NG4 . . . . .**51** B1
West Bridgford NG2 . . . .**76** C3
Belvoir St Hucknall NG15 . . . .**2** B2
Nottingham NG3 . . . .**49** A4
Belward St NG1 . . . .**109** C2
Belwood Cl NG7 . . . .**94** B4
Bembridge Dr NG5 . . . .**70** C2
Bembridge Dr NG5 . . . .**33** C4
Bendigo La NG2 . . . .**61** B2
Benedict Ct 3 NG5 . . . .**22** B3
Benington Dr NG8 . . . .**56** A1
Ben Mayo Ct NG7 . . . .**106** B4
Benner Ave DE7 . . . .**53** B3
Bennerley Ave DE7 . . . .**27** A2
Bennerley Ct NG6 . . . .**20** A2
Bennerley Rd NG6 . . . .**20** A2
Bennett Rd NG3 . . . .**35** B1
Bennett St
Long Eaton NG10 . . . .**89** B4
Nottingham NG3 . . . .**49** A4
Sandiacre NG10 . . . .**79** A3
Benneworth Cl NG15 . . . .**11** A3
Ben St NG7 . . . .**106** B4
Bentinck Ave NG12 . . . .**97** C3
Bentinck Cl NG12 . . . .**60** C2
Bentinck Prim Sch
NG7 . . . .**106** B4
Bentinck Rd Carlton NG4 . . . .**50** A4
Nottingham NG7 . . . .**106** B4
Bentinck St NG15 . . . .**2** B2
Bentley Ave NG3 . . . .**61** C4
Bentwell Ave NG5 . . . .**24** B1
Beresford Dr DE7 . . . .**26** C3
Beresford Rd NG10 . . . .**99** C3
Beresford St NG7 . . . .**106** A3
Berkeley Ave
Long Eaton NG10 . . . .**100** B4
Nottingham NG3 . . . .**48** A2
Berle Ave DE75 . . . .**13** C4
Bernard Ave NG15 . . . .**3** A3
Bernard St NG5 . . . .**47** C3
Bernisdale Cl NG5 . . . .**21** A3
Berridge Adult Ctr The
NG7 . . . .**47** A2
Berridge Inf Sch NG7 . . . . . .**46** C1
Berridge Jun Sch NG7 . . . . . .**46** C1
Berridge Rd NG7 . . . .**47** B2
Berridge Rd W NG7 . . . .**46** C1
Berriedale Cl NG5 . . . .**25** A2
Berry Hill Gr NG4 . . . .**50** C4
Berwick Cl NG5 . . . .**34** A4
Berwin Cl NG10 . . . .**88** C3
Beryldene Ave NG16 . . . .**18** B1
Besecar Ave NG4 . . . .**50** C4
Besecar Cl NG4 . . . .**50** C4
Bessell La NG9 . . . .**79** C3
Bessingham Dr NG11 . . . .**85** B1

Bestwick Ave DE75 . . . .**14** C3
Bestwick Cl DE7 . . . .**53** B2
BESTWOOD **22** C1
Bestwood Ave NG5 . . . .**23** C2
Bestwood Cl NG5 . . . .**23** C2
Bestwood Lodge Dr NG5 . . . .**23** B2
Bestwood Park Drive 4
NG5 . . . .**22** C3
Bestwood Pk Dr NG5 . . . .**22** C2
Bestwood Pk Dr W NG5 . . . . .**23** C2
Bestwood Pk View NG5 . . . . .**23** C3
Bestwood Rd
Hucknall NG15 . . . .**12** A3
Nottingham NG6 . . . .**20** C1
Bestwood Terr NG6 . . . .**21** A2
Bethel Gdns NG15 . . . .**10** A3
Bethnal Wlk 2 NG6 . . . .**20** C1
Betony Cl NG13 . . . .**66** B2
Betula Cl NG11 . . . .**93** B3
Bevel St NG7 . . . .**47** A1
Beverley Cl NG8 . . . .**55** C2
Beverley Dr NG16 . . . .**17** C1
Beverley Gdns NG4 . . . .**51** A1
Beverley Sq NG3 . . . .**48** C1
Bewcastle Rd NG5 . . . .**22** B4
Bewick Dr NG3 . . . .**62** A3
Bexhill Ct NG8 . . . .**72** A3
Bexwell Cl NG11 . . . .**94** A2
Biant Cl NG8 . . . .**31** C1
Bidford Rd NG8 . . . .**45** A3
Biggart Cl 2 NG9 . . . .**91** A4
Big Wood Sch NG5 . . . .**22** C4
Biko Sq 8 NG7 . . . .**47** A2
Bilberry Wlk NG3 . . . .**48** C1
Bilbie Wlk NG1 . . . .**108** A3
BILBOROUGH **44** C1
Bilborough Coll NG8 . . . .**44** A1
Bilborough Rd NG8 . . . .**56** A4
Bilby Gdns 3 NG3 . . . .**61** A3
Billesdon Dr NG5 . . . .**33** A2
BINGHAM **67** A1
Bingham Inf Pk NG13 . . . .**67** A3
Bingham L Ctr NG13 . . . .**67** A1
Bingham Rd
Cotgrave NG12 . . . .**98** B3
Nottingham NG5 . . . .**48** B2
Radcliffe on T NG12 . . . .**65** B2
Bingham Robert Miles Inf
Sch NG13 . . . .**67** A3
Bingham Sta NG13 . . . .**67** B2
Bingley Cl 2 NG8 . . . .**57** C4
BioCity NG8 . . . .**60** C2
Birch Ave Beeston NG9 . . . . . .**83** A2
Carlton NG4 . . . .**50** B1
Ilkeston DE7 . . . .**41** B1
Nuthall NG16 . . . .**29** C4
Birch Cl NG16 . . . .**29** C4
Birchdale Ave NG15 . . . .**11** B3
Birchfield Pk DE75 . . . .**14** A1
Birchfield Rd NG5 . . . .**22** B3
Birch Lea NG5 . . . .**23** B2
Birchover Pl DE7 . . . .**26** C3
Birchover Rd NG8 . . . .**56** A4
Birch Pas NG7 . . . .**106** C3
Birchwood DE75 . . . .**6** A2
Birchwood Ave
Breaston NG10 . . . .**88** C1
Long Eaton NG10 . . . .**100** B3
Birchwood Rd NG8 . . . .**56** A2
Bircumshaw's Rd DE75 . . . . .**13** C4
Birdcroft La DE7 . . . .**53** A3
Birdsall Ave NG8 . . . .**56** C2
Birkdale Cl Ilkeston DE7 . . . . .**40** B3
West Bridgford NG12 . . . . . .**86** C1
Birkdale Way
Nottingham NG5 . . . .**22** A2
9 Nottingham NG5 . . . .**22** B2
Birkin Ave Beeston NG9 . . . . .**90** C4
Nottingham NG7 . . . .**47** A1
Radcliffe on T NG12 . . . .**65** B3
Ruddington NG11 . . . .**95** B2
Birkland Ave
Nottingham, Mapperley
NG3 . . . .**35** B2
Nottingham, St Ann's
NG1 . . . .**108** B4
Birley St NG9 . . . .**79** C3
Birling Cl NG6 . . . .**20** A1
Birrell Rd NG7 . . . .**47** A1
Bisham Dr NG2 . . . .**77** A1
Bishopdale Dr NG10 . . . .**99** C4

Bishopdale Dr NG16 . . . .**18** C1
Bishops Cl NG12 . . . .**104** B4
Bishops Rd NG13 . . . .**66** C3
Bishop St NG16 . . . .**16** A4
Bishops Way NG15 . . . .**3** A2
Bispham Dr NG9 . . . .**90** B4
Bispham Dr Jun Sch
NG9 . . . .**80** A1
Blackacre NG14 . . . .**38** C3
Blackburn Pl DE7 . . . .**26** C1
Blacketts Wlk NG11 . . . .**93** B2
Blackfriars Cl NG8 . . . .**30** B1
Blackhill Dr NG4 . . . .**51** A2
Black Hills Dr DE7 . . . .**53** A4
Blackrod Cl NG9 . . . .**90** C4
Blacksmith Ct NG12 . . . .**98** A4
Blackstone Wlk NG2 . . . .**75** B4
Black Swan Cl NG5 . . . .**34** B2
Blackthorn Cl NG4 . . . .**51** B4
Blackthorn Dr NG6 . . . .**31** C1
Bladon Cl NG3 . . . .**48** C4
Bladon Rd NG11 . . . .**95** A1
Blair Ct 4 NG2 . . . .**75** B3
Blair Gr NG10 . . . .**78** C2
Blaise Cl NG11 . . . .**84** A1
Blake Cl NG5 . . . .**24** B1
Blake Ct NG10 . . . .**100** A3
Blakeney Rd NG12 . . . .**65** C2
Blakeney Wlk NG5 . . . .**35** A3
Blake Rd Stapleford NG9 . . . . .**80** A4
West Bridgford NG2 . . . .**76** C1
Blake St DE7 . . . .**41** A3
Blandford Ave NG10 . . . .**100** A3
Blandford Gdns NG2 . . . .**85** B3
Blandford Rd NG9 . . . .**81** B3
Blankney St NG5 . . . .**32** C2
Blantyre Ave NG5 . . . .**21** C3
Blatherwick's Yd NG5 . . . . . .**24** A2
Bleaberry Cl NG2 . . . .**87** B3
Bleachers Yd NG7 . . . .**47** A3
Bleasby St NG2 . . . .**61** A2
Bleasdale Cl NG4 . . . .**51** B4
Blencathra Cl NG2 . . . .**87** B3
Blenheim Ave NG5 . . . .**50** A4
Blenheim Cl NG11 . . . .**95** A1
Blenheim Dr NG9 . . . .**81** B3
Blenheim Ind Est NG6 . . . . . .**20** A2
Blenheim Cl NG6, NG15 . . . . .**19** C3
Blenheim Ct NG10 . . . .**79** A2
Blessed Robert RC Prim
Sch NG11 . . . .**94** A2
Bildworth Cl NG8 . . . .**44** C4
Bloomgrove Rd DE7 . . . .**41** A4
Bloomsbury Dr NG16 . . . .**30** C1
Bloomsgrove Ind Est
NG7 . . . .**106** B3
Bloomsgrove St NG7 . . . . . .**106** B3
Bluebell Bank NG13 . . . .**66** C1
Bluebell Cl NG15 . . . .**10** A4
Blue Bell Hill Prim Sch
NG3 . . . .**61** A4
Blue Bell Hill Rd NG3 . . . .**60** C4
Bluecoat Cl NG1 . . . .**108** B3
Bluecoat St NG1 . . . .**108** B4
Blundell Cl NG3 . . . .**49** A2
Blyth Gdns NG3 . . . .**48** C4
Blyth St NG3 . . . .**48** C4
Blyton Wlk NG5 . . . .**22** C1
Boatmans Cl DE7 . . . .**41** A4
BOBBERS MILL **46** C1
Bobbers Mill Bridge
NG7 . . . .**46** B1
Bobbers Mill Rd NG7 . . . .**46** C1
Boden Dr NG16 . . . .**30** A4
Boden St NG7 . . . .**106** B3
Bodmin Ave NG15 . . . .**10** A3
Bodmin Dr NG8 . . . .**46** A4
Body Rd NG9 . . . .**91** A4
Bohem Rd NG10 . . . .**79** B1
Bold Cl NG6 . . . .**20** C2
Bolero Cl NG8 . . . .**56** C3
Bolingey Way NG15 . . . .**10** A3
Bolsover St NG15 . . . .**3** A1
Bolton Ave NG9 . . . .**81** B2
Bolton Cl NG2 . . . .**76** C1
Bolton Terr NG12 . . . .**65** A2
Bond St Arnold NG5 . . . .**23** C2
Nottingham NG2 . . . .**60** C2
Bonetti Cl NG5 . . . .**36** A3
Boniface Gdns 4 NG5 . . . . . .**22** B3

Bonington Art Gall★ NG1 108 A3
Bonington Dr NG5 24 A1
Bonington Inf Com Sch NG6 31 C4
Bonington Jun Sch NG6 31 C4
Bonington Rd NG3 35 B1
Bonington Theatre★ NG5 23 C2
Bonner Hill NG14 5 B1
Bonner's Rd NG16 28 A2
Bonnington Cl NG6 31 B4
Bonnington Cres NG5 34 A2
Bonny Mead NG12 98 A2
Bonsall St NG10 90 A2
Bonser Cl NG4 50 C1
Booth Cl NG3 108 C3
Borlace Cres NG9 80 A4
Borman Cl NG6 31 A3
Borrowdale Cl NG2 87 C4
Borrowdale Dr NG10 99 C4
Boscowan Ct DE7 27 A2
Bosden Cl NG8 56 A4
Bosley Sq NG9 72 C2
Bostock's La
Risley NG10, DE72 78 B2
Sandiacre NG10 78 C1
Boston St NG1 108 C3
Bosworth Dr NG16 9 C1
Bosworth Way NG10 101 A3
Bosworth Wlk 10 NG2 75 A3
Botany Ave NG3 49 A1
Botany Cl NG11 95 B4
Botany Dr DE7 27 A3
Bothe Cl NG10 100 B4
Bottle La NG1 109 B2
Boulevard Ind Pk NG7 73 B1
Boundary Cres NG9 72 B3
Boundary La NG16 8 A1
Boundary Rd
Beeston NG9 72 B2
West Bridgford NG2 86 B2
Bourne Cl NG9 71 C3
Bourne Mews NG4 63 B4
Bourne Sq DE72 88 A1
Bourne St NG4 63 B4
Bournmoor Ave NG7 94 A3
Bovill St NG7 106 B4
Bowden Dr NG9 83 A4
Bowers Ave 6 NG3 48 B1
Bowes Well Rd DE7 40 C4
Bowland Cl NG3 49 B1
Bowland Rd NG13 66 B2
Bowling Cl DE7 68 A2
Bowlwell Ave NG5 22 A2
Bowness Ave NG6 46 A4
Bowness Cl NG2 77 B1
Bowscale Cl NG2 87 B3
Boxley Dr NG2 85 B2
Boyce Gdns NG3 49 A3
Boycroft Ave NG3 49 A2
Boyd Cl NG5 24 B3
Boynton Dr NG3 49 A3
Bracadale Rd NG5 22 A3
Bracebridge Dr NG8 44 B1
Bracey Rise NG2 86 A1
Bracken Cl Carlton NG4 50 B4
Long Eaton NG10 89 A3
Nottingham NG8 45 A3
Brackendale Ave NG5 24 A2
Brackenfield Dr NG16 16 C1
Brackenfield Specl Sch NG10 89 A3
Bracken Rd NG10 89 A3
Bracknell Cres NG8 46 B3
Bracton Dr NG3 61 A4
Bradbourne Ave NG11 84 C3
Bradbury Gd NG11 95 A1
Bradbury St NG2 61 B2
Bradden Ave NG9 70 A3
Braddock Cl NG7 107 A2
Bradfield Rd NG8 45 A3
Bradgate Cl NG10 79 A2
Bradgate Rd 2 NG7 47 B2
Bradley St NG10 79 B3
Bradman Gdns NG5 35 C4
BRADMORE 103 C1
Bradmore Ave NG11 95 B2
Bradmore Rise NG5 34 A2
Bradshaw St NG10 100 A3
Bradwell Cl NG16 17 A2
Bradwell Dr NG5 22 B2
Braefell Cl NG2 87 C3
Braefield Cl DE7 52 A3
Braemar Ave NG16 16 A3
Braemar Dr NG4 51 C3
Braemar Rd NG6 21 A1
Brailsford Rd 1 NG7 74 A3
Brailsford Way NG9 91 B3
Bramber Gr NG11 94 A1
Bramble Cl Beeston NG9 91 C4
Long Eaton NG10 89 A3
Nottingham NG6 32 B1
Bramble Ct NG4 51 A3
Bramble Dr NG3 49 C2
Bramble Gdns NG8 45 B2
Brambleway NG12 98 C2
BRAMCOTE 70 C1
Bramcote Ave NG9 81 C4
Bramcote CE Prim Sch NG9 71 A2
Bramcote Dr
Beeston NG9 72 A1
Nottingham NG8 56 B1
Bramcote Dr W NG9 71 C1
BRAMCOTE HILLS 71 B4
Bramcote Hills Prim Sch NG9 71 A3
Bramcote Hills Sp & Com Coll NG9 71 A4
Bramcote La
Beeston NG9 81 B3
Nottingham NG8 56 B1
Bramcote L Ctr NG9 70 C3
Bramcote Park Bus & Ent Sch The NG9 70 C3
Bramcote Rd NG9 72 A1
Bramcote St NG7 106 A3
Bramcote Wlk NG7 106 A3
Bramerton Rd NG8 56 B4
Bramhall Rd NG8 56 A4
Bramley Ct NG16 29 A4
Bramley Rd NG8 44 C3
Brampton Ave DE75 14 B4
Brampton Ct NG2 77 B1
Brampton Dr NG9 80 B3
Brancaster Cl NG6 31 C2
Brandish Cres NG11 93 C3
Brandreth Ave NG3 49 A2
Brandreth Dr NG16 16 B2
Brand St NG2 76 B4
Branklene Cl NG16 17 C1
Branksome Wlk 3 NG2 75 B4
Bransdale Cl NG10 100 A4
Bransdale Rd NG11 93 C3
Branston Gdns NG2 85 C2
Branston Wlk NG5 34 A2
Brantford Ave NG7 94 B3
Brassington Cl NG16 16 C1
Braunton Cl NG15 10 B4
Brayton Cres NG6 32 B3
B Rd NG9 83 C4
Breach Rd DE75 14 B2
Breadsall Ct DE7 27 A1
BREASTON 88 C2
Brechin Cl NG5 24 C3
Breck Hill Rd NG3 35 A2
Brecknock Dr NG10 88 C1
Brecks Plantation Nature Reserve★ NG11 93 C2
Breckswood Dr NG11 94 A1
Brecon Cl
4 Long Eaton NG10 88 C2
Nottingham NG8 31 B1
Bredon Cl 5 NG10 88 C2
Breedon St NG10 89 B4
Brendon Ct NG9 71 A2
Brendon Dr
Kimberley NG16 18 A1
Nottingham NG8 57 B3
Brendon Gdns NG8 57 B3
Brendon Gr NG13 66 B3
Brendon Rd NG8 57 B3
Brendon Way NG10 88 C3
Brentcliffe Ave NG3 49 B1
Brentnall Cl NG10 89 A1
Brett Cl NG15 10 C3
Brettsil Dr NG11 95 A1
Brewery St NG16 29 A4
Brewhouse Yd Mus-The Mus of Nottingham Life★ NG7 109 A1
Brewsters Cl NG13 67 A2
Brewsters Rd NG3 49 A2
Brian Clough Way NG9 79 C3
Briar Ave NG10 79 A1
Briarbank Ave NG3 49 B2
Briarbank Wlk NG3 49 B1
Briar Cl Beeston NG9 72 A3
Hucknall NG15 10 C3
Keyworth NG12 104 C4
Briar Ct NG2 75 A3
Briar Gate Cotgrave NG12 98 C2
Long Eaton NG10 89 A4
Briar Rd NG16 16 C2
Briarwood Ave NG3 49 B1
Briarwood Ct NG3 34 C1
Brickenell Rd NG14 5 B1
Brickyard NG15 12 A4
Brickyard Dr NG15 12 A3
Brickyard La NG12 65 C2
Bridge Ave NG9 82 A3
Bridge Ct NG15 11 B3
Bridge Farm La NG7 94 A4
Bridge Gn Wlk 6 NG8 44 C3
Bridge Gr NG2 76 A2
Bridgend Cl NG9 79 C3
Bridge Rd NG8 56 B3
Bridge St Ilkeston DE7 27 A2
Langley Mill NG16 8 A1
Long Eaton NG10 89 C3
Sandiacre NG10 79 B4
Bridgeway Ct NG2 75 C4
Bridgeway Ctr NG2 75 B4
Bridgford Rd NG2 76 B2
Bridgnorth Dr NG7 94 A4
Bridgnorth Way NG9 80 A1
Bridle Rd Beeston NG9 71 A2
Burton Joyce NG14 38 C3
Bridlesmith Gate NG1 109 B2
Bridlington St NG7 47 A1
Bridport Ave 4 NG8 58 B3
Brielen Rd NG12 65 B2
Brierfield Ave NG11 85 A2
Brierley Gn NG4 51 B1
Brightmoor St NG1 108 C3
Bright St Ilkeston DE7 26 C1
Nottingham NG7 106 A3
Brindley Rd NG8 56 A3
Brinkhill Cres NG11 84 B1
Brinsley Cl NG8 45 B3
Brisbane Dr
Nottingham NG5 21 C2
Stapleford NG9 70 A3
Bristol Rd DE7 40 C3
Britannia Ave NG6 32 C3
Britannia Rd NG10 89 C3
Britten Gdns NG3 61 A4
Brixham Rd NG15 10 B3
Brixton Rd NG7 106 A3
Broad Eadow Rd NG6 20 A1
Broadfields NG14 5 B3
Broadgate NG9 72 C1
Broadgate Ave NG9 72 C1
Broadgate La NG9 72 C1
Broadholme St NG7 107 B1
Broadhurst Ave NG6 46 B4
Broadlands NG10 79 A1
Broadleigh Cl NG11 85 B1
Broad Marsh Sh Ctr NG1 109 B2
Broadmead NG14 39 A3
Broad Meer NG12 98 A3
Broad Oak Cl NG3 48 C1
Broad Oak Dr NG9 79 C4
Broad St Long Eaton NG10 89 C1
Nottingham NG1 108 C3
Broadstairs Rd NG9 90 B4
Broadstone Cl NG2 85 B3
Broad Valley Dr NG6 12 C2
Broadway Carlton NG3 62 B4
Heanor DE75 13 C3
Ilkeston DE7 26 C1
Nottingham NG1 109 C2
Broadway E NG4 62 B4
Broadway Media Ctr★ NG1 109 C2
Broad Wlk NG6 32 A1
Broadwood Ct NG9 72 C2
Broadwood Rd NG5 22 C2
Brockdale Gdns NG12 104 B4
Brockhall Rise DE75 14 B3
Brockhole Cl NG2 87 C3
Brockhurst Gdns NG3 61 A4
Brocklewood Inf Sch NG8 45 A2
Brocklewood Jun Sch NG8 45 A2
Brockley Rd NG2 77 A1
Brockwood Cres NG12 104 B4
Bromfield Cl NG3 50 A1
Bromley Cl NG6 31 C4
Bromley Pl NG1 109 A2
Bromley Rd NG2 86 A4
Brompton Cl NG5 22 B4
Brompton Way NG11 85 B1
Bronte Cl NG10 88 C1
Bronte Ct NG7 106 C4
Brook Ave NG5 24 C2
Brook Cl Eastwood NG16 16 C3
Long Eaton NG10 101 A3
Nottingham NG6 31 C4
Brook Cotts DE7 27 A1
Brook Ct NG16 14 C4
Brookdale Ct NG5 34 B3
Brooke St Ilkeston DE7 53 C4
Sandiacre NG10 79 A3
Brookfield Ave NG15 11 B3
Brookfield Cl NG12 65 A2
Brookfield Ct 8 NG2 75 B4
Brookfield Gdns NG5 24 B1
Brookfield Rd NG5 24 B1
Brookfield Way DE75 14 C3
Brook Gdns NG5 24 B2
Brookhill Cres NG8 56 C1
Brookhill Dr NG8 56 C1
Brookhill Leys Inf Sch NG16 16 B3
Brookhill Leys Jun Sch NG16 16 B4
Brookhill Leys Rd NG16 15 C3
Brookhill St NG9 79 C4
Brook La NG2 77 B1
Brookland Dr NG9 81 C3
Brooklands Ave DE75 14 A4
Brooklands Cres NG4 51 B3
Brooklands Dr NG4 51 B3
Brooklands Prim Sch NG10 89 C1
Brooklands Rd NG3 49 C1
Brooklyn Ave NG14 38 C3
Brooklyn Cl NG6 32 B3
Brooklyn Rd NG6 32 B3
Brook Rd NG9 72 B2
Brooksby La NG11 84 B1
Brookside Eastwood NG16 9 A2
Hucknall NG15 11 C3
Brookside Ave NG8 71 C4
Brookside Cl NG10 89 A2
Brookside Gdns NG11 95 A2
Brookside Rd NG11 95 A2
Brook St Hucknall NG15 2 C1
Nottingham NG1 108 C3
Brookthorpe Way NG11 84 C2
Brook Vale Rd NG16 15 A4
Brook View Ct NG12 104 B1
Brook View Dr NG12 104 B2
Brookwood Cres NG4 50 A1
Broom Cl NG14 5 B3
Broomfield Cl NG10 78 C3
Broomhill Ave DE7 53 B4
Broomhill Jun Sch NG15 11 C3
Broomhill Pk View NG15 12 A3
Broomhill Rd
Hucknall NG15 11 C2
Kimberley NG16 29 B4
Nottingham NG6 32 B4
Broom Rd NG14 5 B3
Broom Wlk NG4 49 C2
Brora Rd NG6 21 B1
Broughton Cl DE7 40 B4
Broughton Dr NG8 58 A1
Broughton St NG9 72 B1
Brownes Rd NG13 67 C3
Browning Cl NG5 23 B1
Brownlow Dr NG5 22 A3
Brown Md Rd NG8 46 C2
Browns Croft NG6 32 B1
Brown's Flats NG16 18 A1
Brown's Rd NG10 90 A2
Brown St NG7 47 A1
Broxton Rise NG8 31 C1
Broxtowe Ave
Kimberley NG16 28 B4
Nottingham NG8 46 A4
Broxtowe Coll
Beeston & Stapleford NG9 82 A3
Kimberley NG16 29 A4
Stapleford NG9 69 C1
Broxtowe Ctry Pk★ NG8 30 C1
Broxtowe Dr NG15 2 C3
Broxtowe Hall Cl NG8 45 B4
Broxtowe La NG8 45 B4
Broxtowe Pk Bsns Ctr NG8 44 C4
Broxtowe St 4 NG5 48 A4
Bruce Cl NG2 75 C4
Bruce Dr NG2 75 C1
Brunel Ave NG16 9 C1
Brunswick Dr NG9 80 A3
Brushfield St NG7 46 C1
Brussels Terr 1 DE7 40 C3
Brusty Pl NG14 38 C3
Buckfast Way NG2 77 A1
Buckingham Ave NG15 3 A2
Buckingham Ct NG10 78 C1
Buckingham Dr DE75 13 A4
Buckingham Rd
Arnold NG5 34 C3
Sandiacre NG10 78 C1
Buckingham Way NG16 18 C1
Bucklee Dr NG14 5 A3
Bucklow Cl NG8 46 B3
Buckminster Rd DE7 52 A2
Budby Rise NG15 3 A1
BULCOTE 39 B4
Bulcote Dr NG14 38 B1
Bulcote Rd NG11 84 A1
Bulgrave Mews NG2 85 B1
Bullace Rd NG3 48 C1
Bull Cl Rd NG7 74 B1
Buller St DE7 53 B4
Buller Terr 2 NG5 34 B1
Bullfinch Rd NG6 32 B2
Bullins Cl NG5 23 A3
Bullivant St NG3 108 C4
BULWELL 31 B4
Bulwell Bsns Ctr NG6 20 B1
Bulwell Hall Pk Nature Reserve★ NG6 20 C4
Bulwell High Rd NG6 20 C1
Bulwell La NG6 32 B2
Bulwell Sta NG6 32 A4
Bulwer Rd NG7 106 B3
Bunbury St NG2 75 C3
Bunny La NG12 104 A2
Bunting Cl DE7 52 A4
Buntings La NG4 50 A1
Bunting St 3 NG7 74 A3
Burford Prim Sch NG5 34 A4
Burford Rd NG7 47 A2
Burford St NG5 23 C2
Burgass Rd NG3 49 B1
Burge Cl NG2 75 B4
Burgh Hall Cl NG9 91 B4
Burhill NG12 98 C2
Burke St NG7 106 C3
Burleigh Cl NG4 51 A1
Burleigh Rd NG2 86 C4
Burleigh Sq NG9 81 B2
Burleigh St 1 DE7 41 A3
Burlington Ave NG5 33 C1
Burlington Rd
Carlton NG4 51 A2
Nottingham NG5 34 A1
Burnaby St NG6 32 B2
Burnbank Cl NG2 87 C3
Burnbreck Gdns NG8 56 C2
Burndale Wlk NG5 21 C2
Burnham Ave NG9 82 B2
Burnham St NG5 48 A4
Burnham Way NG2 109 B1
Burnor Pool NG14 5 B2
Burns Ave NG7 106 C4
Burnside Dr NG9 71 B3
Burnside Gn NG8 56 B4
Burnside Gr NG12 97 C3
Burnside Rd
Nottingham NG8 56 B4

Burnside Rd *continued*
West Bridgford NG2 86 A3
Burns St Heanor DE75 13 B4
Ilkeston DE7 40 C2
Nottingham NG7 106 C4
Burnt House Rd DE75 13 B3
Burnt Oak Cl NG16 30 B1
Burnwood Dr NG8 56 B3
Burr La 12 DE7 41 A3
Burrows Ave NG9 72 B3
Burrows Cres NG9 72 B3
Burrows Ct NG3 61 A3
Burtness Rd NG7 93 C3
Burton Ave NG4 49 B1
Burton Cl NG4 51 B2
Burton Dr NG9 81 B2
BURTON JOYCE 38 C2
Burton Joyce Prim Sch NG14 39 A2
Burton Joyce Sta NG14 38 C1
Burton Manderfield Ct 4 NG2 75 B4
Burton Rd NG4 51 B2
Burton St Heanor DE75 13 C4
Nottingham NG1 108 B3
Burwell St NG7 106 B4
Bush Cl NG5 22 A2
Bushy Cl NG10 99 C4
Bute Ave NG7 107 B2
Butler Ave NG12 65 B3
Butlers Cl NG15 12 A3
Butlers Hill Inf Sch NG15 11 C3
Buttermead Cl NG9 69 C4
Buttermere Cl
Long Eaton NG10 88 C4
West Bridgford NG2 77 C1
Buttermere Ct 1 NG5 48 A4
Buttermere Dr NG9 71 C2
Butterton Cl DE7 41 B1
Butt Rd NG13 67 C2
Butts Cl DE7 53 B2
Butt St NG10 79 A3
Buxton Ave Carlton NG4 50 B3
Heanor DE75 14 A1
Buxton Ct DE7 40 B3
Buxton Gn DE75 14 A1
Byard La NG1 109 B2
Bye Pass Rd NG9 81 C1
Byfield Cl NG7 106 B4
Byford Cl NG3 48 C4
Byley Rd NG8 55 C3
Byrne Ct NG5 35 C3
Byron Ave NG10 79 A1
Byron Cres NG16 28 A2
Byron Ct
7 Nottingham NG2 60 C2
Stapleford NG9 70 A4
Byron Est NG5 24 B1
Byron Gr NG5 34 A1
Byron Rd NG2 76 B1
Byron St Arnold NG5 34 B4
Hucknall NG15 11 B4
Ilkeston DE7 41 A3

C

Caddaw Ave NG15 11 B3
Cadlan Cl NG5 22 B1
Cadlan Ct 5 NG5 22 B1
Caernarvon Pl NG9 81 A2
Caincross Rd NG8 44 B1
Cairngorm Dr NG5 22 C4
Cairns Cl NG5 33 B3
Cairnsmore Cl NG10 88 C3
Cairns St NG1 108 B3
Cairo St NG7 47 A3
Caister Rd NG11 94 A2
Caithness Ct 9 NG5 47 C3
Calcroft Cl NG8 46 A4
Caldbeck Cl NG2 77 B1
Caldbeck Ct NG9 81 A2
Caldbeck Wlk 1 NG5 22 C1
Calderdale NG8 55 C1
Calderdale Dr NG10 99 C4
Calderhall Gdns 2 NG5 23 A2
Calder Wlk 10 NG6 20 C1
Caldon Gn NG6 21 A4
Caledon Rd NG5 33 C1
Calladine Cl DE75 13 B4
Callaway Cl NG8 56 C3
Calstock Rd NG5 34 C3
Calveley Rd NG8 44 C2
Calver Cl NG8 58 A2
Calvert Cl NG16 7 C1
CALVERTON 5 C2
Calverton Ave NG4 49 C3
Calverton Cl NG9 90 C4
Calverton Dr NG8 44 B4
Calverton Folk Mus★ NG14 5 A2
Calverton Forum L Ctr NG4 50 A3
Calverton Rd NG5 24 B4
Cambell Gdns NG5 25 A3
Camberley Ct NG6 20 B2
Camberley Rd NG6 20 B2
Camborne Dr NG8 46 A4
Cambria Mews NG3 48 A1
Cambridge Cres NG9 69 C4
Cambridge Gdns NG5 35 C3
Cambridge Rd
Nottingham NG8 57 B2
West Bridgford NG2 86 C4
Cambridge St NG4 50 C2
Camdale Cl NG9 81 A4
Camden Cl NG2 60 C2
Camelia Ave NG11 93 B3
Camelot Ave NG5 47 B3
Camelot Cres NG11 95 A2
Camelot St NG11 95 A2
Cameo Cl NG4 63 A4
Cameron St NG5 48 A4
Camomile Cl NG5 21 C1
Camomile Gdns 9 NG7 46 C1
Campbell Dr NG4 50 A2
Campbell Gr NG3 108 C3
Campbell St
Langley Mill NG16 8 A2
Nottingham NG3 108 C3
Campden Gn NG7 94 A4
Campion St NG5 23 C2
Campion Way NG13 66 C2
Camrose Cl NG8 45 A2
Canal Side NG9 83 A1
Canal St Ilkeston DE7 41 B3
Long Eaton NG10 89 B3
Nottingham NG1 109 B1
Sandiacre NG10 79 B3
Canberra Cl NG9 70 B3
Canberra Cres NG2 85 C1
Canberra Gdns NG2 85 C1
Candleby Cl NG12 98 B3
Candleby Ct NG12 98 B3
Candleby La NG12 98 B3
Candle Mdw NG2 62 B3
Canning Circ NG7 106 C3
Canning Mews 1 DE7 41 A1
Cannock Way NG10 90 C1
Cannon St NG5 34 A1
Canonbie Cl NG5 24 C3
Canon Cl DE7 27 A3
Cantabury Ave NG7 47 A2
Cantelupe Rd DE7 41 B2
Canterbury Cl NG16 30 B1
Canterbury Ct NG1 108 A4
Canterbury Rd NG8 58 B3
Cantley Ave NG4 50 C4
Cantrell Prim Sch NG6 21 A1
Cantrell Rd NG6 21 A1
Canver Cl NG8 56 A4
Canwick Cl NG8 56 A3
Capenwray Gdns 3 NG5 23 A2
Capitol Ct 1 NG8 57 B3
Caporn Cl NG6 32 A3
Capt Ball Meml Homes NG7 107 A1
Cardale Rd NG3 61 B4
Cardiff St 2 NG3 61 A3
Cardinal Cl NG3 60 C4
Cardington Cl NG5 21 C3
Cardwell St NG7 47 A2
Carew Rd NG7 94 A4
Carey Rd NG6 21 A2
Carisbrooke Ave
Beeston NG9 72 C2
Carlton NG4 51 C3
Nottingham NG3 48 A3
Carisbrooke Dr NG3 48 A3
Carlile Rd NG4 50 C2
Carlin Cl DE72 88 A2
Carlingford Rd NG15 2 C2
Carlin St NG6 20 C1
Carlisle Ave NG6 21 A1
Carlswark Gdns NG5 22 A3
CARLTON 50 B3
Carlton Bsns & Tech Ctr NG4 51 A1
Carlton Central Inf & Jun Schs NG4 50 B2
Carlton Central Jun Sch NG4 50 B2
Carlton Cl DE75 7 B1
Carlton Digby Specl Sch NG3 36 A1
Carlton Fold 6 NG2 61 A1
Carlton Forum L Ctr NG4 50 A3
Carlton Hill NG4 50 A1
Carlton le Willows Comp Sch NG4 51 B3
Carlton Mews NG4 50 A1
Carlton Rd
Long Eaton NG10 100 A3
Nottingham NG3 60 C3
Carlton Sq NG4 50 C1
Carlton St NG1 109 C2
Carlton Sta NG4 51 A1
Carlton Vale Cl NG4 50 B3
Carlyle Pl DE75 6 B1
Carlyle Rd NG2 76 A1
Carlyle St DE75 6 B1
Carman Cl NG16 18 B2
Carmel Gdns NG5 35 A4
Carnarvon Cl NG13 67 A3
Carnarvon Dr NG14 39 B3
Carnarvon Gr
Carlton, Gedling NG4 51 A3
Carlton, Thorneywood NG4 50 B2
Carnarvon Pl NG13 66 C2
Carnarvon Rd NG2 86 B4
Carnarvon St NG4 63 B4
Carnforth Cl NG9 79 C3
Carnforth Ct 1 NG5 23 A2
Carnwood Rd NG5 33 B3
Caroline Ct DE7 53 B4
Carradale Cl NG5 25 A2
Carrfield Ave NG10 90 B3
CARRINGTON 47 C4
Carrington Ct NG5 48 A3
Carrington La NG14 5 C3
Carrington Prim Sch NG5 47 C3
Carrington St NG1 109 B1
Carroll Gdns NG2 75 B3
Cartbridge NG12 98 B2
Carter Ave
Radcliffe on T NG12 65 C2
Ruddington NG11 102 C4
Carter Rd NG9 80 C1
Carters Wood Dr NG16 31 A1
Carver St NG7 47 A2
Carwood Rd NG9 71 C3
Casper Ct 10 NG5 22 B2
Castellan Rise NG5 23 A2
Casterton Rd NG5 22 C1
Castlebridge NG2 74 C4
Castle Bridge Rd NG2 74 C4
Castle Bvd NG7 107 C1
Castle Cl NG14 5 A2
Castlefields NG2 75 B4
Castle Gate NG1 109 B2
Castle Gdns NG7 107 B1
Castle Gr NG7 109 A1
Castle Marina Pk NG2 74 C4
Castle Marina Rd NG2 74 C4
Castle Mdw Rd NG2 109 A1
Castle Mdw Ret Pk NG7 107 C1
Castle Mus & Art Gall★ NG7 109 A1
Castle Pk NG2 75 A4
Castle Pl NG1 109 A2
Castle Quay NG7 109 A1
Castle Rd NG1 109 A2
Castlerigg Cl NG2 87 B3
Castle St Eastwood NG16 16 B3
Nottingham NG2 61 A2
Castleton Ave
Arnold NG5 35 A4
Carlton NG4 50 C3
Ilkeston DE7 26 C3
Castleton Cl
Hucknall NG15 10 B4
8 Nottingham NG2 75 A3
Castleton Ct NG6 31 A4
Castle View Aldercar NG16 7 B2
West Bridgford NG2 85 C4
Caterham Cl NG8 44 B1
Catfoot La NG4 25 C2
Catherine Ave DE7 53 A4
Catherine Cl NG6 20 B1
Catkin Dr NG16 17 A2
Catlow Wlk 4 NG5 23 A2
Cator Cl NG4 36 B1
Cator La NG9 81 C3
Cator La N NG9 81 C4
Catriona Cres NG5 24 B3
Catt Cl NG9 91 A3
Catterley Hill Rd NG3 61 C4
Cattle Mkt Rd NG2 75 C4
Catton Rd NG5 24 B2
Caudale Ct NG2 77 B1
Caulton St NG7 106 B4
Caunton Ave NG3 48 C3
Causeway Mews 4 NG2 75 A3
Cavan Ct 3 NG2 75 B3
Cavell Cl NG11 93 C4
Cavell Ct NG7 73 C4
Cavendish Ave
Carlton NG4 50 B4
Nottingham NG5 34 B1
Cavendish Cl NG15 12 A3
Cavendish Cres
Carlton NG4 50 A4
Stapleford NG9 69 C4
Cavendish Cres N NG7 107 C2
Cavendish Cres S NG7 107 C1
Cavendish Dr NG4 50 C2
Cavendish Pl NG9 82 B4
Cavendish Rd
Carlton NG4 50 A3
Ilkeston DE7 53 A4
Ilkeston DE7 53 B4
Long Eaton NG10 89 B4
Cavendish Rd E NG7 107 C2
Cavendish Rd W NG7 107 C2
Cavendish St Arnold NG5 23 C2
Nottingham NG7 74 A2
Cavendish Vale NG5 34 B1
Cawdron Wlk NG7 94 A4
Cawston Gdns 3 NG6 20 C2
Caxmere Dr NG8 57 A3
Caxton Cl NG4 51 B1
Caxton Rd NG5 47 C3
Caythorpe Cres NG5 34 A1
Caythorpe Rise NG5 34 A1
Cecil St NG7 107 B1
Cedar Ave Beeston NG9 72 C1
Long Eaton NG10 100 B3
Nuthall NG16 31 A2
Cedar Cl NG10 69 A1
Cedar Ct NG9 72 C1
Cedar Dr NG12 104 B2
Cedar Gr Arnold NG5 24 C2
Hucknall NG15 11 C3
Nottingham NG8 57 A2
Cedarland Cres NG16 31 A2
Cedar Pk DE7 40 C1
Cedar Rd Beeston NG9 82 A3
Nottingham NG7 47 B2
Cedars The NG5 34 B2
Cedar Tree Rd NG5 22 C3
Celandine Cl NG5 21 C1
Celandine Gdns NG13 66 B2
Celia Dr NG4 50 B1
Cemetery Rd NG9 70 A1
Central Ave Arnold NG5 24 A1
Beeston, Chilwell NG9 81 C4
Beeston NG9 72 B2
Hucknall NG15 11 B4
Nottingham, Mapperley NG3 35 B2
Nottingham, New Basford NG7, NG5 47 B3
Sandiacre NG10 79 A4
Stapleford NG9 70 B2
West Bridgford NG2 76 B2
Central Ave S NG5 24 A1
Central Ct NG7 74 B3
Central St 3 NG3 60 C4
Central Wlk NG15 2 C1
Centre Way NG12 64 C3
Centurion Way NG11 74 C2
Cernan Ct NG6 31 A3
Cerne Cl NG7 94 A3
Chaceley Way NG11 84 C1
Chaddesden The NG3 48 A1
Chad Gdns NG5 22 B4
Chadwick Rd NG7 46 C1
Chain La NG7 74 A3
Chalfield Cl NG11 93 C3
Chalfont Dr NG8 58 A4
Chalons Cl DE7 41 A3
Chalons Way DE7 41 A2
Chamberlain Cl NG11 93 B3
Chambers Ave DE7 41 C1
Champion Ave DE7 26 A1
Chancery Ct NG11 84 C4
Chancery The NG9 71 B1
Chandos Ave NG4 51 B2
Chandos St Carlton NG4 51 B1
Nottingham NG3 48 C1
Chantrey Cl NG9 81 C2
Chantrey Rd NG2 76 A1
Chantry Cl
Kimberley NG16 29 B3
Long Eaton NG10 99 C2
Chapel Bar NG1 109 A2
Chapel Ct DE7 27 A2
Chapel Ho 3 DE7 40 C2
Chapel La Arnold NG5 23 C2
Bingham NG13 67 A4
Cotgrave NG12 98 B3
Chapel Mews Ct NG9 71 A2
Chapel Pl NG16 29 A4
Chapel Quarter Bsns Development NG1 109 A2
Chapel St Beeston NG9 71 A2
Eastwood NG16 16 A3
Heanor DE75 14 B2
Hucknall NG15 2 C1
8 Ilkeston DE7 41 A3
Kimberley NG16 29 A4
Long Eaton NG10 90 A1
Ruddington NG11 102 C4
Chapman Ct NG8 45 C1
Chapter Dr NG16 29 B3
Chard St NG7 47 A4
Charlbury Ct NG9 55 C2
Charlbury Rd NG8 57 C3
Charlecote Dr NG8 56 B1
Charlecote Pk Dr NG2 85 B2
Charles Ave
Beeston, Chilwell NG9 81 B1
Beeston NG9 72 C3
Eastwood NG16 16 C3
Sandiacre NG10 79 A4
Stapleford NG9 70 B2
Charles Cl Carlton NG4 51 A4
Ilkeston DE7 53 C4
Charles Pk NG6 31 C3
Charles St Arnold NG5 23 C1
Hucknall NG15 2 C1
Long Eaton NG10 100 C4
Ruddington NG11 95 B1
Charlesworth Ave NG7 46 C2
Charlock Cl NG5 21 C1
Charlock Gdns NG13 66 C1
Charlotte Cl NG5 23 C4
Charlotte Gr NG9 71 C3
Charlton Ave NG10 90 B3
Charlton Gr NG9 82 B3
Charnock Ave NG8 58 B1
Charnwood Ave
Beeston NG9 82 A4
Keyworth NG12 104 B2
Long Eaton NG10 100 A2
Sandiacre NG10 78 C2
Charnwood Gr
Bingham NG13 66 C2
Hucknall NG15 2 A1
West Bridgford NG2 76 A1
Charnwood La NG5 35 B4
Charter Pk DE7 40 C1
Chartwell Ave NG11 95 A1
Chartwell Gr NG3 36 A3
Chase Pk NG2 61 B1
Chatham St NG1 108 B4

Chatsworth Ave
Beeston NG9 . . . . **91** B4
Carlton NG4 . . . . **50** C3
Long Eaton NG10 . . . . . . **101** C4
Nottingham NG7 . . . . **47** A4
Radcliffe on T NG12 . . . . . **65** B3
Chatsworth Cl NG10 . . . . **79** A2
Chatsworth Cl NG15 . . . **11** B4
Chatsworth Dr NG15 . . . **11** B4
Chatsworth Rd NG2 . . . . **77** B2
Chatsworth Way DE75 . . . **13** A4
Chaucer Int DE7 . . . . **41** A3
Chaucer St Ilkeston DE7 . . **41** A3
Nottingham NG1 . . . . **108** A3
Chaworth Ave NG16 . . . . **18** B3
Chaworth Rd
Bingham NG13 . . . . **66** C2
Carlton NG4 . . . . **63** A4
West Bridgford NG2 . . . . . **86** A4
Cheadle Cl
Nottingham, Bilborough
NG8 . . . . **44** B2
Nottingham, Portchester
NG3 . . . . **49** C4
Cheapside NG1 . . . . **109** B2
Cheddar Rd NG11 . . . . . . **94** A2
Chedington Ave NG3 . . . . **36** B4
Chediston Vale NG5 . . . . **22** C2
Chedworth Cl 1 NG3 . . . **61** A3
Chelmsford Rd NG7 . . . . **47** A4
Chelmsford Terr NG7 . . . **47** A4
Chelsea Cl NG16 . . . . **30** C1
Chelsea St NG7 . . . . **47** A3
Cheltenham Cl NG9 . . . . **90** B3
Cheltenham St NG6 . . . . **32** C2
Chennel Nook NG12 . . . . **98** C2
Chepstow Rd NG11 . . . . . **94** A2
Cherhill Cl NG11 . . . . **93** C1
Cheriton Dr DE7 . . . . **26** A1
Cherry Ave NG15 . . . . . . **11** C3
Cherry Cl Arnold NG5 . . . . **23** C2
Breaston DE72 . . . . **88** A2
Nottingham NG5 . . . . **22** C1
Cherry Hill NG12 . . . . . . **104** C3
Cherry Orch NG3 . . . . **98** A3
Cherry Orch Mount NG5 . **22** C1
Cherry St NG13 . . . . **67** B2
Cherry Tree Cl
Ilkeston DE7 . . . . **52** B4
Radcliffe on T NG12 . . . . . **65** C1
Risley DE72 . . . . **78** B2
Cherry Tree La NG12 . . . **87** A1
Cherry Wood Dr NG8 . . . **45** C1
Cherrywood Gdns NG3 . . **49** B2
Chertsey Cl NG3 . . . . **49** A3
Cherwell Cl NG6 . . . . **31** A4
Chesham Dr Beeston NG9 . **71** A4
Nottingham NG5 . . . . **47** C3
Chesil Ave 2 NG8 . . . . . **58** B3
Chesil Cotts 3 NG8 . . . . **58** B3
Cheslyn Dr NG8 . . . . **46** A2
Chesterfield Ave
Bingham NG13 . . . . **67** A3
Carlton NG4 . . . . **50** B4
Long Eaton NG10 . . . . **90** B1
Chesterfield Ct NG4 . . . . **36** B1
Chesterfield Dr NG14 . . . **39** B3
Chesterfield St NG4 . . . . **50** B1
Chester Gn NG9 . . . . **90** A4
Chesterman Cl NG16 . . . . **27** C2
Chester Rd NG3 . . . . **61** C3
Chestnut Ave
Beeston NG9 . . . . **82** B4
Bingham NG13 . . . . **67** A2
Nottingham NG3 . . . . **49** C4
Chestnut Bank 2 DE75 . . **13** B3
Chestnut Dr NG16 . . . . . . **29** C4
Chestnut Gr Arnold NG5 . . **24** B2
Burton Joyce NG14 . . . . . . **39** A2
Carlton NG4 . . . . **51** A3
Hucknall NG15 . . . . **11** C2
Nottingham NG3 . . . . **48** A1
Radcliffe on T NG12 . . . . . **65** A3
Sandiacre NG10 . . . . **68** C1
West Bridgford NG2 . . . . . **75** C1
Chestnut Rd NG16 . . . . . . **7** B1
Chestnuts The
Carlton NG4 . . . . **51** C3
Long Eaton NG10 . . . . **88** C2
Nottingham NG3 . . . . **49** A3
Radcliffe on T NG12 . . . . . **64** C2

Chettles Ind Est NG8 . . . **58** B3
Chetwin Rd NG8 . . . . **56** B3
Chetwynd Rd
Beeston, Chilwell NG9 . . . . **81** B1
Beeston, Toton NG9 . . . . . **90** C4
Chetwynd Road Prim Sch
NG9 . . . . **90** C4
Cheverton Ct 7 NG3 . . . . **48** A1
Chevin Gdns 12 NG5 . . . **22** B3
Cheviot Cl NG5 . . . . **22** C4
Cheviot Dr NG6 . . . . **20** A2
Cheviot Rd NG10 . . . . **88** C3
Chewton Ave NG16 . . . . . **16** B3
Chewton St NG16 . . . . . . **16** B3
Cheyny Cl NG2 . . . . **75** B3
Chichester Cl
Ilkeston DE7 . . . . **41** B2
Nottingham NG5 . . . . **21** C1
Chichester Dr NG12 . . . . . **98** A4
Chidlow Rd NG8 . . . . **44** B1
Chigwell Cl NG8 . . . . **30** C1
Chillon Way NG15 . . . . . . **10** B4
Chiltern Cl NG5 . . . . **22** C4
Chiltern Gdns NG10 . . . . . **88** C3
Chiltern Way NG5 . . . . . . **22** C1
Chilton Dr NG16 . . . . **18** B1
Chilvers Cl NG5 . . . . **22** B1
CHILWELL **81** C4
Chilwell Coll House Jun
Sch NG9 . . . . **81** C3
Chilwell Comp Sch NG9 . **81** C1
Chilwell Ct NG6 . . . . **21** B1
Chilwell La NG9 . . . . **81** B4
Chilwell Olympia NG9 . . **81** C1
Chilwell Rd NG9 . . . . **82** B4
Chilwell Ret Pk NG9 . . . . **90** C4
Chilwell St NG7 . . . . **107** B1
Chine Gdns NG2 . . . . **85** B3
Chingford Rd NG8 . . . . . . **44** C2
Chippendale St NG7 . . . **107** B1
Chippenham Rd NG5 . . . . **23** A1
Chisbury Gn NG11 . . . . . . **93** C1
Chisholm Way NG5 . . . . . **33** B4
Christchurch Rd NG15 . . **10** B2
Christina Ave NG6 . . . . . . **32** A2
Christina Cres NG6 . . . . . **32** A2
Christine Cl NG15 . . . . **3** B3
Christopher Cl NG8 . . . . . **57** A4
Christ the King RC Comp
Sch NG5 . . . . **24** C1
Chrysalis Way NG16 . . . . **8** A1
Church Ave Arnold NG5 . . . **23** C1
Long Eaton NG10 . . . . **99** C2
Nottingham NG7 . . . . **107** B1
Church Cl Arnold NG5 . . . . **23** C1
Bingham NG13 . . . . **67** B3
Nottingham NG3 . . . . **108** B4
Radcliffe on T NG12 . . . . . **64** C2
Trowell NG9 . . . . **54** A2
Church Cres Arnold NG5 . . **23** B1
Beeston NG9 . . . . **80** C1
Church Croft NG2 . . . . . . **76** B2
Churchdale Ave NG9 . . . . **70** A3
Church Dr Arnold NG5 . . . . **23** C1
Hucknall NG15 . . . . **2** C1
Ilkeston DE7 . . . . **26** B2
Keyworth NG12 . . . . **104** C3
Nottingham NG5 . . . . **47** C3
Sandiacre NG10 . . . . **69** A1
West Bridgford NG2 . . . . . **76** B1
Church Dr E NG5 . . . . **23** C1
Church Drive Prim Sch
NG5 . . . . **23** C1
Churchfield Ct NG5 . . . . . **22** B3
Churchfield La NG7 . . . . . **106** A4
Churchfield Terr NG7 . . . . **46** C4
Church Gr NG7 . . . . **107** A1
Church Hill NG16 . . . . **29** A4
Churchill Cl NG5 . . . . **35** A4
Churchill Dr
Ruddington NG11 . . . . **95** A1
Stapleford NG9 . . . . **70** A2
Churchill Pk NG4 . . . . **62** A1
Church La Arnold NG5 . . . . **24** A3
Beeston NG9 . . . . **91** C3
Bingham NG13 . . . . **67** B3
Cossall NG16 . . . . **42** A3
Cotgrave NG12 . . . . **98** A3
Hucknall NG15 . . . . **3** A3
Nottingham NG6 . . . . **21** A1
Stanton-by-D DE7 . . . . **68** B3

Church La continued
Stapleford NG9 . . . . **69** C1
Church Mdw NG14 . . . . . . **5** B2
Church Mews 1 NG2 . . . **75** C3
Churchmoor Ct NG5 . . . . **23** C3
Churchmoor La NG5 . . . . **24** A3
Church Rd
Bestwood Village NG6 . . . . **12** C2
Burton Joyce NG14 . . . . . . **39** A2
Nottingham NG3 . . . . **108** C4
Churchside Gdns NG7 . . . **46** C2
Church Sq
1 Heanor DE75 . . . . **14** A3
Nottingham NG7 . . . . **107** A1
Church St Arnold NG5 . . . . **24** A2
Beeston, Bramcote NG9 . . . **71** A2
Beeston NG9 . . . . **82** B4
Bingham NG13 . . . . **67** B2
Carlton NG4 . . . . **50** C1
Eastwood NG16 . . . . **16** A4
Ilkeston DE7 . . . . **26** C2
Nottingham NG7 . . . . **107** A1
Nottingham, Old Basford
NG6 . . . . **46** C4
Ruddington NG11 . . . . **95** B1
Sandiacre NG10 . . . . **69** A1
Stapleford NG9 . . . . **70** A1
Church View Carlton NG4 . . **51** A3
Ilkeston DE7 . . . . **40** C1
Church View Cl NG5 . . . . **22** C3
Church Wlk Carlton NG4 . . **50** C1
Eastwood NG16 . . . . **16** A4
Stapleford NG9 . . . . **70** A1
Churnet CI NG11 . . . . **84** A2
CINDERHILL **31** C2
Cinderhill Gr NG4 . . . . . . **50** C4
Cinderhill Rd NG6 . . . . . . **31** C3
Cinderhill Wlk NG6 . . . . . **31** C4
Cirrus Dr NG16 . . . . **18** B1
Citadel St NG7 . . . . **106** A3
City Gd (Nottingham Forest
FC) The NG2 . . . . **76** A3
City Link NG1, NG2 . . . . . . **61** A1
City of Caves ★ NG1 . . . **109** B2
City of Nottingham Tennis
Ctr NG7 . . . . **73** B2
City Rd Beeston NG9 . . . . . **82** C4
Nottingham NG7 . . . . **73** C3
City The NG9 . . . . **82** C4
Clandon Dr NG5 . . . . **47** C4
Clanfield Rd NG8 . . . . **44** C1
Clapham St NG7 . . . . **106** A3
Clapton La NG7 . . . . **94** A4
Clara Mount Rd DE75 . . . **14** B3
Clarborough Dr NG5 . . . . **35** B4
Clare Cl NG6 . . . . **32** C2
Clarehaven NG9 . . . . **80** A3
Claremont Ave
Beeston NG9 . . . . **71** B1
Hucknall NG15 . . . . **11** B3
Claremont Dr NG11 . . . . . **85** B1
Claremont Prim Sch
NG5 . . . . **47** C3
Claremont Rd NG5 . . . . . . **47** C3
Clarence Rd Beeston NG9 . **81** C1
Long Eaton NG10 . . . . . . **100** B4
Clarence St NG3 . . . . **60** C3
Clarendon Ct 8 NG5 . . . . **47** C2
Clarendon Pk NG5 . . . . . . **47** C2
Clarendon Sixth Form Coll
NG1 . . . . **108** A3
Clarendon St NG1 . . . . . . **108** A3
Clare St NG1 . . . . **108** B3
Clare Valley NG7 . . . . **108** A3
Clarewood Gr NG11 . . . . . **94** A1
Clarges St NG6 . . . . **32** A4
Clarke Ave Arnold NG5 . . . **24** A2
Heanor DE75 . . . . **13** A4
Clarke Dr NG10 . . . . **99** C2
Clarke Rd NG2 . . . . **74** A4
Clarke's La NG9 . . . . **81** C2
Clarkson Dr NG9 . . . . **83** A4
Claude St NG7 . . . . **74** A3
Claxton St DE75 . . . . **13** B4
Claxton Terr 2 DE75 . . . . **13** B4
Clay Ave NG3 . . . . **35** B1
Claye St NG10 . . . . **90** A1
Clayfield Cl NG6 . . . . **31** B4
Claygate NG3 . . . . **49** B1
Clay La NG7 . . . . **14** A4
Claypole Rd 16 NG7 . . . . **47** A1

Clayton Ct NG7 . . . . **106** B3
Clayton Gr DE75 . . . . **6** A2
Claytons Dr 11 NG7 . . . . **74** A4
Clayton's Wharf 12 NG7 . **74** A4
Clether Rd NG8 . . . . **56** B4
Cleve Ave NG9 . . . . **80** A1
Cleveland Ave NG10 . . . . **90** B3
Cleveland Cl NG7 . . . . . . **106** A3
Cleveleys Rd NG9 . . . . . . **80** A1
Clevely Way NG11 . . . . . . **84** A1
Cliff Bvd NG16 . . . . **18** A1
Cliff Cres NG12 . . . . **65** A3
Cliff Dr NG12 . . . . **65** A3
Cliffe Hill Ave NG9 . . . . . **69** C1
Cliffgrove Ave NG9 . . . . . **81** C4
Cliffmere Wlk NG11 . . . . . **93** C3
Clifford Ave NG9 . . . . **72** B2
Clifford Cl
Keyworth NG12 . . . . **104** C3
Long Eaton NG10 . . . . **99** C2
Clifford Ct NG7 . . . . **106** B3
Clifford St
Long Eaton NG10 . . . . **90** A1
Nottingham NG7 . . . . **106** B3
Cliff Rd Carlton NG4 . . . . . **62** B4
Nottingham NG1 . . . . **109** C2
Radcliffe on T NG12 . . . . . **64** C3
Cliff The NG6 . . . . **31** C2
Cliff Way NG12 . . . . **65** A3
CLIFTON **94** B3
Clifton Ave
Long Eaton NG10 . . . . **90** C1
Ruddington NG11 . . . . **95** B1
Clifton Bvd NG7 . . . . **74** B2
Clifton Cres NG9 . . . . **82** A1
Clifton Gr NG4 . . . . **50** C4
Clifton Grove Nature
Reserve ★ NG11 . . . . **83** B1
Clifton La
Ruddington NG11 . . . . **94** C2
Clifton L Ctr NG11 . . . . . . **94** B3
Clifton Rd NG11 . . . . **95** A1
Clifton St NG9 . . . . **82** C4
Clifton Terr NG7 . . . . **107** C1
Clifton Woods Nature
Reserve ★ NG11 . . . . **83** B1
Clinton Ave Brinsley NG16 . **8** B4
Nottingham NG5 . . . . **47** C2
Clinton Ct NG1 . . . . **108** B3
Clinton St E NG1 . . . . **108** B3
Clinton St W NG1 . . . . . . **108** B3
Clinton St Arnold NG5 . . . . **23** C1
Beeston NG9 . . . . **72** A1
Clipstone Ave
Nottingham, Mapperley
NG3 . . . . **35** B2
Nottingham NG1 . . . . **108** A3
Clipstone Cl NG8 . . . . **44** B4
Clive Cres NG16 . . . . **29** B3
Cliveden Gn NG11 . . . . . . **93** C3
Cloister St NG7 . . . . **74** A4
Cloisters The NG9 . . . . . . **72** C2
Close Quarters NG9 . . . . **71** B2
Close The Beeston NG9 . . . **81** C2
Nottingham NG5 . . . . **34** A1
Cloud Ave NG9 . . . . **70** B1
Clouds Hill NG11 . . . . **94** A2
Cloudside Ct NG10 . . . . . . **69** B1
Cloudside Jun Sch
NG10 . . . . **79** A4
Cloudside Rd NG10 . . . . . **68** C1
Clough Ct NG8 . . . . **45** C1
Cloverdale NG12 . . . . **98** C2
Cloverfields NG14 . . . . **5** C3
Clover Gn NG6 . . . . **32** B1
Cloverlands NG11 . . . . **85** B1
Cloverlands Dr NG16 . . . . **18** B1
Clover Rise NG16 . . . . **16** C2
Clumber Ave
Beeston NG9 . . . . **81** C3
Carlton NG4 . . . . **51** B1
Nottingham, Hyson Green
NG5 . . . . **47** C2
Nottingham, Mapperley
NG3 . . . . **35** B2
Clumber Cres N NG7 . . . **107** C1
Clumber Cres S NG7 . . . **107** C1
Clumber Ct Ilkeston DE7 . . **27** A3
Nottingham NG7 . . . . **107** C1
Clumber Dr NG12 . . . . **65** B3

Clumber Rd NG2 . . . . **76** B1
Clumber Rd E NG7 . . . . **107** C2
Clumber Rd W NG7 . . . . **107** C2
Clumber St
Hucknall NG15 . . . . **12** A4
Long Eaton NG10 . . . . **89** C1
Nottingham NG1 . . . . **108** B3
Coach Dr NG16 . . . . **9** A2
Coachmans Croft 2
NG8 . . . . **57** B3
Coates Ave NG15 . . . . **2** B3
Coatsby Rd NG16 . . . . **18** A1
Cobden St
Long Eaton NG10 . . . . **90** A1
Nottingham NG7 . . . . **106** A3
Cockayne Cl NG10 . . . . . . **79** A1
Cockerhouse Rd NG16 . . . **8** C2
Cockington Rd NG8 . . . . . **56** A3
Cockleys NG10 . . . . **100** B4
Codrington Gdns 5
NG5 . . . . **23** A2
Cogenhoe Wlk NG5 . . . . . **24** A4
Cogley La NG13 . . . . **67** C2
Cohen Cl Arnold NG5 . . . . **35** C4
Beeston NG9 . . . . **91** A4
Cokefield Ave NG16 . . . . . **31** A1
Colborn St NG3 . . . . **49** A1
Coleby Ave NG7 . . . . **107** A1
Coleby Rd NG8 . . . . **45** A4
Coledale NG2 . . . . **87** B4
Coleridge Cres NG5 . . . . . **23** B1
Coleridge St NG7 . . . . . . **106** B4
Colesbourne Rd NG7 . . . . **94** B4
Colin Broughton Ct NG6 . **21** B1
Colindale Gdns NG16 . . . . **30** C1
Colinwood Ave NG5 . . . . **21** C3
College Dr
Nottingham NG5 . . . . **84** A1
Nottingham NG11 . . . . **93** C4
College Rd Beeston NG9 . . **82** A3
Carlton NG3 . . . . **36** A1
College St
Long Eaton NG10 . . . . **89** B4
Nottingham NG1 . . . . **109** A2
Colleymoor Leys La NG7 . **94** B4
Colliers Way NG6 . . . . **31** B2
Colliery Cl NG2 . . . . **75** A3
Collin Ave NG10 . . . . **79** A2
Collin Gn NG5 . . . . **34** B2
Collington St NG9 . . . . . . **82** A4
Collington Way NG2 . . . . **85** C4
Collingwood Cl NG11 . . . . **84** A2
Collingwood Rd NG10 . . **101** A4
Collins Cl NG6 . . . . **31** A3
Collin St Beeston NG9 . . . . **82** B4
Nottingham NG1 . . . . **109** B1
Collison St NG7 . . . . **106** B4
Collyer Rd NG14 . . . . **4** C3
Colly Gate NG16 . . . . **29** B3
Collygate Rd NG2 . . . . . . **75** C3
Colmon Cl NG5 . . . . **22** B1
Colmon Wlk 6 NG5 . . . . **22** B1
Colonel Frank Seely Comp
Sch NG14 . . . . **5** A3
Colonsay Cl NG9 . . . . **54** B1
Colston Cres NG2 . . . . **85** C2
Colston Gate NG12 . . . . . . **98** C3
Colston Rd NG6 . . . . **21** A1
Colville St NG1 . . . . **47** C1
Colville Terr 2 NG1 . . . . **47** C1
Colville Villas 1 NG1 . . . **47** C1
COLWICK **63** A3
Colwick Bsns Pk NG4 . . . . **63** B3
Colwick Ctry Pk ★ NG2 . . **62** B3
Colwick Hall ★ NG2 . . . . . **62** A1
Colwick Ind Est NG4 . . . . **63** A3
Colwick Loop Rd NG4 . . . **63** B3
Colwick Manor Farm
NG4 . . . . **62** C3
Colwick Pk Cl NG4 . . . . . . **62** C3
Colwick Rd
Nottingham NG2 . . . . **61** C2
West Bridgford NG2 . . . . . **76** A3
Colwick Woods Nature
Reserve ★ NG2 . . . . **61** C2
Comery Ave NG3 . . . . **61** B4
Comfrey Cl NG5 . . . . **21** C1
Commerce Sq NG1 . . . . **109** C2

Commercial Ave NG9 . . . . 82 B4
Commercial Rd
  Keyworth NG12 . . . . 104 B2
  6 Nottingham NG6 . . . . 20 C1
Commodore Gdns NG8 . . 46 A4
Common La Beeston NG9 . 80 C4
  Hucknall NG15 . . . . 10 B4
  Watnall NG16 . . . . 18 C1
Commons Cl NG16 . . . . 16 B2
COMMON SIDE 13 C3
Common The NG15 . . . . 10 A4
Compton Acres NG2 . . . . . 85 A3
Compton Acres Sh Ctr
  NG2 . . . . 85 B3
Compton Rd NG5 . . . . 33 C1
Comyn Gdns NG3 . . . . 108 C4
Condor Rd DE7 . . . . 53 A2
Conduit Cl NG2 . . . . 75 B4
Conifer Cres NG11 . . . . 94 A1
Conifer Wlk NG3 . . . . 49 B2
Coningsby Gdns E NG5 . . 35 A2
Coningsby Rd NG5 . . . . 35 A3
Coningswath Rd NG4 . . . . 50 A3
Conisborough Terr 10
  NG2 . . . . 75 B3
Conisbrough Ave NG4 . . 51 C3
Coniston Ave NG6 . . . . 46 A4
Coniston Cl NG2 . . . . 77 B1
Coniston Dr DE7 . . . . 52 B3
Coniston Rd Beeston NG9 . 71 C2
  Hucknall NG15 . . . . 2 B2
  Long Eaton NG10 . . . . 88 C4
Connelly Cl NG5 . . . . 36 A4
Connery Mews NG9 . . . . . . 91 A3
Connery The NG15 . . . . 2 C1
Constance St NG7 . . . . 47 B3
Convent St NG1 . . . . 108 C3
Conway Ave NG4 . . . . 51 B1
Conway Cl NG3 . . . . 48 A1
Conway Cres NG4 . . . . 51 B2
Conway Gdns NG5 . . . . 35 A4
Conway Rd Carlton NG4 . . 51 B2
  Hucknall NG15 . . . . 10 B1
Conway St NG10 . . . . 90 B2
Conway Wlk 4 NG3 . . . . 48 A1
Cook Dr DE7 . . . . 53 B4
Cookson Ave NG4 . . . . 50 B4
Coombe Cl NG8 . . . . 58 A1
Coombe Rd NG16 . . . . 9 C2
Co-Operative Ave NG15 . . 3 A2
Co-Operative St NG10 . . 101 A4
Cooper Cl Arnold NG5 . . . . 36 A4
  Nottingham NG6 . . . . 31 A4
Coopers Gn NG8 . . . . 72 A4
Cooper St NG4 . . . . 63 B4
Copeland Ave NG9 . . . . 70 A2
Copeland Gr NG13 . . . . 66 B3
Copeland Rd NG15 . . . . 3 B2
Copenhagen Ct NG3 . . . . . 48 B3
Cope St NG7 . . . . 106 B4
Copestake Cl NG10 . . . . . . 88 C1
Coppice Ave DE7 . . . . 26 B3
Coppice Cl NG15 . . . . 10 C3
Coppice Ct DE75 . . . . 14 A1
Coppice Dr Eastwood NG16 . 8 B1
  Heanor DE75 . . . . 14 A1
Coppice Form Prim Sch
  NG5 . . . . 24 C1
Coppice Gr NG3 . . . . 48 C3
Coppice Mews DE75 . . . . 14 A1
Coppice Prim Sch DE75 . 13 C2
Coppice Rd NG5 . . . . 24 C2
Copplestone Dr NG3 . . . . 36 A4
Copse Cl NG14 . . . . 39 A3
Copseside Cl 3 NG10 . . 88 C2
Copse The Beeston NG9 . . 81 B4
  Hucknall NG15 . . . . 12 A4
  Ilkeston DE7 . . . . 26 B3
Corben Gdns NG6 . . . . 20 A1
Corbiere Ave NG16 . . . . . . 18 B1
Corby Rd NG3 . . . . 48 C3
Corfield Ave DE75 . . . . 14 A1
Corfield CE Inf Sch
  DE75 . . . . 13 B3
Coriander Dr NG6 . . . . 32 B1
Corinth Rd NG7 . . . . 94 A4
Corn Cft NG11 . . . . 84 B3
Corn Cl NG12 . . . . 98 A2

Corncrake Ave NG6 . . . . . . 32 B1
Corncrake Dr NG5 . . . . 25 A1
Cornell Dr NG5 . . . . 25 A2
Cornerhouse The*
  NG1 . . . . 108 B3
Cornfield Rd NG16 . . . . 17 C1
Cornhill Rd NG4 . . . . 49 C1
Cornwall Ave NG7 . . . . 83 B2
Cornwallis Cl NG10 . . . . . 100 C4
Cornwall Rd NG5 . . . . 23 A1
Coronation Ave
  Nottingham NG11 . . . . 75 A2
  Sandiacre NG10 . . . . 68 C1
Coronation Rd
  Arnold NG5 . . . . 35 A1
  Awsworth DE7 . . . . 41 B3
  Bestwood Village NG6 . . . . 12 C2
  Cossall NG16 . . . . 41 C4
  Hucknall NG15 . . . . 2 B2
  Nuthall NG16 . . . . 30 A3
Coronation St 1 DE7 . . . 41 A2
Coronation Wlk NG4 . . . . . 51 B3
Corporation Oaks NG3 . . 48 A1
Corporation Rd DE7 . . . . . 53 B3
Corsham Gdns NG3 . . . . . . 49 B1
Cosby Rd 4 NG2 . . . . 61 A1
COSSALL 42 A3
Cossall Ind Est NG16 . . . . 41 C4
Cossall Rd NG9 . . . . 54 B3
Costock Ave NG5 . . . . 33 C2
Costume & Textile Mus*
  NG1 . . . . 109 B2
Coteswood House Sch
  NG5 . . . . 34 C3
COTGRAVE 98 A2
Cotgrave Ave NG4 . . . . 51 A4
Cotgrave CE Prim Sch
  NG12 . . . . 98 A3
Cotgrave Cl NG8 . . . . 44 C4
Cotgrave Inf Sch NG12 . . 98 B1
Cotgrave L Ctr NG12 . . . . 98 C3
Cotgrave Manvers Jun Sch
  NG12 . . . . 98 B3
COTMANHAY 26 C1
Cotmanhay Rd DE7 . . . . . . 26 C1
Coton Cl NG11 . . . . 84 C1
Cotswold Cl 2 NG10 . . . 89 A2
Cotswold Ct NG9 . . . . 71 C3
Cotswold Rd NG8 . . . . 44 C3
Cottage Cl DE7 . . . . 26 B1
Cottage Garden La DE75 . 13 B4
Cottage Mdw NG4 . . . . 63 A2
Cottage Terr NG1 . . . . 106 C3
Cottam Dr NG5 . . . . 22 B2
Cottam Gdns NG5 . . . . 22 B2
Cottesmore Rd NG7 . . . . . 107 B2
County Bsns Pk NG2 . . . . 76 A4
County Cl NG9 . . . . 82 C3
County Rd Carlton NG4 . . . 36 A1
  Nottingham NG2 . . . . 76 A4
Court Cres NG8 . . . . 57 A2
Courtenay Gdns NG3 . . . . 48 B1
Court Gdns NG11 . . . . 85 A2
Courtlett Way NG6 . . . . . . 31 C3
Courtney Cl NG8 . . . . 56 C3
Court St 11 NG7 . . . . 47 A1
Court Yd NG9 . . . . 71 A2
Covedale Rd NG5 . . . . 34 A3
Coventry Ct NG6 . . . . 32 A3
Coventry La NG9 . . . . 55 B1
Coventry Rd Beeston NG9 . 72 C1
  Nottingham NG6 . . . . 31 C4
Covert Cl
  Burton Joyce NG14 . . . . . . 38 C3
  Hucknall NG15 . . . . 12 A4
  Keyworth NG12 . . . . 104 C4
Covert Rd NG2 . . . . 87 A4
Cowan St NG1 . . . . 108 C3
Cowdrey Gdns NG5 . . . . . . 35 C4
Cow La NG9 . . . . 71 B2
Cowlairs NG5 . . . . 21 C1
Cowley St NG6 . . . . 32 B1
Cowper Rd Arnold NG5 . . . 34 C2
  Eastwood NG16 . . . . 16 B2
Coxmoor Cl NG2 . . . . 87 B2
Coxmoor Ct 14 NG5 . . . . 22 B3
Crabtree Field NG2 . . . . . . 62 B2
Crabtree Rd NG6 . . . . 31 B4
Cragdale Rd NG5 . . . . 34 A3
Cragmoor Rd NG14 . . . . . . 38 C1
Craig Moray NG12 . . . . . . 65 B3

Craig St NG10 . . . . 90 A1
Crammond Cl 8 NG2 . . . 75 A4
Crampton Cl NG5 . . . . 22 B2
Cramworth Dr 4 NG5 . . . 34 B1
Cranberry Cl NG2 . . . . 85 A3
Cranbourne Cl NG9 . . . . . . 69 C4
Cranbourne Gr NG15 . . . . . 2 A1
Cranbrook St NG1 . . . . . . 108 C3
Cranfleet Way NG10 . . . . . 89 A1
Cranford Gdns NG2 . . . . . . 85 B2
Cranmer Gr 8 NG3 . . . . . 48 A1
Cranmer St Ilkeston DE7 . . 41 A3
  Long Eaton NG10 . . . . 89 C3
  Nottingham NG3 . . . . 48 A1
Cranmore Cl NG5 . . . . 24 B4
Cransley Ave NG8 . . . . 71 C4
Cranston Ave NG5 . . . . 24 A3
Cranston Rd NG9 . . . . 71 B3
Cranthorne Dr NG3 . . . . . . 62 A4
Crantock Gdns NG12 . . . 104 C3
Cranwell Ct NG6 . . . . 31 A4
Cranwell Rd NG8 . . . . 44 B4
Craster Dr Arnold NG5 . . . 24 B4
  Nottingham NG6 . . . . 20 A2
Craven Rd NG7 . . . . 46 C1
Crawford Ave NG9 . . . . 69 C2
Crawford Cl NG8 . . . . 56 C3
Crawford Rise NG5 . . . . . . 25 A2
C Rd NG9 . . . . 83 C4
Crescent Ave NG4 . . . . 50 C3
Crescent The Arnold NG5 . 34 C2
  Beeston, Chilwell NG9 . . . . 81 B1
  Beeston, Toton NG9 . . . . . . 90 C4
  Eastwood NG16 . . . . 16 B4
  Nottingham NG3 . . . . 48 B2
  Radcliffe on T NG12 . . . . . . 65 B2
  Stapleford NG9 . . . . 70 A4
Cresswell Rd NG9 . . . . 81 A3
Cressy Rd NG7 . . . . 94 B4
Cresta Gdns NG3 . . . . 48 B4
Crewe Cl NG7 . . . . 106 B4
Cribb Cl NG11 . . . . 75 A1
Crich View NG5 . . . . 48 A4
Cricketers Ct NG2 . . . . 76 B3
Criftin Rd NG14 . . . . 39 B2
Cripps Hill NG7 . . . . 73 B4
Critchley St DE7 . . . . 41 A3
Critch's Flats NG16 . . . . . 29 A4
Crocus St NG2 . . . . 75 C4
Croft Ave NG15 . . . . 11 B4
Croft Cres NG16 . . . . 28 A3
Crofton Cl Beeston NG9 . . 81 C1
  3 Nottingham NG8 . . . . . 57 C4
Crofton Rd NG9 . . . . 91 C4
Croft Rd Arnold NG5 . . . . . 24 A2
  Keyworth NG12 . . . . 104 A3
  West Bridgford NG12 . . . . . 86 C2
Crofts The NG13 . . . . 67 A2
Cromarty Ct 2 NG2 . . . . . 75 A4
Cromdale Cl NG5 . . . . 25 A3
Cromer Rd NG3 . . . . 48 C1
Cromford Ave NG4 . . . . . . 50 B2
Cromford Cl
  Aldercar NG16 . . . . 7 C2
  Long Eaton NG10 . . . . 99 C3
Cromford Rd Heanor NG16 . 6 C3
  Langley Mill NG16 . . . . 7 C2
  West Bridgford NG2 . . . . . . 86 B4
Crompton Rd DE7 . . . . 53 C1
Cromwell Ave DE7 . . . . . . 53 B3
Cromwell Rd NG9 . . . . 82 A4
Cromwell St Carlton NG4 . 50 C1
  Eastwood NG16 . . . . 17 A2
  Nottingham NG7 . . . . 106 C3
Crookdole La NG14 . . . . . . 5 B2
Cropston Cl NG2 . . . . 86 A2
Cropton Cres NG8 . . . . 57 C4
Cropton Gr NG13 . . . . 66 B2
Cropwell Gdns NG12 . . . . 65 B1
Cropwell Gn NG3 . . . . 61 A4
Cropwell Rd NG12 . . . . 65 B1
Crosby Rd NG2 . . . . 76 B2
Crossdale Dr NG12 . . . . . 104 B4
Crossdale Drive Prim Sch
  NG12 . . . . 104 B4
Crossdale Wlk NG5 . . . . . . 21 C2
Crossfield Dr
  Nottingham NG5 . . . . 22 B2
  13 Nottingham NG5 . . . . . 22 B2
Crossgate Dr NG2 . . . . 74 C3
Crosshill NG12 . . . . 98 C3

Crosshill Dr DE7 . . . . 52 A3
Crossland Rd NG5 . . . . 33 B3
Crosslands Mdw NG4 . . . . 63 A2
Crossley St NG5 . . . . 47 C4
Crossman St NG5 . . . . 48 A4
Cross St Arnold NG5 . . . . . 23 C2
  Beeston NG9 . . . . 72 B1
  Carlton, Netherfield NG4 . . 51 B1
  Carlton, Thorneywood
  NG4 . . . . 50 B2
  Eastwood NG16 . . . . 16 B4
  Long Eaton NG10 . . . . 90 A2
  Sandiacre NG10 . . . . 79 B4
Cross The NG12 . . . . 64 B2
Crowborough Ave NG8 . . 72 A4
Crowcroft Way NG10 . . . . 89 A4
Crow Ct NG13 . . . . 67 C2
Crow Hill Rd NG4 . . . . 51 A1
Crowley Cl NG8 . . . . 56 A4
Crown Cl NG10 . . . . 88 C1
Crown Way NG16 . . . . 7 C2
Crow Pk Dr NG14 . . . . 38 C1
Crowthorne Cl NG5 . . . . . . 21 C3
Crowthorne Gdns NG5 . . 21 C3
Croxall Cl NG11 . . . . 84 A2
Croxley Gdns NG16 . . . . . 30 B1
Croydon Rd NG7 . . . . 106 A3
Crummock Cl NG9 . . . . 71 B2
Cudworth Dr NG3 . . . . 49 A4
Cuillin Cl NG10 . . . . 88 C3
Cullen's Ct NG5 . . . . 48 A4
Cullin Cl NG5 . . . . 22 A4
Cumberland Ave NG9 . . . . 81 C4
Cumberland Pl NG1 . . . . 109 A2
Curie Ct NG7 . . . . 73 C4
Curlew Cl NG3 . . . . 62 A3
Curlew Wharf 5 NG7 . . . 74 B4
Cursley Way NG9 . . . . 91 B4
Curtis St NG15 . . . . 11 B4
Curzon Ave NG4 . . . . 49 C1
Curzon Ct NG3 . . . . 108 C4
Curzon Gdns NG3 . . . . 108 C4
Curzon Pl NG3 . . . . 108 C3
Curzon St Carlton NG4 . . . 51 B1
  Long Eaton NG10 . . . . 89 A4
  Nottingham NG3 . . . . 108 C3
Cuxton Cl NG8 . . . . 44 B3
Cycle Rd NG7 . . . . 107 A2
Cypress Ct NG15 . . . . 10 A3
Cyprus Ave NG9 . . . . 72 B1
Cyprus Dr NG9 . . . . 72 B1
Cyprus Rd NG3 . . . . 48 A3
Cyril Ave Beeston NG9 . . . 72 A1
  Nottingham NG8 . . . . 46 B2
  Stapleford NG9 . . . . 69 C1
Cyril Rd NG2 . . . . 76 C1

D

Dabell Ave NG6 . . . . 20 A2
Dagfa House Sch NG9 . . . 72 C1
Dagmar Gr Beeston NG9 . 82 C4
  Nottingham NG3 . . . . 48 B3
Daisy Cl NG12 . . . . 98 A2
Daisy Farm Rd NG16 . . . . 16 C2
Daisy Rd NG3 . . . . 49 B3
Dakeyne St NG3 . . . . 60 C3
Dalbeattie Cl NG5 . . . . 24 C2
Dalby Sq NG8 . . . . 58 A1
Dale Ave Carlton NG4 . . . . 50 A1
  Long Eaton NG10 . . . . 89 C3
  Nottingham NG3 . . . . 49 B4
Dalebrook Cres NG15 . . . 10 A3
Dale Cl Hucknall NG15 . . . 10 A3
  West Bridgford NG2 . . . . . . 77 A1
Dale Farm Ave NG3 . . . . . 61 B3
Dale Gr NG2 . . . . 61 A2
Dalehead Rd NG11 . . . . . . 93 C4
Dale La NG9 . . . . 82 A3
Dalemoor Gdns NG8 . . . . 45 C2
Dale Rd Carlton NG4 . . . . . 50 B2
  Keyworth NG12 . . . . 104 B3
  Kimberley NG16 . . . . 29 A3
Daleside NG12 . . . . 98 A2
Daleside Rd NG2 . . . . 61 B1
Daleside Rd E NG2, NG3 . 62 A2
Dale St Ilkeston DE7 . . . . . 41 A3
  Nottingham NG2 . . . . 60 C2
Dale View DE7 . . . . 40 C1
Dale View Rd NG3 . . . . 49 C1
Dalkeith Terr 10 NG7 . . . 47 A1

Dallas York Rd NG9 . . . . . 83 A4
Dalley Cl NG9 . . . . 70 B1
Dallimore Prim Sch DE7 52 B2
Dallimore Rd DE7 . . . . 52 B2
Dalton Cl NG9 . . . . 80 A3
Daltons Cl NG16 . . . . 7 B2
Damson Wlk NG3 . . . . 49 C2
Dane Cl NG3 . . . . 108 C4
Dane Ct NG3 . . . . 108 C4
Danes Cl NG5 . . . . 23 B2
Danethorpe Vale NG5 . . . 34 A2
Daniel Mews NG10 . . . . . . 78 C3
Daniels Way NG15 . . . . . . 11 A2
Darfield Dr DE75 . . . . 14 B4
Darkey La NG9 . . . . 80 A3
Dark La NG13 . . . . 67 C2
Darley Ave Beeston NG9 . 80 B1
  Carlton NG4 . . . . 50 C3
  Nottingham NG7 . . . . 46 C1
Darley Dr NG10 . . . . 99 C3
Darley Rd NG7 . . . . 46 C1
Darley Sq DE7 . . . . 26 C3
Darlton Dr NG5 . . . . 24 C1
Darnal Cl NG5 . . . . 21 C1
Darnhall Cres NG8 . . . . . . 44 B1
Daron Gdns 10 NG5 . . . . 22 B1
Darvel Cl 6 NG8 . . . . 57 C4
Darwin Ave DE7 . . . . 40 C1
Darwin Cl NG5 . . . . 21 C2
Darwin Rd NG10 . . . . 100 A3
David Gr NG9 . . . . 72 A3
David La NG6 . . . . 32 B1
Davidson Cl NG5 . . . . 25 A1
Davidson Gd NG11 . . . . . . 94 C1
Davidson St 8 NG2 . . . . . 61 A1
Davies Rd NG2 . . . . 76 C1
Davis Rd NG9 . . . . 81 A1
Davy Cl NG15 . . . . 3 A4
Dawes Way NG7 . . . . 106 A3
Dawlish Cl NG15 . . . . 10 B4
Dawlish Ct NG16 . . . . 8 B1
Dawlish Dr NG5 . . . . 33 C3
Dawn Cl NG15 . . . . 3 B3
Dawn View NG9 . . . . 69 C4
Dawson Cl NG16 . . . . 16 B3
Dawver Rd NG16 . . . . 29 A4
DAYBROOK 23 B1
Daybrook Ave 4 NG5 . . . 34 A1
Daybrook St NG5 . . . . 34 A1
Dayncourt Sch NG12 . . . . 65 B2
Deabill St NG4 . . . . 63 B4
Dead La NG16 . . . . 42 B3
Deakins Pl NG7 . . . . 106 A3
Deal Gdns NG6 . . . . 20 A1
Dean Ave NG3 . . . . 35 B1
Dean Cl NG8 . . . . 56 B3
Dean Rd NG5 . . . . 34 C3
Deanscourt NG12 . . . . 98 C3
Deans Croft NG9 . . . . 71 A3
Dean St Langley Mill NG16 . 8 A1
  Nottingham NG1 . . . . 109 C2
Debdale La NG12 . . . . 104 B3
Deddington La NG9 . . . . . 71 B4
Deeley Cl NG16 . . . . 18 B1
Deepdale Ave NG9 . . . . . . 79 C4
Deepdale Cl NG2 . . . . 77 B1
Deepdale Ct DE75 . . . . 13 C3
Deepdale Rd
  Long Eaton NG10 . . . . 99 C3
  Nottingham NG8 . . . . 56 B2
Deepdene Cl NG8 . . . . 45 B4
Deepdene Way NG8 . . . . . 45 B4
Deep Furrow Ave NG4 . . . 50 B2
Deerleap Dr NG5 . . . . 23 A1
Deer Pk NG8 . . . . 56 C2
Deer Pk Dr Arnold NG5 . . 23 A3
  Nottingham NG5 . . . . 22 C2
Delia Ave NG15 . . . . 3 B3
Dell Way NG7 . . . . 94 B4
Dellwood Cl NG4 . . . . 50 A4
Delta St NG7 . . . . 47 A3
Deltic Cl NG16 . . . . 18 B1
Delves Ct DE75 . . . . 13 C2
Delves Rd DE75 . . . . 13 B2
Delville Ave NG12 . . . . . . 104 B4
Denacre Ave NG10 . . . . . . 90 B3
Denehurst Ave NG8 . . . . . 46 A3
Denewood Ave NG9 . . . . . 71 B4
Denewood Cres NG8 . . . . 44 C2
Denholme Rd NG8 . . . . 56 B3
Denison St Beeston NG9 . 72 A1

Denison St continued
Nottingham NG7.........**106** B4
Denman St Central
NG7................**106** B3
Denman St E NG7.......**106** B3
Denman St W NG7.....**106** A3
Denmark Gr 1 NG3 ... **48** B2
Dennett Cl NG3........**60** C4
Dennis Ave NG9.......**72** A2
Dennis St NG4.........**51** B1
Denstone Rd NG3......**60** C3
Dentdale Dr NG8 ......**55** C2
Denton Ave NG10......**78** C4
Denton Dr NG2........**85** C2
Denton Gn NG8.........**45** A4
Denver Ct NG7.........**70** A3
Depedale Ave DE7.....**52** B3
Deptford Cres NG6 ....**32** A3
Derby Gr NG7.........**106** B3
Derby Rd Beeston NG9 ..**71** C3
  Eastwood NG16.......**15** C4
  Heanor DE75 ....**13** B3
  Ilkeston DE7...........**40** B1
  Langley Mill NG16 ......**8** A1
  Long Eaton NG10......**89** A2
  Nottingham NG7......**107** B2
  Sandiacre NG10.......**78** C3
Dereham Dr NG5 ....**35** B4
Derry Dr NG5..........**24** A4
Derry Hill Rd NG5 .....**23** C3
Derrymount Sch NG5 ...**24** A3
Derwent Ave DE7......**40** B4
Derwent Cl Beeston NG9 ..**82** A1
  West Bridgford NG2....**77** B1
Derwent Cres NG5 .....**35** B4
Derwent Ct NG7 ......**106** C4
Derwent Dr NG15......**11** B2
Derwent Ind Est
NG10................**100** C4
Derwent St NG10......**100** B4
Derwent Terr 5 NG5....**48** A4
Derwent Way
  Nottingham NG7.......**58** B2
  Nottingham NG7......**107** A2
Desford Cl NG5.........**33** B2
De Vere Gdns NG5 .....**35** B2
Devitt Dr NG15 ....**3** B3
Devon Cir NG5.........**23** B3
Devon Cl Eastwood NG16 ..**16** C4
  Sandiacre NG10 ....**79** A3
Devon Dr Nottingham NG5 ..**48** A4
  Ruddington NG11.......**95** C2
Devonshire Ave
  Beeston NG9..........**82** B4
  Long Eaton NG10 ......**90** C2
Devonshire Cl DE7.....**26** C3
Devonshire Cres NG5 ..**47** C4
Devonshire Dr
  Eastwood NG16........**16** A4
  Stapleford NG9.........**69** C4
Devonshire Prom NG7 ..**107** A1
Devonshire Rd
  Nottingham NG5........**47** C4
  West Bridgford NG2....**86** B4
Devon St Ilkeston DE7 ...**53** B3
  Nottingham NG3........**61** A3
Dewberry La NG12......**65** C1
DH Lawrence Birthplace
Mus ★ NG16............**9** A1
Dial The NG12..........**98** A1
Dickens Ct NG16........**9** C1
Dickson Dr NG11 ......**103** A4
Didcot Dr NG8..........**46** B3
Digby Ave NG3 ....**36** A1
Digby Ct NG7..........**107** B1
Digby Hall Dr NG4.......**36** A1
Digby St Cossall DE7 ....**41** B3
  Kimberley NG16.........**17** B1
Dirca Cl NG11 ....**93** B2
Diseworth Gr 3 NG2 ...**73** C3
Disraeli Cres DE7.......**41** A2

Distillery St NG11......**102** C4
Djanogly City Acad NG7 ..**47** B3
Dockholm Rd NG10......**89** B4
Dodford Ct DE75........**14** B3
Dogwood Ave NG6......**20** B1
Dolphin Ct 7 NG5......**22** B2
Donbas Cl NG6.........**31** C2
Doncaster Ave NG10 ....**79** A4
Doncaster Gr NG10 .....**90** B3
Doncaster Terr 11 NG2 ..**75** B3
Donington Rd NG7......**94** A3
Donkey La NG11........**103** B1
Donner Cres DE7 ....**26** C3
Dooland Dr NG3........**49** A3
Dorchester Gdns NG2 ...**86** A1
Dorchester Rd NG16 ....**18** A1
Doris Rd DE7...........**41** B1
Dorket Cl NG5..........**24** B3
Dorket Dr NG8..........**58** B1
Dorking Rd NG7 ....**106** B4
Dormy Cl Beeston NG9 ...**71** B1
  Radcliffe on T NG12 .....**65** C2
Dormy Ct NG6..........**21** B1
Dornoch Ave NG5.......**48** B4
Dorothy Ave
  Eastwood NG16..........**9** B1
  Hucknall NG15 ....**3** A3
  Sandiacre NG10 ....**79** A3
Dorothy Gr 1 NG8 ......**58** B4
Dorset Gdns NG2.......**85** B3
Dorset St NG8..........**58** B3
Dorterry Cres DE7......**53** B3
Douglas Ave
  Awsworth NG16.........**28** A3
  Carlton NG4............**62** C4
  Heanor DE75 ....**13** A4
Douglas Cl NG12.......**64** C1
Douglas Cres NG4......**62** C4
Douglas Ct NG9.........**90** C4
Douglas Prim Sch NG7 ..**106** B3
Douglas Rd
  Long Eaton NG10 ......**89** A3
  Nottingham NG7......**106** B3
Douro Dr NG5...........**24** C3
Dove Cl NG13............**67** B1
Dovecote Dr NG8 ....**56** C2
Dovecote La NG9.......**82** C3
Dovecote Prim Sch
NG11................**84** B1
Dovecote Rd NG16......**16** C4
Dovedale Ave NG10 .....**99** C4
Dovedale Cir DE7.......**26** C3
Dovedale Ct NG10 .....**100** A4
Dovedale Prim Sch
NG10................**99** C4
Dovedale Rd
  Nottingham NG3........**62** A4
  West Bridgford NG2....**86** C3
Dove La NG10 ....**89** B2
Dovenby Rd NG7 ....**94** B4
Dover Beck Cl NG14 .....**5** C2
Doveridge Ave NG4.....**51** B2
Doveridge Rd NG4......**51** B2
Dove St NG6............**20** C1
Dovey's Orch NG14 ......**4** C2
Downes Cl NG6.........**20** B1
Downham Cl NG5.......**35** B4
Downing Cl NG6.........**20** C2
Downing Gdns 7 NG6 ...**20** C2
Downing St NG6.........**20** C2
Downs The NG11 ....**84** C1
Dowson Cl NG12........**65** C3
Dowson St NG3.........**61** A4
Doyne Ct 2 NG2.........**75** B3
Drakemyre Cl NG5......**24** C3
Drake Rd NG4...........**63** C4
Draycott Cl DE75........**6** A2
Draycott Ct DE7........**27** A1
Draycott Rd NG10......**99** C2
Draymans Ct NG7.......**47** A3
Drayton St 3 DE75......**48** A4
Drift The Hucknall NG15....**3** A3
  Nottingham NG11.......**84** A1
Drive The NG9...........**82** A1
Drmonde Terr 7 NG3 ....**48** A4
Dronfield Pl DE7........**26** B3
Drummond Ave NG4.....**51** C1
Drummond Dr NG16.....**30** C2
Drummond Rd DE7......**40** C3
Dryden Ct NG9.........**70** A3
Dryden St NG1 ....**108** A4

Drysdale Cl NG6........**31** C3
Duchess Gdns 8 NG6....**20** C2
Duchess St NG6.........**20** C2
Dudley Ct NG9..........**70** C2
Duffield Cl NG10........**99** C3
Duffield Ct NG5.........**22** A2
Duke Cl NG6............**31** B3
Duke Cres NG16........**17** A3
Dukes Pl DE7 ....**26** C2
Duke's Pl NG1.........**109** C2
Duke St Arnold NG5......**23** C1
  Hucknall NG15 ....**3** A1
  Ilkeston DE7...........**27** A1
5 Ilkeston DE7.........**27** A1
Duke William Mount
NG7................**107** C2
Dulverton Vale NG8 .....**31** C1
Dulwich Rd NG7.......**106** A3
Dumbles Cl DE7.........**52** A4
Dunblane Rd NG11 .....**102** C4
Duncombe Cl NG3 ......**48** C1
Duncroft Ave NG4.......**51** A3
Dundas Cl NG1 ....**108** B3
Dunelm Dr NG14 ....**5** C2
Dungannon Rd NG11 ....**94** A2
Dunholme Cl NG6.......**20** C2
Dunkery Rd NG11.......**94** B2
DUNKIRK............**74** A4
Dunkirk Ind Est NG7....**73** C1
Dunkirk Prim Sch NG7 ..**74** A3
Dunkirk Rd 4 NG7......**74** A4
Dunlin Wharf 2 NG2 ....**74** C4
Dunlop Ave NG7 ....**107** A2
Dunoon Cl NG5.........**21** C3
Dunsby Cl NG7 ....**94** A3
Dunsford Dr NG3........**36** A4
Dunsil Dr NG11 ....**74** C2
Dunsil Rd NG16..........**9** C2
Dunsmore Cl NG9 ....**83** A2
Dunstan St NG4.........**51** B1
Dunster Rd
  Eastwood NG16........**16** C3
  West Bridgford NG2....**86** C4
Dunston Cl NG10 ....**90** B1
Dunvegan Dr NG5......**22** A4
Durban House Heritage
Ctr ★ NG16.............**9** A1
Durham Ave NG2 ....**61** A2
Durham Cl 1 NG2.......**61** A2
Durham Cres NG6.......**32** A4
Durham St 3 DE7.......**41** A3
Durlston Cl NG2 ....**85** A3
Durnford St NG7.........**47** A4
Dursley Cl NG6..........**31** C3
Dyce Cl NG6............**20** A1
Dylan Thomas Rd NG5 ...**23** A2

E

Eagle Cl Arnold NG5 .....**24** B1
  Beeston NG9 ....**71** C2
Eagle Ct NG6............**21** B1
Eagle Rd DE7...........**53** A2
Ealing Ave NG6.........**32** B2
Eardley Rd NG5.........**32** C4
Earl Cres NG4...........**37** A1
Earl Dr NG16 ....**17** A3
Earlham Cl DE7.........**52** A4
Earls Cl NG8............**56** A3
Earlsfield Dr NG5.......**21** C3
Earlswood Dr NG12.....**87** A2
Easedale Cl NG2........**77** B1
Easegill Ct NG5.........**22** A2
East Acres NG12........**98** B3
East Cir St NG1 ....**109** A2
East Cl NG12 ....**104** B2
Eastcliffe Ave NG4......**36** B1
Eastcote Ave NG9.......**71** A4
East Cres NG9 ....**83** A3
Eastdale Rd NG3........**62** A4
East Dr NG7............**73** B3
Eastham Cl NG3........**60** C4
Eastham Rd NG5.......**36** A4
Eastholme Croft NG2 ...**62** B3
Easthorpe St NG11......**95** B1
East Moor NG12 ....**98** C1
Eastmoor Dr NG4.......**51** A2

East Nelson St DE75.....**13** B4
East St Bingham NG13 ....**67** B2
  Heanor DE75 ....**14** B2
  Ilkeston DE7...........**41** A2
  Long Eaton NG10 ......**90** B2
  Nottingham NG1......**108** C3
East View NG2..........**85** C4
Eastwell St NG15 ....**2** C2
Eastwold NG12 ....**98** C2
EASTWOOD............**8** C1
Eastwood Cl NG15 ......**10** C2
Eastwood Comp Sch
NG16.................**8** C1
Eastwood Com Sports Ctr
NG16.................**8** C1
Eastwood Inf Sch NG16 ..**15** C4
Eastwood Jun Sch NG16 ..**15** C4
Eastwood & Kimberley Coll
NG16................**16** A4
Eastwood Rd
  Kimberley NG16........**28** C4
  Radcliffe on T NG12 .....**65** B2
Eastwood St NG6.......**32** A3
Eaton Ave Arnold NG5....**24** B1
  Ilkeston DE7...........**52** B4
Eaton Cl NG9...........**83** A4
Eaton Grange Dr NG10 ..**88** C2
Eatons Rd NG9.........**79** C4
Eaton St NG3...........**49** A4
Eaton Terr NG3.........**49** A4
Ebenezer St Ilkeston DE7 ..**27** A1
  Langley Mill NG16 ......**17** C2
Ebers Gr NG3...........**48** A2
Ebers Rd NG3...........**48** A2
Ebony Wlk NG3.........**49** C2
Ebury Rd NG5...........**47** C3
Eckington Terr 12 NG2 ...**75** B3
Ecton Cl NG5............**24** C3
Edale Cl Hucknall NG15....**10** A4
  Long Eaton NG10 .....**100** A4
Edale Rd NG2...........**61** B3
Edale Rise NG9.........**80** A1
Edale Sq DE7...........**26** C3
Eddleston Dr NG7.......**94** B3
Edenbridge Ct NG8 .....**71** C4
Eden Cl NG5............**35** B4
Edenhall Gdns NG7......**94** B4
Edern Cl NG5...........**22** B1
Edern Gdns 9 NG5......**22** B1
Edgbaston Gdns 1 NG8 ..**46** B2
Edgcote Way NG5.......**33** B4
Edge Hill Ct NG10......**100** C2
Edge Way NG5..........**44** B3
Edgewood Dr NG15 .....**10** B3
Edgewood L Ctr NG15 ...**10** B2
Edgewood Prim Sch
NG15................**10** A2
Edgewood Rd NG16.....**29** A4
Edginton Cl NG12 ....**98** C1
Edginton St NG3........**49** A1
Edgware Rd NG6........**21** B1
Edinbane Cl NG5........**22** A3
Edinburgh Dr NG13 .....**66** C3
Edingale Ct NG9.........**55** C2
Edingley Ave NG5.......**34** A2
Edingley Sq NG5........**33** C1
Edison Way NG5.........**25** A1
Edlington Dr NG8.......**56** A1
Edmond Gr NG15 ....**3** B1
Edmonds Cl NG5........**22** B4
Edmonton Ct NG2......**85** C4
Edna G Olds Prim Sch
NG7................**107** B1
Ednaston Rd NG7.......**73** C3
Edwald Rd NG12........**87** A1
Edwaltam Ave NG2......**76** A1
EDWALTON............**87** A1
Edwalton Cl 1 NG12.....**87** A1
Edwalton Ct NG6........**32** C4
Edwalton Lodge Cl
NG12................**86** C1
Edwalton Prim Sch
NG12................**87** B2
Edward Ave NG8........**46** B2
Edward Cl NG15 ....**10** B2
Edward Rd
  Eastwood NG16........**16** B4
  Long Eaton NG10 ......**89** C2
  Nuthall NG16 ....**30** A3
  West Bridgford NG2....**76** B2
Edwards La NG5.........**34** A3

Edward St Aldercar NG16....**7** C1
  Stapleford NG9.........**69** C1
Edwin St NG3...........**34** B4
Edwinstowe Dr NG5.....**34** A2
Eelwood Rd NG15 ......**10** B2
Egerton Dr NG9.........**69** C4
Egerton Rd NG5........**34** C2
Egerton St NG3.........**48** A1
Egerton Wlk 2 NG3 .....**48** A1
Egling Croft NG4........**63** A2
Egmont Ct 1 NG2......**75** B3
Egreaves Ave DE75 ......**6** A2
Egypt Rd NG7...........**47** A3
Eighth Ave NG9.........**83** B3
Eisele Cl NG6...........**31** A4
Ekowe St NG7...........**47** A3
Eland St NG7............**47** A3
Elder Cl NG5............**24** B3
Elder Gdns 8 NG5.......**22** B2
Elder Gr NG15 ....**11** C2
Eldon Rd NG9...........**91** B3
Eleanor Ave DE7........**53** B3
Eleanor Cres NG9.......**70** B1
Electric Ave NG11......**74** C2
Eley Cl NG7.............**40** A4
Elford Rise NG3.........**61** A3
Elgar Dr NG10 ....**100** A3
Elgar Gdns NG3.........**49** A1
Eliot Cl NG10 ....**100** A3
Eliot Dr DE7............**52** B3
Eliot Wlk NG11 ....**93** B2
Elizabeth Cl NG15 ......**10** C3
Elizabeth Ct DE7........**40** B3
Elizabeth Gr NG4.......**50** C4
Ella Bank Rd DE75......**14** B3
Ella Rd NG2............**76** B3
Ellastone Ave NG5......**23** A2
Ellerby Ave NG7........**94** A4
Ellerslie Gr NG10 ....**78** C3
Ellesmere Bsns Pk NG5 ..**47** C4
Ellesmere Cl NG5.......**24** C1
Ellesmere Dr NG9.......**54** A3
Ellesmere Rd NG2......**86** B2
Ellington Rd NG5.......**24** B4
Elliott Durham Comp Sch
NG3.................**48** C3
Elliott Durham Swimming
Pool NG3..............**48** C3
Elliott St NG7..........**106** C3
Ellis Ave NG15 ....**11** C4
Ellis Cl NG10 ....**100** B4
Ellis St NG3............**108** C4
Ellis Gr NG9............**82** B3
Ellis Guilford Comp Sch
NG6.................**46** A4
Ellsworth Rise NG5.....**33** A4
Ellwood Cres NG8......**57** B3
Elm Ave
  Beeston, Attenborough
NG9..................**91** C4
  Beeston, Chilwell NG9 ..**82** A4
  Bingham NG13 ....**67** C2
  Carlton NG4...........**51** A1
  Hucknall NG15 ....**10** C3
  Keyworth NG12.......**104** C2
  Long Eaton NG10 ......**89** B2
  Nottingham NG3........**48** A1
  Nuthall NG16 ....**29** C4
  Sandiacre NG10 ....**69** A1
Elm Bank NG3..........**48** A1
Elm Bank Dr NG3.......**48** A2
Elmbridge NG5.........**22** C1
Elm Cl Keyworth NG12...**104** C2
  Nottingham NG3........**48** A1
Elmdale Gdns NG8......**45** C2
Elm Dr NG4.............**51** A1
Elm Gr NG5.............**24** B3
Elmhurst Ave NG5......**50** A4
Elmore Ct NG7.........**106** B4
Elms Cl NG11 ....**103** A4
Elmsfield Ave DE75......**14** B4
Elms Gdns NG11.......**102** C4
Elmsham Ave NG5......**21** C3
Elms Jun Sch The NG10 ..**89** B2
Elms Pk NG11 ....**103** A4
Elms Prim Sch NG3......**48** A1
Elms The Carlton NG4 ...**63** A4
  Watnall NG16 ....**18** A2

Elmsthorpe Ave NG7....107 A2
Elmswood Gdns NG5 ....34 B1
Elm Tree Ave NG2........75 C1
Elmtree Rd NG14 ....4 C2
Elnor St NG16 ....8 A1
Elson St NG7 ....47 A2
Elston Gdns NG11 ....84 A2
Elswick Cl NG5 ....22 C2
Elswick Dr NG9 ....83 B2
Elterwater Dr NG2 ....87 B4
Eltham Cl NG8 ....31 A1
Eltham Dr NG8 ....45 B4
Eltham Rd NG2 ....76 C1
Elton Cl NG9 ....69 C2
Elton Rd 🟥 NG5 ....47 C3
Elton Rd N NG5 ....47 B3
Elton Terr NG7 ....47 A1
Elvaston Dr NG10 ....99 C2
Elvaston Rd NG8 ....57 C3
Elveden Dr DE7 ....26 A1
Emerys Rd NG4 ....51 C2
Emmanuel Ave
Nottingham, Portchester
NG3...................49 B3
Nottingham, Rise Park
NG5...................22 B3
Emneth Cl NG3 ....49 A2
Empingham Cl NG9 ......91 A4
Empire Ct DE75..........13 C4
Emsworth Cl DE7 ....26 B1
Ena Ave NG2 ....61 A3
Enderby Gdns NG5 ......23 C3
Enderby Sq NG9 ....72 B2
Endsleigh Gdns
Beeston NG9 ....72 B1
West Bridgford NG12....86 C2
Enfield St NG9 ....72 A1
Engine La NG16 ....9 C2
England Cres DE75 ......14 B4
English Martyrs RC Prim
Sch NG10 ....89 A3
Ennerdale Cl NG2........77 B1
Ennerdale Rd
Long Eaton NG10 ....89 A4
Nottingham NG5.........34 B3
Ennismore Mews NG11 ..95 B4
Enthorpe St 🟦 NG8......57 C4
Epperstone Rd NG2 ......76 A2
Epsom Rd NG9 ....80 A1
Erdington Way NG9.......80 A1
Erewash Ct DE7 ....40 B3
Erewash Dr DE7 ....53 C4
Erewash Gdns NG5 ......22 B2
Erewash Gr NG9 ....80 A1
Erewash Mus★ DE7 .....41 A2
Erewash Sq DE7 ....53 B4
Erewash St NG10 ....90 A2
Eric Ave NG15 ....2 B3
Erith Cl NG8 ....44 B3
Ernehale Jun & Inf Sch
NG5....................35 B4
Ernest Rd NG4 ....49 C3
Erskine Rd 🟦 NG5.......47 C3
Esher Gr NG3 ....48 A3
Eskdale Cl NG10 ....100 A3
Eskdale Ct NG2 ....77 B1
Eskdale Dr Beeston NG9 ..81 A3
Nottingham NG8.........45 C2
Eskdale Jun Sch NG9 ....81 A3
Eskhouse Cl NG2 ....87 B2
Essex St 🟦 DE7 ....41 A3
Estwic Ave NG16 ....9 A1
Ethel Ave Hucknall NG15...3 B3
Nottingham NG3.........49 B3
Ethel Rd NG2 ....76 B1
Eton Gr NG8 ....57 C2
Eton Rd NG2 ....86 A4
Eucalyptus Ave NG11 ....93 B3
Eugene Gdns NG2 ....75 C4
Eugene St NG2 ....109 C1
Europa Way NG2 ....85 B1
Evans Rd NG6 ....32 B1
Evedon Wlk NG5 ....22 C3
Evelyn St Beeston NG9 ...73 A1
🟥 Nottingham NG2.....60 C2
Eversley Wlk NG5 ....22 C2
Evesham Ct NG9 ....90 C3
Ewart Rd NG7 ....47 B2

Ewe Lamb Cl NG9........70 B3
Ewe Lamb La NG9 ....70 B3
Ewell Rd NG8 ....56 C3
Exbourne Rd NG8........45 A3
Exbury Gdns NG2 ....85 A2
Exchange Arc NG1 ......109 B2
Exchange Rd NG2 ....76 B1
Exchange Wlk NG1 .....109 B2
Exeter Cl NG4 ....51 A4
Exeter Rd
Nottingham NG7.........47 B2
West Bridgford NG2.....86 B4
Exton Rd NG5 ....33 B1
Eyam Cl NG9 ....71 B4
Eyre's Gdns DE7 ....41 A4
Eyre St NG2 ....60 C2

F

Fabis Dr NG11 ....84 A2
Factory La Beeston NG9...82 A3
Ilkeston DE7 ....40 C4
Failsworth Cl NG11 ......84 A1
Fairbank Cres NG5 ......84 B4
Fairburn Cl NG8 ....56 A2
Faircroft Ave NG10 ......79 A3
Fairdale Dr NG16 ....16 C4
Fairfax Cl NG7 ....47 A4
Fairfield Cl NG11 ....85 A3
Fairfield Cres NG10 ......99 C2
Fairfield Prim Sch NG9..79 C4
Fairfield St NG13 ....67 A2
Fairham Cl NG11 ....95 A2
Fairham Com Coll NG11 .94 B2
Fairham Dr NG8 ....58 B2
Fairham Rd NG12 ......104 A3
Fairisle Cl NG11 ....94 C3
Fairland Cres NG2 ....85 C2
Fairlawn Pl NG5 ....48 B4
Fair Lea Cl NG10 ....100 C4
Fairlight Way NG5 ....22 C1
Fairmaid Gr NG7 ....94 A4
Fairmead Cl NG3 ....49 B2
Fairnley Rd NG8 ....44 B2
Fairview Ct NG11 ....95 C4
Fairview Rd NG5 ....34 C2
Fairway NG12 ....105 A2
Fairway Dr Beeston NG9 ..81 C4
Nottingham NG4.........50 A2
Nottingham NG6.........21 B1
Fairway The NG4 ....36 C1
Falcon Cl NG7 ....107 A2
Falcon Ct DE7 ....40 B3
Falconers Wlk 🟦 NG5 ...23 A2
Falcon Gr NG7 ....47 B3
Falcon St 🟦 NG7 ....47 B3
Falconwood Gdns NG11..93 B3
Fallow Cl NG7 ....94 A4
Fall Rd DE75.............6 C1
Falston Rd NG8 ....45 B4
Faraday Ct NG9 ....70 A3
Faraday Rd NG7 ....107 A2
Farfield Ave NG9 ....72 A2
Farfield Gr NG9 ....72 A2
Farfield Rd DE7 ....41 B2
Farleys Gr NG15 ....11 B3
Farleys La NG15 ....11 B3
Farley St NG6 ....20 C1
Farm Ave NG15 ....10 B2
Farm Cl Ilkeston DE7.....41 B2
Long Eaton NG10 ......101 A3
Nottingham NG7.........94 A4
Farmer St NG11 ....103 B1
Farm Rd Arnold NG5 ....24 C1
Beeston NG9 ....81 C3
Farn'boro Sch & Tech Coll
NG11..................94 C4
Farnborough Rd NG11...94 C4
Farndale Cl NG10 ....99 C3
Farndale Dr NG8 ....55 C2
Farndon Dr NG9 ....80 B1
Farndon Gn NG8 ....58 A1
Far New Cl NG10 ....79 A3
Farnsfield Ave NG9 ......39 B3
Farnsworth Cl NG16 ....18 B3
Far Pasture Cl NG12 ...104 B2
Farriers Croft DE7 ......26 A1
Farriers Gn NG11 ....93 B4
Farringdon Cl NG8.......30 B1
Far Rye NG8.............57 A4

Far St NG11 ....103 B1
Farthing Ct NG10 ....89 A1
Farwells Cl NG6 ....32 A1
Faulconbridge Cl NG6 ...31 C4
Fearn Chase NG4 ....50 C1
Fearn Cl DE72 ....88 C1
Fearnleigh Dr NG6.......46 B4
Featherstone Cl NG4 ....36 B1
Feignes Ct NG12 ....104 B3
Felen Cl NG5 ....22 B1
Fellbarrow Cl NG2 ....87 B3
Fellows Rd NG9 ....72 A1
Fell Side NG5 ....35 B3
Fellside Cl NG2 ....87 B4
Felly Cl NG15 ....10 C3
Felstead Ct NG9 ....71 B3
Felton Cl NG9 ....81 A3
Felton Rd NG2 ....75 C3
Fenchurch Cl NG5 ....22 B3
Fenimore Cl NG12 ....65 C2
Fenroth Cl NG6 ....20 A2
Fenton Dr NG6 ....21 A4
Fenton Rd NG5 ....33 A2
Fenwick Cl NG8 ....45 A4
Fenwick Rd NG8 ....45 A4
Ferguson Cl 🟥 NG9......91 B4
Fern Ave 🟦 NG5 ....47 C3
Fern Cl NG9 ....71 B1
Fern Cres NG16..........8 B1
Ferndale Cl NG9 ....92 A4
Ferndale Gr NG3 ....61 C4
Ferndale Rd NG3 ....61 C4
Fernden Dr NG10 ....88 C1
Ferngill Cl 🟦 NG2 ....75 A3
Fern Lea Ave NG12 ......98 A2
Fernleigh Ave NG3.......49 C4
Fernwood Comp Sch
NG8....................56 B2
Fernwood Cres NG8 .....56 B2
Fernwood Dr NG12 ......65 A3
Fernwood Inf & Jun Sch
NG8....................56 B2
Ferny Hollow Cl NG5.....21 C2
Ferous Cl NG11 ....94 B2
Ferrers Wlk NG3.........60 C3
Ferriby Terr 🟦 NG2 ......75 B3
Festival Rd DE7 ....52 A3
Festus Cl NG3 ....108 C4
Festus St NG4 ....51 B1
Field Ave NG15 ....10 B2
Field Cl Beeston NG9.....81 A2
Breaston DE72 ....88 B1
Carlton NG4 ....51 A4
Field House Cl NG8 ......56 B3
Field House Inf Sch DE7 .53 A4
Field La NG9 ....81 A2
Field Maple Dr NG7 ......46 C2
Field Rd DE7 ....41 A1
Fields Ave NG11 ....102 C3
Fields Farm Rd NG10 ...101 A3
Fieldway NG11 ....85 A2
Fiennes Cres NG7 ......107 C1
Fifth Ave NG9 ....83 C4
Filey St NG6 ....21 A2
Finch Cl NG7 ....74 B2
Finchley Cl NG11 ....93 B3
Findern Gn NG3 ....61 B4
Fingal Cl NG7 ....94 A4
Finsbury Ave NG2 ....61 A2
Finsbury Pk Cl NG2 .....85 B3
Finsbury Rd Beeston NG9.56 A1
Nottingham NG5.........22 B4
Firbank Ct NG9 ....81 A2
Firbeck Prim Sch NG8..55 C2
Firbeck Rd Arnold NG5...24 B2
Nottingham NG8.........56 A2
Fir Cl NG6..............20 A1
Fircroft Ave NG8 ....45 A2
Fircroft Dr NG15 ....10 A3
Fir Dale NG12 ....98 C3
Firecrest Way NG6.......32 B1
Firfield Ave DE72 ....88 A1
Firfield Prim Sch DE72 .88 A1
Firs Ave NG9 ....72 B1
Firsby Rd NG8 ....45 A4
Firs Rd NG12 ....87 A2
Firs St NG10 ....99 C2
First Ave Beeston NG9 ...83 B4
Carlton, Colwick NG4 ....62 C3
Carlton, Gedling NG4 ....51 A3

First Ave continued
Carlton, Thorneywood
NG4...................50 A2
Nottingham NG6.........20 C1
Risley NG10 ....78 B3
Firs The 🟦 NG5 ....34 B1
Firth Cl NG5 ....25 A3
Firth Dr NG9 ....91 B4
Firth Way NG5 ....20 B3
Fisher Ave NG5 ....35 A3
Fisher Ct DE7 ....27 A2
Fisher Gate NG1 ....109 C2
Fisher La NG13 ....67 A2
Fisher St 🟦 NG7 ....47 A2
Fish Pond Dr NG7 ......109 A1
Five Acres NG11 ....84 C2
Flaghome NG12..........98 B2
Flake La DE7 ....68 A3
Flamingo Ct 🟦 NG2 .....74 C4
Flamstead Ave DE75 .....6 A2
Flamstead Rd DE7 ......41 A3
Flamsteed Rd NG8 ......44 B3
Flatts La NG14...........5 A4
Flatts The NG9 ....81 A3
Flawforth Ave NG11 ....103 A4
Flawforth La NG11 ......96 A1
Flaxendale NG12 ....98 C2
Flaxton Way NG5 ....22 A1
Fleam Rd NG11 ....84 A2
Fleeman Gr NG2 ....76 C3
Fleet Cl NG7 ....58 B4
Fleetway Cl NG16 ....16 C3
Fleetwith Cl NG2 ....87 B3
Fleming Cl NG16 ....18 B2
Fleming Dr NG4 ....50 A1
Fleming Gdns NG11 .....93 B3
Fletcher Gate NG1 .....109 B2
Fletcher Rd NG9 ....72 C1
Fletcher St Heanor DE75 .13 C4
Long Eaton NG10 ....89 C2
Fletcher Terr NG3........48 C4
Flewitt Gdns NG3 ....60 C4
Flinthamn Dr NG5 ....34 A2
Flixton Rd NG16 ....18 A1
Floralands Gdn Village★
NG4...................25 C2
Florence Ave NG10 ......90 B3
Florence Boot Cl NG9 ...73 A2
Florence Cres NG4 ......51 C2
Florence Ct DE7 ....41 A3
Florence Gr NG3 ....49 B1
Florence Rd Carlton NG4 .51 C2
Nottingham NG3.........49 B3
West Bridgford NG2.....76 C2
Florence St NG15 ....11 B3
Florey Ct 🟦 NG7.........74 A4
Florey Wlk NG11 ....93 B2
Florin Gdns NG10 ....88 C1
Flowers Cl NG5 ....35 C4
Flying Horse Wlk NG1 ..109 B2
Foljambe Terr NG3.....108 C3
Folkton Gdns NG3 ......49 A3
Forbes Cl NG10 ....101 A3
Ford Ave DE75............6 A2
Fordham Gn NG11 ......94 A2
Ford St N NG7 ....47 B3
Ford St NG7 ....47 B3
Forest Ct NG12 ....98 A3
Forester Cl NG9 ....81 B2
Forester Gr NG4 ....50 B2
Forester Rd NG3 ....49 B2
Forester St NG4 ....51 B1
Forest Fields Prim Sch
NG7....................47 B2
Forest Gr NG1 ....108 A4
Forest Rd Bingham NG13..66 C2
Calverton NG14 ....4 C3
Forest Rd E NG1 ....47 C1
Forest Rd W NG7 ......106 C4
Forest View Dr NG15 .....2 A1
Forge Ave NG14 ....5 B3
Forge Hill NG9 ....81 C2
Forge The NG9 ....53 C3
Forman St NG1 ....108 B3
Forster St NG7 ....106 A3
Forsythia Gdns NG7 ....74 A4
Forum Rd NG5 ....32 C4
Fosbrooke Dr NG10 ....100 C3
Fosse Wlk NG12 ....98 C1

Foster Ave NG9.........82 B[?]
Fosters Dr NG5 ....34 B[?]
Fosters La NG13 ....67 B[?]
Fothergill Ct 🟦 NG3 .....48 A[?]
Fountain Dale Ct 🟦 NG3..48 B[?]
Fountains Cl NG2 ....87 A[?]
Fourth Ave Beeston NG9 .83 C[?]
Carlton NG4 ....49 C[?]
Fowler St NG3 ....48 B[?]
Fox Cl NG10 ....100 C[?]
Fox Covert NG4..........63 A[?]
Fox Covert La NG11 .....93 B[?]
Foxearth Ave NG11 .....94 C[?]
Foxes Cl NG7 ....107 C[?]
Foxglove Rd NG16 ......16 C[?]
Foxgloves The NG13 ....66 C[?]
Fox Gr NG5.............32 C[?]
Fox Gr Ct NG5 ....32 C[?]
Foxhall Bsns Ctr NG7....47 C[?]
Foxhall Rd NG7 ....47 B[?]
Fox Hill NG12...........98 A[?]
Foxhill Ct NG4 ....50 C[?]
Foxhill Rd
Burton Joyce NG14 .....38 C[?]
Carlton NG4 ....50 A[?]
Foxhill Rd Central NG4..50 A[?]
Foxhill Rd E NG4........50 B[?]
Foxhill Rd W NG4.......49 C[?]
Foxhollies Gr NG5 ....33 C[?]
Fox Mdw NG15 ....11 A[?]
Fox Rd NG2 ....76 A[?]
Foxton Cl NG6..........20 A[?]
Foxwood Found Sch &
Tech Coll NG9...........71 A[?]
Foxwood Gr NG14 ....5 B[?]
Fradley Cl NG6 ....21 A[?]
Frampton Rd NG8 ....45 B[?]
Frances Gr NG15 ....3 A[?]
Francis Gr NG6 ....32 C[?]
Francis Rd NG4 ....51 A[?]
Francis St NG7 ....106 C[?]
Franklin Cl NG5 ....23 A[?]
Franklin Dr NG12 ....97 C[?]
Franklyn Gdns
Keyworth NG12 ....104 B[?]
Nottingham NG8.........58 A[?]
Fraser Cres NG4 ....49 C[?]
Fraser Rd Carlton NG4 ...49 C[?]
Nottingham NG2.........75 C[?]
Fraser Sq NG4 ....49 C[?]
Frearson Farm Ct NG16 .16 A[?]
Freckingham St NG1 ...109 C[?]
Freda Ave NG4 ....50 B[?]
Freda Cl NG4 ....36 B[?]
Frederic Ave DE75 ......14 A[?]
Frederick Ave
Carlton NG4 ....49 C[?]
Ilkeston DE7............53 B[?]
Frederick Harrison Inf Sch
NG9....................70 B[?]
Frederick Rd NG9 ....69 C[?]
Frederick St NG10 ......90 B[?]
Freeland Cl NG9 ....80 B[?]
Freemans Rd NG4 ......51 B[?]
Freemans Terr NG4 .....51 B[?]
Freemantle Wlk NG5 ....21 C[?]
Freeston Dr NG6 ....20 A[?]
Freeth St NG2 ....76 B[?]
Freiston St 🟦 NG7.......46 C[?]
Fremount Dr NG8........45 B[?]
French St DE7 ....53 B[?]
Fretwell St 🟦 NG7......46 C[?]
Friar La NG1 ....109 A[?]
Friars Ct Ilkeston DE7....52 A[?]
Nottingham NG7........107 C[?]
Friar St Long Eaton NG10 .89 C[?]
🟦 Nottingham NG7.....74 A[?]
Friary Cl 🟥 NG7.........74 A[?]
Friary The NG7 ....74 A[?]
Friday La NG4 ....51 A[?]
Friesland Dr NG10 ......78 B[?]
Friesland Sch NG10 .....78 B[?]
Frinton Rd NG8..........44 C[?]
Frisby Ave NG10 ....101 A[?]
Frobisher Gdns NG5 ....34 B[?]
Frogmore St NG1 ......108 B[?]
Front St NG5 ....24 A[?]
Frost Ave NG16 ....7 B[?]
Fryar Rd NG16..........9 A[?]
Fulforth St NG1.........108 B[?]
Fuller St NG11 ....102 C[?]

Fullwood Ave **4** DE7 .... 40 C3
Fullwood Cl NG9 .... 81 B2
Fullwood St **6** DE7 .... 40 C3
Fulwood Cres NG8 .... 45 C3
Fulwood Dr NG10 .... 88 C1
Furlong Ave NG5 .... 23 C2
Furlong Cl NG9 .... 69 C2
Furlong St NG5 .... 23 C2
Furnace La DE7 .... 6 B2
Furnace Rd DE7 .... 53 C4
Furness Cl NG2 .... 76 C1
Furness Rd NG6 .... 32 A1
Furzebrook Rd NG4 ...... 62 C4
Furze Gdns NG3 .... 48 B1
Fylde Cl NG9 .... 90 B4
Fylingdale Way NG8 ...... 56 A2

G

Gabor Cl NG11 .... 93 B2
Gabrielle Cl NG6 .... 32 B2
Gadd St NG7 .... 106 B4
Gadsby Cl DE7 .... 53 B2
Gainsborough Cl
  Long Eaton NG10 ...... 101 A3
  Stapleford NG9 .... 80 A4
Gainsford Cl NG5 .... 33 A3
Gainsford Cres NG5 ...... 33 A3
Gala Way NG5 .... 32 C4
Gale Cl NG9 .... 83 A4
Galena Dr NG3 .... 49 B1
Galen Ct **2** NG7 .... 74 A4
Galleries of Justice★
  NG1 .... 109 C2
Gallows Inn Cl DE7 .... 53 B3
Galway Rd Arnold NG5 ... 23 C2
  Nottingham NG7 .... 107 B1
Gamble St NG7 .... 106 C3
GAMSTON 77 C1
Gamston Cres NG5 ...... 34 A1
Gamston Lings Bar Rd
  NG12 .... 87 B1
Ganton Cl NG3 .... 49 A3
Garden Ave Carlton NG4 .. 50 B2
  Ilkeston DE7 .... 53 A3
Garden City NG4 .... 50 C2
Gardendale Ave NG11 .... 99 C3
Gardenia Cres NG3 ...... 49 C4
Gardenia Gr NG3 .... 49 C4
Garden Rd Bingham NG13 .66 C2
  Eastwood NG16 .... 9 B1
  Hucknall NG15 .... 2 B1
Gardens Ct NG2 .... 76 C1
Garden St NG7 .... 106 B3
Gardens The DE75 .... 6 A2
Gardinia Cl NG9 .... 90 C4
Garfield Cl NG9 .... 70 A3
Garfield Rd NG7 .... 106 B3
Garforth Cl NG8 .... 46 C2
Garners Hill NG1 .... 109 B2
Garnet Cl NG3 .... 60 C3
Garnet St NG4 .... 51 A1
Garnett Ave DE75 .... 14 A4
Garrett Gr NG11 .... 93 C4
Garsdale Cl NG2 .... 87 B4
Garsdale Dr NG11 .... 84 C1
Garton Cl Beeston NG9 .. 81 A3
  Nottingham NG6 .... 31 C3
Gas St NG10 .... 79 B4
Gatcombe Cl NG12 ...... 65 B2
Gatcombe Gr NG10 ...... 78 C1
Gateford Cl NG9 .... 71 B4
Gateside Rd NG2 .... 74 C3
Gatling St NG7 .... 106 A3
Gaul St NG6 .... 20 C1
Gauntley Ct **1** NG7 .... 47 A2
Gauntley St NG7 .... 46 C2
Gautries Cl NG5 .... 22 B2
Gawthorne St NG7 ...... 47 B3
Gayhurst Gn NG6 .... 32 C3
Gayhurst Rd NG6 .... 32 C3
Gaynor Ct NG8 .... 57 C4
Gayrigg Ct NG9 .... 81 A2
Gayton Cl NG8 .... 44 B2
Gayton Rd DE7 .... 40 B3
Gaywood Cl NG11 ...... 94 B2
GEDLING 51 A4
Gedling Gr NG7 .... 106 C4
Gedling Rd Arnold NG5 .. 35 C3
  Carlton NG4 .... 51 A2
Gedling Sch The NG4 .... 36 C1

Gedling St NG1 .... 109 C2
Gedney Ave NG3 .... 49 A2
Gelding Gr NG5 .... 24 A1
Gelding House Woods
  Nature Reserve★ NG4 .51 C4
Gell Rd NG7 .... 80 C1
George Ave Beeston NG9 .82 B3
  Long Eaton NG10 .... 90 B3
George Rd Carlton NG4 .. 50 C1
  West Bridgford NG2 .... 76 A1
George's La NG14 ...... 4 C1
George Spencer Sch &
  Tech Ctr NG9 .... 80 A3
George St Arnold NG5 ... 34 C4
  Hucknall NG15 .... 2 C2
  Langley Mill NG16 ..... 7 C1
  Nottingham NG1 .... 108 B3
Georgia Dr NG5 .... 23 C4
Georgina Rd NG9 .... 82 B3
Gerrard Cl NG5 .... 22 B4
Gertrude Rd NG2 .... 76 C3
Gervase Gdns NG11 .... 95 C4
Ghost House La NG9 .... 81 A2
Gibbons Ave NG9 ...... 79 C4
Gibbons St NG7 .... 74 A3
Gibb St NG10 .... 90 A1
Gibson Rd NG7 .... 47 B2
Gifford Gdns NG2 ...... 75 A4
Gilbert Ave NG9 .... 90 C4
Gilbert Bvd NG5 .... 25 A1
Gilbert Gdns NG3 ...... 61 B4
Gilead St NG6 .... 20 C1
Giles Ave NG2 .... 85 C4
Gillercomb Cl NG2 ..... 87 C3
Gillot St DE75 .... 14 B2
Gillotts Cl NG13 .... 67 A3
Gill St NG1 .... 108 A4
Gilpet Ave NG3 .... 49 A2
GILTBROOK 17 A2
Giltbrook Cres NG16 ... 17 A2
Gilt Hill NG16 .... 17 B1
Gilthill Prim Sch NG16 .17 B1
Giltway NG16 .... 17 A1
Gimson Cl DE7 .... 26 A1
Gin Cl Way NG16 ...... 28 A4
Girton Rd NG5 .... 33 B1
Gisburn Cl NG11 ...... 84 C2
Glade Ave NG8 .... 58 A3
Glade Hill Prim Sch
  NG5 .... 23 A2
Gladehill Rd NG5 ...... 23 A1
Glade The NG11 .... 94 A1
Gladstone Ave DE75 ... 14 A4
Gladstone St W DE7 ... 41 A1
Gladstone St
  Beeston NG9 .... 82 B4
  Carlton NG4 .... 50 B1
  Heanor DE75 .... 13 C4
  Langley Mill NG16 .... 8 A2
  Long Eaton NG10 ..... 100 C4
  Nottingham NG7 ...... 47 B2
Gladys St NG7 .... 47 A1
Glaisdale Dr E NG8 .... 56 C4
Glaisdale Drive Ind Est
  NG8 .... 56 B4
Glaisdale Dr W NG8 .... 56 B3
Glaisdale Parkway NG8 . 56 B3
Glamis Rd NG5 .... 47 B4
Glanton Way NG5 ..... 24 B4
Glapton Prim Sch NG11 .93 C4
Glapton Rd NG2 ...... 75 B3
Glapton Wood Nature
  Reserve★ NG11 ...... 93 C2
Glaramara Cl **1** NG2 ..75 A3
Glasshouse St NG1 .... 108 B3
Glebe Cres DE7 .... 41 B1
Glebe Dr NG14 .... 38 B1
Glebe Farm Cl NG2 ... 85 B2
Glebe Farm View NG4 ..41 A1
Glebe Rd Carlton NG4 .. 50 A4
  Nuthall NG16 .... 30 A4
  West Bridgford NG2 .. 76 B1
Glebe St Beeston NG9 .. 82 A4
  Hucknall NG15 .... 2 C1
Glebe The NG16 .... 27 C2
Glen Ave NG16 .... 16 C3
Glenbrook Cres NG8 ... 45 B1
Glenbrook Prim Sch
  NG8 .... 45 A1
Glencairn Dr NG8 .... 45 B2
Glencoe Rd NG11 .... 94 C3

Glencoyne Rd NG11 .... 94 A2
Glendale Cl NG4 .... 50 B4
Glendale Gr NG9 ...... 82 A1
Glendale Gdns NG5 ... 24 A1
Glendoe Gr NG13 ..... 66 B2
Glendon Dr
  Hucknall NG15 .... 11 B3
  Nottingham NG5 ..... 33 B1
Glendon Rd DE7 ...... 52 A2
Gleneagles Cl NG12 .. 87 B1
Gleneagles Dr NG5 ... 24 C3
Glenfield Ave NG16 .. 17 B1
Glenfield Rd NG10 ... 100 C3
Glen Helen NG4 ...... 63 A4
Glenlivet Gdns NG7 .. 94 B3
Glenloch Dr NG11 .... 94 B2
Glenmore Rd NG2 .... 87 A4
Glenorchy Cres NG5 .. 21 C2
Glen Parva Ave NG5 .. 23 C3
Glen Rd NG14 .... 38 C3
Glenridding Cl NG2 .. 87 C3
Glensford Gdns NG5 .. 21 C4
Glenside NG5 .... 35 C3
Glenside Rd NG9 .... 71 B3
Glenstone Ct **1** NG7 ..47 A2
Glen The NG7 .... 94 B4
Glentworth Rd NG7 .. 106 A4
Glenwood Ave NG8 ... 56 B1
Glinis Rd NG5 .... 22 A2
Gloucester Ave
  Beeston NG9 .... 82 B3
  Nottingham NG7 .... 107 A2
  Nuthall NG16 .... 31 A2
  Sandiacre NG10 ..... 78 C2
Glover Ave NG8 ..... 56 B2
Goatchurch Ct **8** NG5 .22 B3
Goathland Cl **3** NG5 ..22 C2
Godber Rd NG15 .... 10 C3
Godfrey Dr DE7 ..... 52 B4
Godfrey St Carlton NG4 .63 B4
  Heanor DE75 .... 13 C3
Godkin Dr NG16 ..... 7 B2
Goldcrest Cl NG13 ... 67 C1
Goldcrest Rd NG6 ... 31 C2
Goldham Rd NG8 ... 44 B2
Goldsmith Sq NG1 .. 108 A3
Goldsmith St NG1 .. 108 A3
Goldswong Terr NG3 .48 A1
Golf Club Rd DE7 ... 69 A3
Golf Course Rd NG12 .105 B2
Golf Rd NG12 .... 65 B2
Goodall Cres NG15 .. 12 A3
Goodall St **1** NG7 .. 47 A1
Goodliffe St **6** NG7 ..47 A2
Goodman Cl NG16 ... 17 A2
Good Shepherd RC Prim
  Sch The NG5 .... 35 B3
Goodwin Cl NG10 ... 78 C4
Goodwin Dr NG16 ... 28 C4
Goodwin St NG7 .... 106 C4
Goodwood Ave NG5 .23 C2
Goodwood Cres DE7 .52 B2
Goodwood Dr NG9 .. 90 B4
Goodwood Rd NG8 .. 57 A2
Goole Ave DE7 ...... 52 B3
Goose Gate
  Cotgrave NG12 ..... 98 A3
  Nottingham NG1 .... 109 C2
Gordon Cl NG9 ..... 91 C4
Gordon Rd
  Burton Joyce NG14 .. 39 B3
  Nottingham NG3 .... 61 A4
  West Bridgford NG2 . 76 B1
Gordon Rise NG3 ... 48 C4
Gordon Sq NG2 ..... 76 B1
Gordon St Ilkeston DE7 .41 B3
  Nottingham NG6 .... 32 B2
Gorman Ct NG5 .... 24 C1
Gorse Cl Calverton NG14..4 C2
  Eastwood NG16 .... 16 C2
  Long Eaton NG10 ... 89 A4
Gorse Ct NG6 ...... 32 C1
Gorse Rd NG12 .... 104 A3
Gorsey Rd NG3 ..... 48 B2
Gosforth Ct NG2 ... 75 C3
Goshawk Rd DE7 .. 53 B1
Gothic Cl NG6 ..... 32 C2
Goverton Sq NG6 .. 32 B3
Gowan Cl **7** NG9 .. 91 B4
Goyden Cl NG5 .... 22 B2
Grace Ave NG9 .... 83 A4

Grace Cres DE75 .... 14 A4
Grace Dr NG8 ...... 46 B2
Grafton Ave NG5 ... 34 C3
Grafton Ct NG7 .... 106 C3
Graham St Ilkeston DE7 ..41 A1
  Nottingham NG7 .... 106 B3
Grainger Ave NG2 .. 86 A1
Grainger St NG2 ... 74 A4
Graingers Terr NG15 . 11 C4
Grampian Dr NG5 .. 22 C4
Grampian Way NG10 .88 C2
Granby Dr NG13 ... 66 C2
Granby St DE7 ..... 40 C4
Grandfield Ave NG12 ..65 A3
Grandfield Cres NG12 .65 A3
Grandfield St DE75 . 6 A2
Grange Ave Beeston NG9 .82 B4
  Ruddington NG11 ... 95 B2
Grange Cl NG11 .... 75 A2
Grange Cres NG4 .. 37 A1
Grange Ct NG2 .... 95 B4
Grange Dr NG10 ... 90 B2
Grange Farm Cl NG9 .90 C3
Grangelea Gdns NG9 ..71 A2
Grange Pk NG2 .... 87 B3
Grange Prim Sch NG10 .90 B2
Grange Rd Arnold NG5 .34 C2
  Long Eaton NG10 ... 90 B2
  Nottingham NG6 .... 32 B1
  West Bridgford NG2 ..86 C2
Grange The DE75 .. 13 A2
Grange View NG16 .. 9 A1
Grange View Rd NG4 .51 B4
Grangewood Ave **3**
  DE7 .... 41 A1
Grangewood Ct NG8 .56 A1
Grangewood Rd NG8 .56 A1
Grannis Dr NG8 .... 45 B2
Grantham Cl NG16 .. 17 A1
Grantham Rd NG4 .. 65 A1
Grantleigh Cl NG8 .. 57 A3
Granton Ave NG11 .. 94 B2
Grant St NG7 ...... 106 B3
Granville Ave NG10 .. 89 C3
Granville Cres NG12 .64 C1
Granville Ct **4** NG3 .. 61 A4
Granville Gr **4** NG3 .. 61 A3
Grasmere Cl NG15 .. 2 B2
Grasmere Rd
  Beeston NG9 .... 71 C2
  Long Eaton NG10 ... 89 A4
Grasmere St NG10 .. 79 B3
Grassingdale Cl NG4 .50 B4
Grassington Rd NG8 .46 B1
Grassmere NG12 ... 98 C3
Grass St DE7 ...... 26 C1
Grassy La NG9 ..... 82 C3
Graveney Gdns NG5 .36 A4
Graylands Rd NG8 .. 56 C4
Grayson Ms NG9 ... 91 A4
Graystones Cl NG2 .. 87 B3
Grazingfield NG11 .. 84 C2
Greasley Ave NG16 .. 17 A4
Greasley Beauvale DH
  Lawrence Int Sch NG16 ..9 C1
Greasley Beauvale Jun Sch
  NG16 .... 16 C4
Greasley St NG6 .... 20 C1
Great Freeman St NG3 .108 B4
Great Hoggett Dr NG9 ..81 A4
Great Northern Cl The
  NG2 .... 109 C1
Great Northern Rd NG16 .15 B4
Great Northern Way
  NG4 .... 63 C4
Greaves Cl Arnold NG5 .35 C3
  Nottingham NG8 .... 44 B3
Greek St NG7 ...... 106 C3
Greenacre NG14 .... 38 C3
Green Acre
  Nottingham NG8 .... 55 C3
  West Bridgford NG2 .87 A2
Greenacre Ave DE75 .7 B1
Greenacres Cl NG16 .17 A4
Green Ap NG4 ..... 50 A2
Green Ave NG4 .... 51 B1
Greenbank NG4 ... 62 B4
Greenburn Cl NG2 .. 87 C4
Green Cl Hucknall NG15 .12 A3
  Keyworth NG12 .... 104 C4
Greencroft NG11 ... 94 B4

Greendale Gdns NG8 ... 45 C2
Greendale Rd Arnold NG5 .35 A4
  Nottingham NG3 .... 62 A4
Greenfield Com Prim Sch
  NG2 .... 75 C3
Greenfield Gr NG4 .. 50 A2
Greenfields NG16 ... 7 B2
Greenfields Dr NG12 .98 B2
Greenfield St NG7 .. 73 C3
Greenford Cl NG16 .. 30 C1
Greengates Ave NG3 .35 A1
Greenhill Cres NG4 . 62 C4
Greenhill Rd NG4 ... 62 C4
Greenhill Rise NG4 .. 50 C1
Greenhills Ave NG16 .9 B1
Greenhills Rd NG16 . 9 A1
Greenholme Sch NG7 .107 A2
Green La Ilkeston DE7 ..41 B1
  Nottingham NG7 .... 94 A3
Greenland Cres NG9 .81 B2
Green Leys NG2 .... 85 B2
Green Platt NG12 ... 98 A3
Greens Ct DE7 ..... 40 B3
Green's Farm La NG4 .51 B4
Greenside Cl NG10 .. 90 A1
Greens La NG16 .... 29 B4
Green St Barton in F NG11 .92 C1
  Nottingham NG2 ... 75 C3
Green The Beeston NG9 .82 A2
  Radcliffe on T NG12 ..64 C2
Greenway Cl NG12 .. 64 C2
Greenway The NG10 .79 A4
Greenwich Ave NG6 .32 A2
Greenwich Pk Cl NG2 .85 B3
Greenwood Ave
  Hucknall NG15 ..... 2 B2
  Ilkeston DE7 .... 41 B1
  Nottingham NG3 ... 62 B3
Greenwood Cres NG4 .62 C4
Greenwood Dale Tech Sch
  NG2 .... 61 B2
Greenwood Gdns NG11 .103 A4
Greenwood Inf Sch NG2 .61 B2
Greenwood Jun Sch
  NG2 .... 61 B2
Greenwood Rd NG3 .62 B3
Greenwood Vale NG15 ..2 B2
Greetwell Cl **1** NG8 .57 B4
Gregg Ave DE75 ... 14 A4
Gregory Ave Aldercar NG16 .7 B2
  Nottingham, New Lenton
    NG7 .... 107 A3
  Nottingham, Portchester
    NG3 .... 49 B4
Gregory Bvd NG7 .. 47 B1
Gregory Cl NG9 .... 70 B2
Gregory Ct Beeston NG9 ..81 A2
  Nottingham NG7 ... 107 A1
Gregory St Ilkeston DE7 ..40 C2
  9 Ilkeston DE7 .... 40 C3
  Nottingham NG7 ... 74 A4
Gregson Gdns NG9 .91 A3
Gregson Rd NG9 ... 91 A4
Grenville Dr Ilkeston DE7 ..27 A1
  Stapleford NG9 .... 70 A2
Grenville Rd NG4 .. 83 A2
Grenville Rise NG5 .24 A3
Gresham Cl NG2 ... 75 B1
Gresham Gdns
  Arnold NG5 .... 35 B3
  West Bridgford NG2 .75 C1
Gresley Dr NG2 .... 61 A1
Gresley Rd **11** DE7 .41 A3
Gretton Rd NG3 ... 35 B2
Greyfriar Gate NG1 .109 B1
Greyfriars Cl **4** DE75 .14 A3
Greyhound St NG1 .109 B2
Greys Rd NG5 .... 35 A4
Grey St NG16 ..... 16 B3
Greystoke Dr NG8 .44 A1
Greythorn Dr NG2 .85 C2
Greythorn Prim Sch
  NG2 .... 85 C3
Grierson Ave NG5 .22 C2
Griffon Rd DE7 ... 53 A2
Griffs Hollow NG4 .50 C1
Grimesmoor Rd NG14 ..5 C3
Grimsby Terr NG3 .108 B4

Grimston Rd NG7......106 A4
Grindon Cres NG6 ......21 A4
Grinsbrook NG7 ....107 A2
Gripps Comm NG12.......98 B1
Grisedale Ct NG9 ....80 C2
Gritley Mews NG2 ....75 A4
Grizedale Ct NG13.......66 A2
Groome Ave DE75 ....6 A2
Grosvenor Ave
　Breaston DE72...........88 B2
　Long Eaton NG10 ....99 C2
　Nottingham NG3.........48 A3
Grosvenor Rd NG16.......16 A4
Grosvenor Sch NG12 ...86 C2
Grouville Dr NG9 ....35 B3
Grove Ave Beeston NG9 ...82 A4
　Nottingham NG7........106 C4
Grove Cl NG14..........39 A3
Grove Mews NG16 ....15 C3
Grover Ave NG3 ....35 B1
Grove Rd NG7 ....107 B1
Groveside Cres NG11 ....83 B1
Grove St NG9............82 C3
Grove The Breaston DE72...88 B2
　Calverton NG14 ....5 C2
　Nottingham, Carrington
　　NG5..................47 C4
　Nottingham NG7........106 B4
Grundy St NG7 ....46 C1
Guinea Cl NG10.........88 C1
Gunn Cl NG6 ....20 B1
Gunnersbury Way NG8...30 C1
Gunthorpe Cl NG5.......33 C1
Gunthorpe Dr NG5.......33 C1
Gunthorpe Rd NG4 ....36 B1
Gutersloh Ct NG9.......70 B2
Guy Cl NG9.............80 A4
Gwenbrook Ave NG9....82 A3
Gwenbrook Rd NG9.......81 C3
Gwndy Gdns [3] NG5 ....22 B1

H

Hackworth Cl NG16.......9 C1
Hadbury Rd NG5.........33 A1
Hadden Ct NG8..........56 B3
Hadden Pk High Sch
　NG8..................45 B1
Hadderley Wlk NG5...108 C4
Haddon Cl Carlton NG4...50 B4
　Heanor DE75 ....13 A4
　Hucknall NG15 ....11 B4
Haddon Cres NG9 ....91 B4
Haddon Nurseries DE7...26 C1
Haddon Prim Sch NG4...50 B3
Haddon Rd NG2 ....86 B4
Haddon St Ilkeston DE7 ..26 C1
　Nottingham NG5.........47 C4
Haddon Way
　Long Eaton NG10 ....99 B2
　Radcliffe on T NG12 ....65 B3
Hadleigh Cl NG9........90 A4
Hadley St DE7 ....53 B3
Hadrian Gdns NG5.......22 B4
Hadstock Cl NG10 ....79 A2
Hagley Cl NG3..........61 B4
Haileybury Cres NG2...86 B3
Haileybury Rd NG2 ....86 B3
Haise Ct NG6 ....31 A3
Halberton Dr NG2 ....85 C2
Hales Cl NG12 ....98 A3
Haley Cl NG16 ....28 B4
Halifax Ct NG8.........44 B4
Halifax Pl NG1 ....109 B2
Hallam Fields Jun Sch
　DE7..................53 A3
Hallam Fields Rd DE7 ...53 C2
Hallam Rd Beeston NG9...82 B4
　Nottingham NG3.........49 B4
Hallams La NG9 ....81 C3
Hallam's La NG5.......24 A1
Hall Cl NG12............64 C2
Hall Croft NG9.........82 B3
Hallcroft Rd [2] DE7......41 A2
Hall Dr Beeston NG9 ....81 C3
　Nottingham NG8.........56 C1
　Sandiacre NG10 ....79 A4
Hall Farm Ct DE7 ....68 B2

Hallfields NG12..........87 A1
Hall Gdns NG9..........71 A1
Hallington Dr DE75 .....13 B3
Hall La NG16 ....8 B4
Hallowell Dr NG8........57 A3
Hall Rd NG16 ....8 A2
Halls La NG16 ....16 B2
Halls Rd NG9 ....79 C4
Hall St NG5.............34 B1
Hallum Ct DE7..........27 A1
Hall View Dr NG8 ....56 B4
Halstead Cl Beeston NG9...81 B2
　Nottingham NG8.........31 C1
Haltham Wlk NG11 ....93 C2
Hambledon Dr NG8.......57 C3
Hambleton Cl NG10.......88 C3
Hambling Cl NG6 ....20 B1
Hamilton Cl Arnold NG5...25 A3
　Beeston NG9 ....90 B4
Hamilton Dr
　Nottingham NG7........109 A1
　Radcliffe on T NG12 ....65 A3
Hamilton Gdns [11] NG5...47 C3
Hamilton Rd
　Long Eaton NG10 ....89 C3
　Nottingham NG5.........47 C2
Hamlet The DE75 ....6 C1
Hammersmith Cl NG16...30 C2
Hampden Gr NG9.........82 A4
Hampden St
　Eastwood NG16 ....16 C2
　Nottingham NG1.......108 A3
Hampshire Dr NG10 .....79 A3
Hampstead Rd NG3.......48 C3
Hampton Cl NG9 ....80 A1
Hampton Ct [4] DE75....13 B4
Hampton Rd NG2 ....86 A4
Handel St NG3..........60 C3
Hand's Rd DE75 ....14 B3
Hankin St NG15.........12 A4
Hanley Ave NG9 ....71 A2
Hanley St NG1.........108 A3
Hannah Cres NG11.......75 A1
Hanover Ct NG8 ....56 B4
Hanslope Cres NG8 .....44 B1
Hanson Cres NG15.......2 C1
Hanworth Gdns NG5 ....23 B2
Harberton Cl NG5 ....23 C3
Harby Dr NG8 ....58 A2
Harcourt Cl DE7 ....40 B3
Harcourt Cres NG16 ....31 A1
Harcourt Rd NG7 ....47 B2
Harcourt St NG9 ....82 A4
Harcourt Terr NG3 .....108 C3
Harden Ct NG11 ....93 B2
Hardstaff Rd NG2.......61 B2
Hardwick Cl NG10 ....99 B2
Hardwicke Rd NG9 ....81 B1
Hardwick Gr
　Nottingham NG7........107 B2
　West Bridgford NG2....76 B3
Hardwick Pl DE7 ....52 A3
Hardwick Rd
　[1] Nottingham, Carrington
　　NG5..................34 A1
　Nottingham, The Park
　　NG7.................107 C1
Hardwood Cl
　Nottingham NG6........20 A1
　[1] Nottingham NG6....20 A1
Hardy Barn DE75 ....14 B1
Hardy Cl Kimberley NG16...18 A1
　Long Eaton NG10 ....100 C4
Hardy's Dr NG4.........51 A3
Hardy St Kimberley NG16...18 A1
　Nottingham NG7........106 C4
Harewood Ave NG6......32 B3
Harewood Cl
　Radcliffe on T NG12 ....65 B2
　Sandiacre NG10 ....79 A2
Hargreaves Ct [5] DE7...41 A1
Harkstead Rd NG5.......22 C3
Harlaxton Dr
　Long Eaton NG10 ....90 C2
　Nottingham NG7........107 B2
Harlaxton Wlk NG3....108 B4
Harlech Cl DE7 ....26 A1
Harlech Rise NG9.......81 A2
Harlequin Cl NG12......65 C2
Harlequin Ct NG16.......8 B1
Harley St NG7 ....107 B1

Harlow Gr NG4 ....50 C4
Harmston Rise NG5.....33 A2
Harold Ave NG16 ....7 C2
Harold St NG2..........60 C2
Harpenden Sq NG8 .....31 C1
Harpole Wlk NG5 ....24 A4
Harrier Gr NG15 ....10 C2
Harriett St NG9 ....69 C1
Harrimans Dr DE72.....88 B2
Harrimans La NG7 .....74 B2
Harrington Cl NG4.....51 C3
Harrington Dr NG7.....107 B2
Harrington Jun Sch
　NG10.................100 A3
Harrington St NG10....100 A3
Harris Cl NG8 ....57 A3
Harrison Ct NG13 ....66 B2
Harrison Rd NG9 ....69 C2
Harrison's Plantation
　Nature Reserve* NG8...57 A3
Harris Rd NG8 ....81 C4
Harrogate Rd NG3.......62 A3
Harrogate St NG4.......51 A1
Harrowby Rd NG7 .....107 B2
Harrow Dr DE7 ....53 B2
Harrow Gdns NG8 .....58 A2
Harrow Rd Hucknall NG15...10 B3
　Nottingham NG8........57 C2
　West Bridgford NG2....86 A3
Hart Ave NG10.........78 C3
Hartcroft Rd NG5.......33 A2
Hartford Cl [2] NG2.....75 C4
Harthill Cl [10] NG9.....91 B4
Hartington Ave
　Carlton NG4 ....50 B3
　Hucknall NG15 ....10 A4
Hartington Pl DE7 .....26 C2
Hartington Rd NG5.....34 A1
Hartley Ct NG7 ....106 B4
Hartley Dr NG9 ....83 A4
Hartley Rd NG7 ....106 B4
Hartness Rd NG11 .....93 B2
Hartside Cl NG2 ....77 B1
Hartside Gdns [1] NG10...88 C2
Hart St NG7 ....107 B1
Hartwell St NG3 ....108 C4
Hartwood Dr NG9 ....69 C3
Harvest Cl Bingham NG13...66 C2
　Nottingham NG5........22 A2
Harvey Cl NG11.......103 A3
Harvey Croft NG9 .....54 A2
Harvey Ct [3] NG7......74 A1
Harvey Hadden Sports Ctr
　NG8....................45 A1
Harvey Rd
　Nottingham, Bilborough
　　NG8..................45 A1
　Nottingham, Dunkirk NG7...74 A4
Harwich Cl NG6 ....20 B2
Harwill Cres NG8 ....45 C4
Harwood Cl NG5.......24 C2
Haslam St NG7 ....109 A1
Haslemere Rd
　Long Eaton NG10 ....89 A2
　Nottingham NG8........45 B3
Hassock La N DE75.....14 C1
Hassock La S DE75.....26 A4
Hassocks La NG9 ....73 A1
Hastings St NG4 ....50 A1
Haswell Rd NG6 ....31 C3
Hatfield Ave NG10 .....79 A2
Hatfield Dr NG2 ....85 B2
Hatfield Rd NG3........48 A3
Hatherleigh Cl NG3.....36 A4
Hathern Cl NG10.......100 C3
Hathern Gn NG9 ....72 C2
Hathersage Ave
　Long Eaton NG10 ....99 B3
　Long Eaton NG10 ....99 C3
Hatley Cl [7] NG5.......75 A3
Hatton Cl NG5..........22 B4
Hatton Crofts NG10....100 A4
Hatton Gdns NG6.......30 C1
Havelock Gdns NG3....108 B4
Havelock St DE7 ....41 A1
Haven Cl NG2..........85 C3
Havenden Gdns [2] NG7...44 A4
Havenwood Rise NG11...93 C2
Haverhill Cres NG5.....21 B3
Haversham Cl NG6 .....46 A4
Hawarden Terr [9] NG7...47 A1

Hawkhurst Dr NG8......71 C4
Hawkins Ct DE7 ....27 A2
Hawk Ridge Gdns [1]
　NG3..................60 C3
Hawkshead Cl NG2.....87 C3
Hawksley Gdns NG11...93 B4
Hawksley Rd [14] NG7...47 A1
Hawkswood NG9.......81 A2
Hawksworth Ave NG5...34 B2
Hawksworth Rd NG2...76 B3
Hawksworth St [10] NG3...60 C3
Hawthorn Ave
　Breaston DE72...........88 B2
　Hucknall NG15 ....2 B1
　Stapleford NG9..........79 C4
Hawthorn Cl
　Keyworth NG12.........104 B2
　[5] Nottingham NG2....75 A3
　West Bridgford NG12...87 A2
Hawthorn Cres NG5 ....24 B3
Hawthorn Ct [6] NG2...75 A3
Hawthorne Ave NG10...100 B4
Hawthorne Gr NG9 .....83 A4
Hawthorne Prim Sch
　NG6..................12 C2
Hawthorne Rise NG16...27 C2
Hawton Cres NG8.......58 A1
Hawton Spinney NG8...58 A2
Hayden La NG15........3 A3
Haydn Ave NG5.........47 C4
Haydn Prim Sch NG5...48 A4
Haydn Rd NG5.........47 C4
Haydock Cl NG16.......17 C1
Hayes Rd NG12 ....104 B3
Hayles Cl NG5 ....33 C4
Hayling Cl DE7 ....26 A1
Hayling Dr NG8.........46 B3
Haynes Ave NG9 ....54 A3
Haynes Cl NG11.......84 B1
Hays Cl DE7 ....40 B4
Haywood Ct [2] NG2...60 C2
Haywood Rd NG3.......35 B1
Haywood Sch NG5.....34 A3
Haywood St NG2 ....60 C2
Hazelbank Ave NG3.....49 A3
Hazel Cl Bingham NG13...67 C2
　Heanor DE75 ....13 B3
Hazel Dr NG16.........29 C4
Hazel Gr Hucknall NG15...11 B3
　Nottingham NG3........35 B2
Hazel Hill Cres NG5.....22 C2
Hazelhurst Gdns [3] NG6...20 C1
Hazel Hurst Prep Sch
　NG3..................35 B1
Hazel Mdws NG15 .....11 B3
Hazelmere Gr NG7.....107 A2
Hazel St NG6 ....20 C2
Hazel Way NG15 ....3 A4
Hazelwood NG12 ....98 C3
Hazelwood Cl NG16....16 C4
Hazelwood Dr NG15....10 A4
Hazelwood Rd NG7.....46 C1
Headingley Gdns [3]
　NG8..................46 B2
Healey Cl NG2.........75 B4
HEANOR 13 A4
　14 C4
HEANOR GATE 13 A2
Heanor Gate [3] DE75...13 B3
Heanor Gate Ind Est
　DE75.................13 B2
Heanor Gate Rd DE75...13 B2
Heanor Gate Science Coll
　DE75.................13 A3
Heanor Langley Mill &
　District Meml Hosp
　DE75.................14 A3
Heanor Rd DE7 ....26 B1
Heanor Rd, DE75 ....13 B3
Heard Cres NG9 ....72 B2
Heathcoat St NG1 .....108 C3
Heather Cl
　Eastwood NG16 ....17 A4
　Nottingham NG3........48 B1
Heather Cres DE72 .....88 B1
Heather Croft NG2.....85 B2
Heather Ct DE75 ....14 C3
Heatherley Dr NG6 ....33 A2
Heather Rd NG4 ....50 B3
Heather Rise NG9 .....72 A3
Heathervale NG2 ....85 A4

Heathfield Ave DE7 ....41 B2
Heathfield Gr NG9 .....81 B1
Heathfield Prim Sch
　NG5..................33 A1
Heathfield Rd NG5.....33 A2
Heath Gdns DE72 ....88 C2
Heathrington Gdns [9]
　NG5..................22 B3
Heath The NG16 ....16 C2
Heaton Cl NG3.........49 A3
Heckington Dr NG8.....57 C3
Heddington Gdns [1]
　NG5..................23 B2
Hedges Dr DE7 ....53 B3
Hedley St NG7 ....47 B2
Hedley Villas [5] NG7 ...47 B3
Helen Cl NG9...........81 C4
Hellebore Cl NG5.......21 C1
Helm Cl NG6 ....20 A1
Helmsdale Cl NG5......24 C3
Helmsdale Gdns NG5...22 A3
Helston Dr NG8.........44 C3
Helvellyn Cl [7] NG2....75 B4
Helvellyn Way NG10....89 A4
Hemingway Cl
　Carlton NG4 ....50 A1
　Eastwood NG16 ....17 A3
Hemlock Ave
　Long Eaton NG10 ....89 C3
　Stapleford NG9..........70 A2
Hemlock Gdns NG6 ....31 A4
Hemlock La DE7 ....52 B3
Hempshill Hall Prim Sch
　NG6..................31 A3
Hempshill La NG6 .....31 B4
HEMPSHILL VALE 30 C4
Hemsby Gdns [5] NG6...20 C2
Hemscott Cl NG2 ......20 A2
Hemsley Dr NG16.......8 B1
Hemswell Cl NG3.......61 B3
Hendon Rise NG3.......49 A2
Hendre Gdns [1] NG5...22 B1
Henley Cl NG4...........63 B4
Henley Gdns NG9 .....70 A3
Henley Rise NG5 ....33 B1
Hennessey Cl [1] NG9...91 B4
Henning Gdns [13] NG5...22 B2
Henrietta St NG6 ....32 A4
Henry Ct NG2..........75 B4
Henry Mellish Comp Sch
　NG6..................32 B3
Henry Rd Beeston NG9...82 C4
　Nottingham NG7........107 A1
　West Bridgford NG2....76 A2
Henry St Arnold NG5....23 B2
　Hucknall NG15 ....11 C4
　[6] Nottingham NG2...60 C2
Henry Whipple Inf Sch
　NG5..................33 A4
Henry Whipple Jun Sch
　NG5..................33 A4
Henshaw Ave DE7 .....52 B3
Henshaw Pl DE7 ....26 C2
Henson's Sq NG9 ....71 A2
Hepple Dr NG6 ....20 A1
Herald Cl NG9 ....73 A1
Herbert Rd NG5 ....47 C3
Hereford Rd Arnold NG5...34 C3
　Carlton NG4 ....51 A4
　Nottingham NG3........61 C3
Hermitage Sq [1] NG2...61 A1
Hermitage Wlk
　Ilkeston DE7...........53 A4
　Nottingham NG7.......107 C1
Hermon St NG7........106 C3
Heron Dr NG7 ....107 A2
Herons Ct NG2 ....87 B2
Heron Wharf [2] NG7...74 B4
Hervey Gr NG7 ....94 A4
Heskey Cl NG3.........108 B4
Heskey Wlk NG3.......108 B4
Heslington Ave NG8 ...46 C2
Hethbeth Ct [5] NG2....75 B4
Hethersett Gdns [4] NG6...20 C2
Hetley Rd NG9.........72 B2
Hexham Ave DE7 ....53 B2
Hexham Cl NG2.........86 C4
Hexham Gdns [1] NG5...22 B3
Heyford Ct DE75 ....14 B3
Heymann Prim Sch NG2...85 C2
Hey St NG10 ....100 B2

Hickings La NG9 . . . . .70 A2
Hickling Rd NG3. . . . . .49 B4
Hickling Way NG12 . . . . . .98 C1
Hickton Dr NG9 . . . . .91 A3
Hide Hill View NG12 . . . . .97 C3
Highbank Dr NG11. . . . . . .94 A1
Highbank Prim Sch
  NG11. . . . . .93 C1
Highbury Ave NG6 . . . . . . .32 B3
Highbury Cl NG8 . . . . .30 C1
Highbury Hospl NG6. . . . . .32 A3
Highbury Rd
  Keyworth NG12 . . . . .104 B4
  Nottingham NG6. . . . . . . .32 A4
Highbury Wlk NG6. . . . . . . .32 A4
High Church St NG7 . . . . . .47 B3
High Church Street 1
  NG7. . . . . .47 B2
Highclere Dr NG4. . . . . . . .51 A2
Highcliffe Rd NG3 . . . . . . .61 B3
Highcroft NG3. . . . . .35 A2
Highcroft Cl NG10 . . . . . .101 A3
Highcroft Dr NG8 . . . . .55 C3
Highcross Ct NG7. . . . . . .106 B4
High Cross St NG1 . . . . . .108 C3
Highfield Ct NG9 . . . . .82 B4
Highfield Dr Carlton NG4. .49 C2
  Nuttall NG16. . . . . .31 A2
Highfield Gr NG2 . . . . .76 B1
Highfield Prim Sch
  Cotgrave NG12. . . . . .98 B3
  Long Eaton NG10 . . . . . . .89 B4
Highfield Rd
  Beeston NG9 . . . . .80 C1
  Keyworth NG12 . . . . .104 B4
  Nottingham NG7. . . . . . . .73 C3
  Nuttall NG16. . . . . .30 C2
  West Bridgford NG2. . . . . .76 B1
Highfields Ct NG15 . . . . . .11 B4
Highfield St NG10 . . . . . . .89 B3
Highgate Cl NG4. . . . . .50 A4
Highgate Dr DE7 . . . . .26 A1
Highgrove Ave NG9 . . . . . .81 C4
Highgrove Ct NG15 . . . . . .13 A3
Highgrove Gdns NG12 . . . .86 C2
High Hazles Cl NG4. . . . . .36 C1
High Holborn DE7 . . . . . . .26 C1
High Hurst NG14 . . . . .5 A2
High Leys Rd NG15 . . . . . .11 A3
High Mdw NG12 . . . . .97 C3
High Pavement NG1 . . . . .109 C2
High Pavement Sixth Form
  Coll NG1. . . . . .108 A3
High Rd
  Beeston, Chilwell NG9 . . . .81 C2
  Beeston NG9 . . . . .72 C1
  Beeston, Toton NG9 . . . . . .90 C3
High St NG5 . . . . .23 C1
High St Pl NG1 . . . . .109 B2
High St Arnold NG5 . . . . . .23 C1
  Hucknall NG15 . . . . .3 A1
  Ilkeston DE7. . . . . .41 A2
  Kimberley NG16 . . . . .29 A4
  Long Eaton NG10 . . . . . . .90 A2
  Nottingham NG1. . . . . . . .109 B2
  Ruddington NG11 . . . . . . .95 B1
  Stapleford NG9. . . . . .70 A1
Highurst St NG7 . . . . .106 C3
High View Ave NG12 . . . . .105 A3
Highwood Ave NG8 . . . . . .45 A2
Highwood Player Inf Sch
  NG8. . . . . .45 A2
Highwood Player Jun Sch
  NG8. . . . . .44 C2
Highwray Gr NG11. . . . . . .93 C3
Hilary Cl NG8 . . . . .56 B1
Hilcot Dr NG8 . . . . .46 A3
Hillbeck Cres NG8 . . . . . . .56 A2
Hill Cl Eastwood NG16 . . . .17 A3
  West Bridgford NG2. . . . . .87 A4
Hillcrest Cl NG16 . . . . .29 B4
Hillcrest Dr NG15. . . . . . . .10 B4
Hillcrest Gdns NG14 . . . . .38 C3
Hill Crest Gr NG5 . . . . .33 C1
Hillcrest Rd NG12. . . . . . .104 B4
Hillcrest View NG4. . . . . . .49 C3
Hill Dr NG13. . . . . .66 C3
Hill Farm Cl NG10. . . . . . . .97 C3
Hill Farm Ct NG12 . . . . . . .96 C4
Hillfield Gdns NG5 . . . . . . .21 C3

Hillfield Rd NG9 . . . . .70 B3
Hillgrove Gdns 14 NG5 . . .22 B2
Hilliers Ct NG5 . . . . .22 A2
Hillington Rise NG5. . . . . . .23 A1
Hill Rd Beeston NG9 . . . . . .91 A4
  Bestwood Village NG6 . . . .12 C2
  Heanor DE75 . . . . .13 B3
Hill Rise NG9 . . . . .54 A2
Hillsford Cl NG8 . . . . .57 B3
Hillside NG16. . . . . .7 B1
Hill Side NG7. . . . . .58 B1
Hillside Ave NG3. . . . . .35 B2
Hillside Cres NG9. . . . . . . .72 A2
Hillside Dr
  Burton Joyce NG14 . . . . . .39 A3
  Long Eaton NG10 . . . . . . .89 A2
Hillside Gr NG10 . . . . .78 C4
Hillside Rd
  Beeston, Bramcote
    NG9. . . . . .71 C2
  Beeston, Chilwell NG9 . . . .81 A1
  Radcliffe on T NG12 . . . . . .65 B2
Hills Rd NG5 . . . . .35 A2
Hillview Ave NG3 . . . . .48 B4
Hill View Rd NG4 . . . . .49 B3
Hill View Rd NG9 . . . . .90 C4
Hilton Cl NG10. . . . . .99 B2
Hilton Cres NG2 . . . . .87 A3
Hilton Ct NG2 . . . . .87 A3
Hilton Rd NG3. . . . . .35 B1
Hinchin Brook NG7 . . . . . .107 A2
Hinsley Cl NG5 . . . . .24 C2
Hirst Cres NG8 . . . . .56 C2
Hobart Cl NG2 . . . . .75 B3
Hobart Dr NG9 . . . . .70 B3
Hobson Dr DE7 . . . . .52 C4
Hockerwood NG11. . . . . . . .84 A2
Hockley NG1 . . . . .109 C2
Hodgkin Cl NG11 . . . . .93 B3
Hodgkinson St NG4. . . . . . .63 B4
Hoefield Cres NG6. . . . . . . .31 B4
Hoewood Rd NG6. . . . . . . .20 B2
Hogan Gdns NG5 . . . . .22 B3
Hogarth Cl NG9 . . . . .80 A4
Hogarth Prim Sch NG3 . . .49 B1
Hogarth St NG3 . . . . .61 A4
Hogbarn La DE75,NG16. . . .9 B3
Hoggetts Cl NG9. . . . . .81 A3
Hogg La NG12 . . . . .64 C2
Hoggs Field NG16 . . . . .5 C2
Holbeck Rd Hucknall NG15 . .3 A3
  Nottingham NG8. . . . . . . .58 B4
Holborn Ave NG2 . . . . .61 A2
Holborn Cl NG16. . . . . .30 B1
Holborn Pl NG6 . . . . .21 A1
Holbrook Ct NG11 . . . . . . .94 A2
Holbrook St DE75. . . . . . . .14 B4
Holby Cl NG5 . . . . .22 A2
Holcombe Cl NG8 . . . . .45 C4
Holdale Rd NG3 . . . . .61 C4
Holden Cres NG16 . . . . . . .30 A4
Holden Gdns NG9 . . . . .80 A4
Holden Rd NG9 . . . . .72 A1
Holden St NG7 . . . . .106 C3
Holgate NG11 . . . . .93 B4
Holgate Rd NG2 . . . . .75 B3
Holgate Sch NG15. . . . . . . .10 C4
Holgate Wlk NG15. . . . . . . .10 C4
Holkham Ave NG9 . . . . . . .81 B3
Holkham Cl Arnold NG5. . . .35 B4
  Shipley DE7 . . . . .26 A1
Holland Mdw NG10 . . . . . .100 C3
Holland St NG7 . . . . .47 A1
Holles Cres NG7 . . . . .107 C1
Hollies Dr NG12 . . . . .86 C2
Hollies The
  Eastwood NG16 . . . . .16 A4
  Sandiacre NG10 . . . . .78 C3
Hollington Rd NG8. . . . . . . .57 C4
Hollingworth Ave NG10 . . .79 A1
Hollins The NG14 . . . . .5 C3
Hollinwell Ave NG8 . . . . . .58 A3
Hollinwell Ct NG12. . . . . . .87 A1
Hollinwood Lane NG14. . . . .4 B1
Hollis St NG7 . . . . .47 B3
Hollows The
  Long Eaton NG10 . . . . .90 C2
  Nottingham NG11. . . . . . . .84 C2
Hollow Stone NG1 . . . . . . .109 C2
Holly Ave Breaston DE72 . .88 B3
  Carlton NG4 . . . . .50 B2

Holly Ave continued
  Nottingham, Wilford
    NG11. . . . . .75 A2
Hollybrook Gr NG16 . . . . . .18 C1
Holly Cl Bingham NG13 . . . .67 C2
  Hucknall NG15 . . . . .11 C3
Hollycroft NG2 . . . . .86 C2
Holly Ct NG9 . . . . .71 B2
Hollydale Rd NG3. . . . . . . .61 C4
Hollydene Cl NG15. . . . . . .10 A3
Hollydene Cres NG6 . . . . . .31 C2
Holly Farm Ct NG16 . . . . . .17 A3
Hollygate Ind Pk NG12. . . .98 C4
Holly Gdns NG3. . . . . .49 A1
Hollygirt Sch NG3 . . . . .48 A1
Holly La NG9 . . . . .82 A3
Holly Rd NG16 . . . . .18 B1
Hollythorpe Pl NG15 . . . . .10 A3
Hollywell Prim Sch
  NG16. . . . . .18 A1
Holme Cl DE7 . . . . .40 B4
Holmefield Cres DE7 . . . . .41 B2
Holme Gr NG2 . . . . .77 A4
Holme La NG12 . . . . .64 A2
HOLME PIERREPONT 63 C1
Holme Pierrepont Ctry
  Pk* NG12. . . . . .63 A1
Holme Pierrepont Hall*
  NG12. . . . . .63 C1
Holme Pit Nature
  Reserve* NG11 . . . . .83 B1
Holme Rd Bingham NG13 . . .67 C2
  West Bridgford NG2. . . . . .76 C3
Holmes Cl NG16 . . . . .7 B1
Holmefield Dr DE75. . . . . .14 B1
Holmes St DE75 . . . . .13 B4
Holme St NG2 . . . . .76 A4
Holmewood Cres NG5 . . . .33 C4
Holmewood Dr NG16 . . . . .16 C2
Holmfield Rd NG9 . . . . .81 B1
Holmsfield NG12 . . . . .104 B2
Holroyd Ave NG2 . . . . .61 A2
Holt Gr NG14 . . . . .5 B2
Holwood Ct NG6. . . . . .31 B4
Holy Cross RC Prim Sch
  NG15. . . . . .3 A3
Holyoake Rd NG3 . . . . .36 A1
Holyrood Ct NG9 . . . . .71 B3
Holywell Rd DE7 . . . . .26 A1
Home Cl NG5. . . . . .23 B2
Home Croft The NG8 . . . . . .71 A1
Homefield Ave NG5. . . . . . .24 B3
Homefield Rd NG8. . . . . . . .46 B1
Homestead NG16 . . . . .7 B2
Honeysuckle Cl 4 NG8 . . .44 C3
Honeysuckle Gr
  Bingham NG13 . . . . .66 C1
  Nottingham NG6. . . . . .31 C2
Honeywood Dr NG3. . . . . . .49 B1
Honeywood Wlk NG3 . . . . .49 B1
Honingham Cl NG5 . . . . . . .35 B4
Honingham Rd DE7. . . . . . .26 A1
Honister Cl
  Nottingham NG11. . . . . . . .93 C1
  West Bridgford NG2. . . . . .77 B1
Honiton Cl NG9 . . . . .90 C4
Honiton Rd NG8 . . . . .44 C3
Hood St NG5 . . . . .48 B4
Hook Cl 8 NG6 . . . . .91 B4
Hooley Cl NG10. . . . . .100 A4
Hooley Pl 3 NG5. . . . . .34 B1
Hoopers Wlk 6 NG2. . . . . .75 B4
Hooton Rd NG4 . . . . .50 A1
Hooton St NG3 . . . . .61 A3
Hope Cl NG2 . . . . .75 A4
Hopedale Cl NG7 . . . . .106 A3
Hope Dr NG7 . . . . .109 A1
Hope St Beeston NG9 . . . . .72 A1
  2 Ilkeston DE7. . . . . .41 A1
Hopewell Cl NG12 . . . . . . .65 B3
Hopewell Wlk DE7 . . . . . . .27 A3
Hopkins Ct NG16 . . . . .9 A1
Horace Ave NG9 . . . . .79 C4
Hornbeam Cl DE7 . . . . .41 C1
Hornbeam Gdns NG6 . . . . .20 A1
Hornbuckle St NG7. . . . . . .106 B3
Hornchurch Rd NG8 . . . . . .44 B2
Hornsby Wlk NG5. . . . . . . .21 C2
Horridge St DE7 . . . . .27 A2
Horsecroft Cl DE7 . . . . . . .27 A4
Horsendale Ave NG16 . . . .31 A2

Horsendale Prim Sch
  NG16. . . . . .30 C1
Horsham Dr NG5 . . . . .22 A2
Horsley Cres NG16. . . . . . . .7 B1
Hoselett Field Rd NG10 .101 A3
Hoten Rd 7 NG2 . . . . .61 A1
Hotspur Cl NG6. . . . . .32 C3
Houghton Ave DE7. . . . . . .26 A1
Houghton Cl NG16. . . . . . . .30 C2
Houldsworth Rise NG5. . . .23 C4
Hound Rd NG2 . . . . .76 A2
Hounds Gate NG1 . . . . . . .109 A2
Houseman Gdns NG2 . . . . .75 B4
Houston Cl NG5 . . . . .21 C3
Hove Rd NG5 . . . . .32 C3
Howard Cl NG10 . . . . .90 A3
Howard St NG1 . . . . .108 B3
Howbeck Rd NG5. . . . . .24 C2
Howden Rd NG6 . . . . .21 A3
Howell-Jones Rd NG9 . . . .81 A1
Howells Cl NG5 . . . . .23 A2
Howick Dr NG6. . . . . .20 A2
Howitt St Heanor DE75. . . .14 A4
  Heanor DE75 . . . . .14 B4
  Long Eaton NG10 . . . . . . .90 A1
Hoylake Cres NG8 . . . . . . .44 B1
Hoyland Ave NG7 . . . . .74 A4
Hubert St NG7 . . . . .106 B4
Huckerby Rd DE7 . . . . .40 A4
Huckerbys Field NG4 . . . . .50 A3
HUCKNALL 10 C4
Hucknall Annie Holgate
  Jun Sch NG15. . . . . .11 A4
Hucknall La NG6. . . . . .44 B4
Hucknall Cres NG4 . . . . . . .50 C4
Hucknall Ind Pk NG15 . . . .10 C2
Hucknall La NG6. . . . . .21 B4
Hucknall Rd NG6. . . . . .32 C4
Hucknall L Ctr NG15. . . . . . .3 A2
Hucknall Rd NG6. . . . . .32 C4
Hucknall Sta NG15 . . . . . . .11 A3
Hudson St NG3 . . . . .61 A4
Hudson Wy NG12 . . . . .65 C3
Hufton's Ct DE75 . . . . .14 B1
Hufton's Dr DE75 . . . . .14 B1
Hugessen Ave NG15 . . . . . .3 B2
Hugget Gdns 4 NG5. . . . . .22 B2
Humber Cl NG2 . . . . .75 B4
Humber Rd Beeston NG9 . .72 C1
  Long Eaton NG10 . . . . . . .89 B3
Humber Rd S NG9 . . . . . . .83 A4
Humberston Rd NG8. . . . . .56 A1
Hungerhill Rd NG3 . . . . . . .48 B1
Hungerton St NG7 . . . . . . .107 B1
Hunston Cl NG8 . . . . .45 B1
Hunt Ave DE75. . . . . .13 C4
Hunt Cl NG12 . . . . .65 A2
Hunter Rd NG5 . . . . .36 A4
Hunters Cl NG11. . . . . .84 C4
Huntingdon Dr NG7. . . . . .109 A2
Huntingdon Prim Sch
  NG3. . . . . .108 B4
Huntingdon St NG1 . . . . . .108 B3
Huntingdon Way NG9 . . . . .71 A4
Huntingdon Wlk NG10 . . . .79 A3
Huntly Cl NG7 . . . . .94 B3
Hurcomb St NG3 . . . . .49 A1
Hurts Croft NG9 . . . . .81 C2
Hurt's Yd NG1 . . . . .109 B2
Huss's La NG10 . . . . .90 B2
Hutchinson Gn NG3. . . . . .108 C4
Hutton Cl NG9 . . . . .71 C3
Hutton St NG2 . . . . .61 A1
Huxley Cl NG8 . . . . .44 B1
Hyde Cl NG11. . . . . .84 B2
Hyde Pk Cl NG2. . . . . .85 B3
Hyson Cl 10 NG7 . . . . .47 A2
HYSON GREEN 47 A1
Hyson St 12 NG7. . . . . .47 A1

I

Ian Gr NG4 . . . . .51 A2
Ilam Sq DE7 . . . . .26 C3
Ilford Cl DE7 . . . . .26 B1
ILKESTON 40 C1
  41 C1
Ilkeston Com Hospl DE7 .26 B2
Ilkeston Rd Heanor DE75 . .14 A2
  Sandiacre NG10 . . . . .69 B2
  Stanton-by-D DE7. . . . . . . .53 A1
  Stapleford NG9. . . . . .70 B4

Ilkeston Rd continued
  Trowell NG9 . . . . .54 A3
Ilkeston Sch DE7 . . . . .40 B2
ILS Nottingham NG5. . . . . .47 C2
Imperial Ave
  Beeston NG9 . . . . .82 A4
  Carlton NG4 . . . . .50 C3
Imperial Rd Beeston NG9. .82 A4
  Nottingham NG6. . . . . .32 B4
Inchwood Cl NG9 . . . . .90 B4
Incinerator Rd NG2 . . . . . .76 A4
Independent St NG7. . . . . .106 A4
Industrial Mus & Yd Gall*
  NG8. . . . . .57 B1
Ingham Gr NG7 . . . . .107 A1
Ingham Rd NG10 . . . . .89 B4
Ingleborough Gdns 6
  NG10. . . . . .88 C2
Ingleby Cl Cotgrave NG12. .98 A2
  Nottingham NG8. . . . . .55 C2
Ingleby Rd NG10 . . . . .99 B2
Inglefield Rd DE7. . . . . . . .53 B4
Inglewood Rd NG7. . . . . . .94 A3
Ingram Rd NG6 . . . . .32 B4
Ingram Terr NG6. . . . . .32 A4
Inham Cir NG9 . . . . .81 B4
Inham Cl NG9 . . . . .80 C3
Inham Rd NG9 . . . . .81 A3
Innes Rd NG4. . . . . .50 A1
Instow Rise NG3 . . . . .108 C4
Intake Rd NG12 . . . . .104 A3
Iona Dr NG9 . . . . .69 C4
Iona Gdns NG5 . . . . .22 B3
Iona Sch NG3 . . . . .61 B3
Ipswich Cir NG3 . . . . .61 B3
Ireland Ave NG9 . . . . .82 C3
Ireland Cl NG9 . . . . .82 C3
Iremonger Rd NG2. . . . . . .75 C4
Irene Terr NG7. . . . . .47 A4
Ireton Gr NG9 . . . . .91 C4
Ireton St Beeston NG9. . . . .82 A4
  Nottingham NG7. . . . . . . .106 C3
Irwin Dr NG6 . . . . .31 B4
Isaac's La NG9 . . . . .69 C1
Isabella St NG7 . . . . .109 B1
Island Bsns Quarter
  NG1. . . . . .109 C1
Islay Cl Arnold NG5 . . . . . .24 A3
  Stapleford NG9. . . . . .54 B1
Ivatt Dr NG2 . . . . .61 A1
Ives Cl NG2. . . . . .85 B2
Ivy Cl NG16 . . . . .18 A3
Ivy Gr Carlton NG4 . . . . . . .50 B1
  Nottingham NG7. . . . . .47 B2
Ivy La NG16. . . . . .15 C4

J

Jacklin Gdns NG5 . . . . . . .22 B3
Jackson Ave Ilkeston DE7 .40 C2
  8 Ilkeston DE7. . . . . .40 C3
  Sandiacre NG10 . . . . .78 C4
James Peacock Inf Sch
  NG11. . . . . .95 A1
James St Arnold NG5 . . . . .23 C2
  Kimberley NG16 . . . . .29 A4
Jamia Al Hudaa Ind Sch
  NG3. . . . . .48 A2
Japonica Dr NG6 . . . . .31 C2
Jardines The NG9. . . . . . . .71 B3
Jarrow Gdns NG5. . . . . . . .22 A4
Jarvis Ave NG3 . . . . .61 C4
Jasmine Cl Beeston NG9 . .71 C3
  Nottingham, Broxtowe
    NG8. . . . . .44 C4
  Nottingham, Glapton
    NG11. . . . . .93 B3
Jasmine Rd NG5. . . . . .32 C1
Jasper Cl NG12 . . . . .64 C1
Jayne Cl Carlton NG4 . . . . .51 B4
  Nottingham NG8. . . . . .56 C3
Jedburgh Cl NG3 . . . . .108 C4
Jedburgh Wlk NG3 . . . . . .108 C4
Jenned Rd NG5 . . . . .24 B4
Jenner St 14 NG5 . . . . .47 C3
Jenness Ave NG5 . . . . .21 C3
Jennison St NG6. . . . . .21 A1
Jenny Burton Way NG15 . .12 A3

Jensen Way NG5 . . . . 47 C3
Jermyn Dr NG5 . . . . 22 B3
Jersey Gdns NG3 . . . . 60 C4
Jervis Ct DE7 . . . . 27 A1
Jesmond Rd NG6 . . . . 32 B4
Jesse Boot Prim Sch
NG3 . . . . 61 C3
Jesse Gray Prim Sch
NG2 . . . . 86 A2
Jessop's La NG4 . . . . 51 A4
Joan Ave DE75 . . . . 13 C4
John Carroll Ct **2** NG3 . . 61 A4
John Carroll L Ctr NG7 . 106 B3
John Clifford Prim Sch
NG9 . . . . 82 C4
Johnson Ave NG15 . . . . . . 11 C3
Johnson Dr DE75 . . . . 14 A4
Johnson Rd NG7 . . . . . . 107 A2
Johns Rd NG12 . . . . 65 C2
John St Heanor DE75 . . . . 13 B4
Ilkeston DE7 . . . . 41 A3
Nottingham NG7 . . . . 47 A3
John Wright Cl NG5 . . . . . 21 B3
Joyce Ave Beeston NG9 . . 80 C1
Nottingham NG5 . . . . 34 B3
Joyce Cl NG5 . . . . 34 B3
Jubilee Ave NG5 . . . . 73 A2
Jubilee Rd NG5 . . . . 34 C4
Jubilee St
Kimberley NG16 . . . . 17 C1
3 Nottingham NG2 . . . . . 61 A2
Judson Ave NG9 . . . . 80 B4
Julian Cl DE7 . . . . 53 B4
Julian Rd NG2 . . . . 77 A3
Julie Ave DE75 . . . . 14 B3
Jumelles Dr NG14 . . . . 4 C2
Junction Rd NG10 . . . . . 101 C4
Juniper Cl NG11 . . . . 93 B3
Juniper Cl NG16 . . . . 17 A2
Juniper Gdns NG13 . . . . . 67 C2

K

Kansington Ct **5** NG5 . . . 34 A1
Kappler Cl NG4 . . . . 51 B1
Karen Rise NG5 . . . . 24 B3
Katherine Dr NG9 . . . . 80 B2
Kayes Wlk NG1 . . . . 109 C2
Keats Cl Arnold NG5 . . . . . 23 B1
Long Eaton NG10 . . . . 100 A3
Nuthall NG16 . . . . 29 C4
Keats Dr NG15 . . . . 10 B4
Kedleston Cl
Beeston NG9 . . . . 81 B3
Long Eaton NG10 . . . . 99 C3
Kedleston Dr
Heanor DE75 . . . . 13 A4
Ilkeston DE7 . . . . 26 B1
Keeling Cl NG16 . . . . 16 C3
Keepers Cl NG6 . . . . 12 C2
Keighton Hill NG7 . . . . . . 73 B3
Keilder Dr NG13 . . . . 66 B2
Kelfield Cl NG6 . . . . 32 C3
Kelham Gn NG3 . . . . 61 A4
Kelham Way NG16 . . . . 8 C1
Kelling Cl NG5 . . . . 33 B4
Kelly Wlk NG2 . . . . 75 A1
Kelsey Cl NG9 . . . . 82 A1
Kelso Gdns NG2 . . . . 75 A4
Kelstern Cl NG8 . . . . 32 A1
Kelvedon Gdns NG3 . . . . . 60 C4
Kelvin Cl NG9 . . . . 79 B3
Kelvin Rd NG3 . . . . 49 B1
Kemmel Rd NG6 . . . . 32 B3
Kempsey Cl NG5 . . . . 21 C2
Kempson St NG11 . . . . . . 102 C4
Kempton Cl NG16 . . . . 17 C1
Kempton Dr NG5 . . . . 24 B3
Kendal Cl NG15 . . . . 2 B2
Kendal Ct NG2 . . . . 77 A2
Kendal Dr NG9 . . . . 71 C2
Kendale Ct NG3 . . . . 49 A3
Kenia Cl NG4 . . . . 50 B2
Kenilworth Ct
Beeston NG9 . . . . 72 C1
Nottingham NG7 . . . . 109 A1
Kenilworth Dr DE7 . . . . . . 52 B3

Kenilworth Rd
Beeston NG9 . . . . 72 C2
Nottingham NG7 . . . . 109 A1
Ken Martin Swimming Ctr
NG6 . . . . 21 A3
Kenmore Gdns NG3 . . . . 108 C4
Kennedy Ave NG10 . . . . . 100 B3
Kennedy Cl NG5 . . . . 23 C1
Kennedy Dr NG9 . . . . 70 A3
Kenneth Rd NG5 . . . . 24 A4
Kennington Rd NG8 . . . . . 58 B3
Kenrick Rd NG3 . . . . 49 B4
Kenrick St NG4 . . . . 51 B1
Kensington Ave DE75 . . . 13 A3
Kensington Cl NG9 . . . . . . 90 C3
Kensington Gdns
Carlton NG4 . . . . 50 C1
Ilkeston DE7 . . . . 41 A1
Ilkeston DE7 . . . . 41 B1
Kensington Pk Cl NG2 . . . 85 B3
Kensington Rd NG10 . . . . 78 C2
Kensington St NG7 . . . . . . 53 A4
Kenslow Ave **10** NG7 . . . 46 C1
Kent Ave NG9 . . . . 82 B2
Kentmere Cl NG2 . . . . 77 B1
Kenton Ave NG16 . . . . 30 B1
Kenton Ct **6** NG2 . . . . . . 75 C3
Kent Rd Eastwood NG16 . . 17 A2
Nottingham NG3 . . . . 35 B1
Kent St NG1 . . . . 108 C3
Kentwood Rd NG2 . . . . . . 61 A2
Kenyon Rd NG7 . . . . 58 B1
Keppel Ct DE7 . . . . 27 A1
Kersall Ct NG6 . . . . 32 B3
Kersall Dr NG6 . . . . 32 B3
Kersall Gdns NG15 . . . . . . 3 A1
Kestral Dr NG13 . . . . 67 B1
Kestrel Cl Carlton NG4 . . . 49 C3
Ilkeston DE7 . . . . 57 A2
West Bridgford NG2 . . . . . 77 B1
Keswick Ct
Long Eaton NG10 . . . . 89 A4
3 Nottingham NG2 . . . . . 60 C2
Keswick St NG2 . . . . 60 C2
Kett St NG6 . . . . 31 C4
Keverne Cl NG8 . . . . 46 A4
Kevin Rd NG8 . . . . 71 C4
Kew Cl NG11 . . . . 85 B1
Kew Cres DE75 . . . . 14 C3
Kew Gdns NG8 . . . . 30 C1
Keys Cl NG6 . . . . 20 B1
Key St NG3 . . . . 61 A3
KEYWORTH 104 C2
Keyworth L Ctr NG12 . . . 104 C2
Keyworth Prim Sch
NG12 . . . . 104 B3
Keyworth Rd NG4 . . . . 36 B1
Kibworth Cl NG5 . . . . 33 A2
Kiddier Ave NG5 . . . . 24 C1
Kilbourne Rd NG5 . . . . . . 24 C1
Kilbourn St NG3 . . . . 108 B4
Kilburn Cl NG9 . . . . 71 A4
Kilby Ave NG3 . . . . 61 B4
Kildare Rd NG3 . . . . 49 A2
Kildonan Cl NG8 . . . . 44 B4
Killerton Gn NG11 . . . . 94 A1
Killerton Pk Dr NG11 . . . . 85 A2
Killisick Jun Sch NG5 . . . . 24 C2
Killisick Rd NG5 . . . . 24 C2
Kilnbrook Ave NG5 . . . . . . 24 C3
Kilnwood Cl NG3 . . . . 61 B4
Kilsby Rd NG7 . . . . 94 B4
Kilverton Rd NG10 . . . . . . 78 C4
Kilverton Cl NG8 . . . . 58 B2
Kilvington Rd NG5 . . . . . . 24 C1
Kimber Cl NG8 . . . . 56 B4
KIMBERLEY 17 C2
Kimberley Cl NG16 . . . . . . 29 A3
Kimberley Comp Sch
NG16 . . . . 29 A4
Kimberley L Ctr NG16 . . . 29 B4
Kimberley Prim Sch
NG16 . . . . 29 A4
Kimberley Rd
Nottingham NG6 . . . . 61 B2
Nuthall NG16 . . . . 30 A3
Kimbolton Ave NG7 . . . . 107 B2
Kindlewood Dr NG9 . . . . . 91 A3
King Charles St NG1 . . . . 109 A2

King Edward Gdns NG10 . 79 A4
King Edward St
Hucknall NG15 . . . . 11 B4
Nottingham NG1 . . . . 108 C2
Sandiacre NG10 . . . . 79 A4
Kingfisher Cl NG6 . . . . 32 B2
Kingfisher Ct
Beeston NG9 . . . . 83 A3
Ilkeston DE7 . . . . 53 A2
Kingfishers Ct NG2 . . . . . 87 B2
Kingfisher Wharf
4 Nottingham NG7 . . . . . 74 B4
1 Nottingham NG7 . . . . . 74 C4
King George Ave DE7 . . . 40 C2
King Johns Arc NG1 . . . . 109 B2
Kinglake Pl NG2 . . . . 75 B4
Kingrove Ave NG9 . . . . . . 81 C4
Kings Ave NG4 . . . . 50 C4
Kingsbridge Ave NG3 . . . . 36 A4
Kingsbridge Way NG9 . . . 81 B4
Kingsbury Dr NG8 . . . . 45 B2
Kings Cl DE75 . . . . 13 A3
Kingsdale Cl NG10 . . . . . . 99 C3
Kingsdown Mount NG8 . . 72 A4
Kingsford Ave NG7 . . . . . 106 A4
Kingsley Cres NG10 . . . . . 100 A2
Kingsley Dr NG4 . . . . 51 B1
Kingsley Rd NG2 . . . . 61 B1
King's Mdw Rd NG2 . . . . . 74 C4
Kingsmead Ave NG9 . . . . 69 C4
Kings Moor NG5 . . . . 21 C1
King's Pl NG1 . . . . 109 C2
Kings Rd NG10 . . . . 79 A4
Kings Sch The NG2 . . . . . . 75 C3
King St Beeston NG9 . . . . 82 C4
Eastwood NG16 . . . . 16 A4
Ilkeston DE7 . . . . 41 A3
Long Eaton NG10 . . . . 89 C2
Nottingham NG1 . . . . 108 B3
Kingsthorpe Cl NG3 . . . . . 49 A3
Kingston Ave DE7 . . . . 53 B2
Kingston Ct **14** NG2 . . . . 60 C2
Kingston Dr NG12 . . . . 98 B1
Kingston Rd NG2 . . . . 86 A4
Kingsway Heanor DE75 . . . 13 B4
Ilkeston DE7 . . . . 53 B4
Radcliffe on T NG12 . . . . . 64 C1
Kingsway Gdns NG15 . . . . 10 C2
Kingsway Rd NG15 . . . . . . 10 C2
Kingswell Rd NG5 . . . . 35 A4
King's Wlk NG1 . . . . 108 B3
Kingswood Rd
Nottingham NG8 . . . . 57 C3
West Bridgford NG2 . . . . . 85 C3
Kinlet Rd NG5 . . . . 33 B4
Kinsdale Wlk NG11 . . . . . . 84 A1
Kipling Cl NG11 . . . . 93 B2
Kipps St NG1 . . . . 108 C3
Kirby Cl NG16 . . . . 9 B1
Kirby Rd NG16 . . . . 9 B1
Kirkbride Ct NG9 . . . . 81 A2
Kirkby Ave DE7 . . . . 53 A4
Kirkby Gdns NG2 . . . . 75 C4
Kirk Cl NG9 . . . . 81 C2
Kirkdale Cl NG8 . . . . 55 C2
Kirkdale Gdns NG10 . . . . 100 A4
Kirkdale Rd
Long Eaton NG10 . . . . 100 A4
Nottingham NG3 . . . . 61 C4
Kirkewhite Ave NG10 . . . . 89 C1
Kirkfell Cl NG2 . . . . 87 B3
KIRK HALLAM 52 B4
Kirk Hallam Com Tech Coll
DE7 . . . . 52 B4
Kirkham Cl **5** DE75 . . . . 13 B3
Kirkham Dr NG9 . . . . 90 B4
Kirkhill NG13 . . . . 67 A3
Kirk La NG11 . . . . 95 B1
Kirkland Dr NG9 . . . . 71 B4
Kirkley Dr DE75 . . . . 13 A3
Kirkley Gdns NG5 . . . . 24 B2
Kirkman Rd DE75 . . . . 4 B2
Kirk Rd NG3 . . . . 49 B4
Kirk's Bldgs NG4 . . . . 50 B1
Kirkstead Gdns **7** NG7 . . 47 A1
Kirkstead St **6** NG7 . . . . 47 A1
Kirkstone Ct NG10 . . . . . . 89 A4
Kirkstone Dr NG2 . . . . 77 B1
Kirk White Ct **5** NG2 . . . 85 A4
Kirtle Cl NG8 . . . . 45 C2
Kirtley Dr NG2 . . . . 74 C4

Kirton Ave NG10 . . . . 89 C1
Kittiwake Mews NG7 . . . 107 A2
Kiwi Cl NG15 . . . . 10 B3
Knapp Ave NG16 . . . . 16 A3
Kneesall Gr NG15 . . . . 3 A1
Kneeton Cl Carlton NG4 . . 36 B2
Nottingham NG5 . . . . 34 A2
Kneeton Vale NG5 . . . . . . 34 A2
Knighton Ave NG7 . . . . . 106 A4
Knighton Rd NG5 . . . . 34 B3
Knightsbridge Dr
Nuthall NG8 . . . . 30 C1
West Bridgford NG2 . . . . . 85 B2
Knightsbridge Gdns NG15. 2 B3
Knights Cl
Nottingham NG5 . . . . 22 A2
West Bridgford NG2 . . . . . 85 B1
Knight St NG4 . . . . 63 B4
Kniveton Pk DE7 . . . . 40 A1
Knole Rd NG8 . . . . 56 C3
Knoll Ave NG15 . . . . 10 B3
Knowle Hill NG16 . . . . 29 B3
Knowle La NG16 . . . . 29 B3
Knowle Pk NG16 . . . . 29 B3
Knowles Wlk **3** NG5 . . . . 23 B2
Krebs Cl NG11 . . . . 93 B3
Kyle View NG5 . . . . 22 B3
Kyme St NG7 . . . . 106 B3
Kynance Gdns NG11 . . . . 85 A3

L

Labray Rd NG14 . . . . 5 A3
Laburnum Ave NG12 . . . . 105 A4
Laburnum Cl NG10 . . . . . . 69 A1
Laburnum Gr
Beeston NG9 . . . . 83 A3
Hucknall NG15 . . . . 11 C3
Laburnum St NG3 . . . . 48 B1
Lace Ctr The* NG1 . . . . . . 109 A2
Lace Market Theatre The*
NG1 . . . . 109 B2
Lace Mkt Ctr The*
NG1 . . . . 109 B2
Lace Rd NG9 . . . . 72 B1
Lace St NG7 . . . . 73 C3
Lace Wy NG1 . . . . 60 C1
Lacey Ave NG15 . . . . 11 B3
Lacey Cl DE7 . . . . 26 A1
Lacey Fields Rd DE75 . . . . 14 C3
Ladbrooke Cres NG6 . . . . 32 A1
Ladybank Rise NG5 . . . . . 25 A2
Lady Bay Ave NG2 . . . . . . 76 B3
Lady Bay Bridge NG2 . . . . 76 A4
Lady Bay Prim Sch NG2 . . 76 C3
Lady Bay Rd NG2 . . . . 76 C3
Lady Bay Ret Pk NG2 . . . . 60 C1
Ladybridge Cl NG9 . . . . . . 82 A1
Ladycroft Ave NG15 . . . . . . 2 C1
Ladycross Inf Sch NG10 . . 79 A4
Ladylea Rd NG10 . . . . 99 C2
Ladysmith Rd NG2 . . . . . . 61 B2
Ladysmock Gdns NG2 . . . 75 C4
Ladywood Prim Sch DE7 . 52 B3
Ladywood Rd DE7 . . . . . . 52 A3
Lake Ave DE75 . . . . 6 A2
Lake Gdns DE75 . . . . 6 A2
Lakeland Ave NG15 . . . . . 12 A3
Lakeside Arts Ctr* NG7 . . 73 C3
Lakeside Ave NG10 . . . . . 100 B2
Lakeside Cres NG10 . . . . 100 B3
Lakeside Inf Sch NG10 . . 100 A2
Lake St NG7 . . . . 106 B4
Lakeview Sixth Form Coll
NG9 . . . . 81 C1
Lamartine Cl NG3 . . . . . . 108 C3
Lamartine St NG3 . . . . . . 108 C3
Lamb Cl Dr NG16 . . . . 9 C2
Lambert Ct NG9 . . . . 73 A1
Lambert Gdns NG8 . . . . . . 46 A2
Lambert St NG7 . . . . 46 C1
Lambeth Rd NG5 . . . . 22 B4
Lambie Cl NG8 . . . . 58 A3
Lambley Ave NG3 . . . . 35 C1
Lambley Bridle Rd NG14 . 38 B4
Lambley La
Burton Joyce NG14 . . . . . . 38 C3
Carlton NG4 . . . . 37 A1
Lambourne Dr NG8 . . . . . 57 B3
Lambourne Gdns NG5 . . . 35 B3
Lambton Cl DE7 . . . . 26 C1

Lamcote Gdns NG12 . . . . 64 C1
Lamcote Gr NG2 . . . . 75 C2
Lamcote Mews NG4 . . . . . 64 C1
Lamcote St NG2 . . . . 75 C2
Lammas Gdns NG2 . . . . . . 75 C2
Lamorna Gr NG11 . . . . 85 A4
Lamplands NG12 . . . . 98 A1
Lamp Wood Cl NG14 . . . . . 5 A3
Lanark Cl NG8 . . . . 58 A1
Lancaster Ave
Sandiacre NG10 . . . . 78 C2
Stapleford NG9 . . . . 70 A1
Lancaster Rd
Bestwood Village NG6 . . . 12 C2
Hucknall NG15 . . . . 10 B2
Nottingham NG3 . . . . 49 C1
Lancaster Way NG8 . . . . . 44 B4
Lancelot Dr NG16 . . . . 18 B3
Lancelyn Gdns NG2 . . . . . 86 A2
Landcroft Cres NG5 . . . . . 33 B4
Landmere Cl DE7 . . . . 26 A1
Landmere Gdns NG3 . . . . 49 A3
Landmere La
West Bridgford NG11 . . . . 85 B3
West Bridgford NG11,
NG12 . . . . 96 A3
Landsdowne Rd NG5 . . . . 32 C2
Landsdown Gr NG10 . . . . 90 B3
Landseer Cl NG7 . . . . 106 A4
Laneham Ave NG5 . . . . . . 24 B1
Laneside Ave NG9 . . . . 90 A4
Lane The NG16 . . . . 28 A2
Laneward Cl DE7 . . . . 26 B2
Langar St NG5 . . . . 34 A2
Langar Rd NG13 . . . . 67 A2
Langdale Dr NG10 . . . . 99 C4
Langdale Gr NG13 . . . . . . 66 A2
Langdale Rd NG3 . . . . 62 A3
Langdon Cl NG10 . . . . 88 C3
Langdown Cl NG6 . . . . 20 B2
Langford Rd NG5 . . . . 24 C1
Langham Ave NG3 . . . . . . 61 B4
Langham Dr NG14 . . . . . . 39 A3
Langley Ave Arnold NG5 . . 35 A4
Ilkeston DE7 . . . . 26 B3
LANGLEY MILL 7 C1
Langley Mill Business Park
NG16 . . . . 14 C4
Langley Mill CE Inf Sch
NG16 . . . . 7 C1
Langley Mill Jun Sch
NG16 . . . . 7 B2
Langley Mill Sta NG16 . . . 14 C4
Langley Pk NG16 . . . . 7 C1
Langstrath Dr NG2 . . . . . . 87 B2
Langstrath Rd NG7 . . . . . . 94 A3
Langton Cl NG4 . . . . 62 C4
Langtree Gdns NG13 . . . . 67 B3
Langtry Gr NG7 . . . . 47 B3
Lansdown Cl NG9 . . . . 81 A2
Lansdowne Dr NG2 . . . . . 85 C2
Lansing Cl NG11 . . . . 94 B2
Lanthwaite Cl NG7 . . . . . . 94 B3
Lanthwaite Rd NG7 . . . . . 94 B3
Lapford Cl NG3 . . . . 36 B4
Larch Cl Bingham NG13 . . 67 C2
Hucknall NG15 . . . . 11 C3
Nottingham NG5 . . . . 23 A2
Larch Cres Beeston NG9 . . 71 C1
Eastwood NG16 . . . . 15 C4
Larchdene Ave NG8 . . . . . 56 B1
Larch Dr NG10 . . . . 69 A1
Larch Gdns NG6 . . . . 20 B1
Larch Way NG12 . . . . 105 A2
Largs Cl NG5 . . . . 21 C3
Lark Cl NG9 . . . . 80 C3
Larkdale St NG7 . . . . 106 C4
Larkfield Rd NG16 . . . . . . 29 A2
Larkfields Inf Sch NG16 . . 29 C4
Larkfields Jun Sch
NG16 . . . . 29 C3
Larklands Ave DE7 . . . . . . 41 B1
Larkspur Ave NG5 . . . . . . 23 C4
Larwood Gr NG5 . . . . 34 A2
Lascelles Ave NG4 . . . . . . 50 B4
Latham St NG6 . . . . 20 C1
Lathkill Cl DE7 . . . . 26 C3
Lathkill Dr NG16 . . . . 20 C1
Lathkilldale Cres NG10 . . . 99 C3
Latimer Cl NG6 . . . . 32 A4
Latimer Dr NG9 . . . . 55 C1

Laughton Ave NG2........85 B2
Laughton Cres NG15.....10 C2
Launceston Cres NG11...84 C2
Launder St NG2 ....75 B4
Laurel Ave NG12..........104 C2
Laurel Cres
  Long Eaton NG10.......100 B4
  Nuthall NG16 ....29 C4
Laurel Rd NG4.............50 A2
Laurie Ave NG7............47 B2
Laurie Cl ◢ NG7..........47 B2
Lauriston Dr NG2..........32 B2
Lavender Cl ◼ NG8......44 C3
Lavender Cres NG4........50 B3
Lavender Gdns DE75......14 C3
Lavender Gr NG9..........83 A3
Lavender Wlk NG3.........48 B1
Laver Cl NG5...............24 C1
Lawdon Rd NG5............24 B3
Lawley Ave NG9...........72 C3
Lawn Cl DE75..............14 A4
Lawn Mill Rd NG16........17 C1
Lawrence Ave
  Awsworth NG16............28 A2
  Carlton NG4..............62 C3
  Eastwood NG16 ....16 A4
Lawrence Ct NG12........98 B3
Lawrence St
  Long Eaton NG10.........89 C2
  Sandiacre NG10 ....69 A1
  Stapleford NG9...........79 C4
Lawrence Way ◢ NG2...74 C4
Lawson Ave NG10.........90 A1
Lawson St NG7...........106 C4
Lawton Dr NG6.............21 A3
Laxton Ave NG5...........32 B3
Laxton Dr NG15............10 C4
Leabrook Cl NG11.........83 B1
Leabrook Gdns NG15 .....3 B2
Leacroft Rd NG8..........46 B2
Leadale Ave NG15 ....3 B2
Leaf Cl NG15...............3 A3
Leafe Cl NG9...............91 B4
Leafield Gn NG7...........94 A4
Leafy La DE75..............14 A3
Leahurst Gdns NG2.......87 A4
Leahurst Rd NG2..........87 A3
Leamington Dr NG9.......81 B2
Leander Cl NG11...........85 A4
Leas The NG14.............39 C3
Lechlade Rd NG5..........33 B4
Ledbury Vale NG8..........45 C2
Leech Ct NG16.............16 C1
Lee Cres DE7..............41 B2
Lee La DE75................14 C3
Leen Cl NG15................3 B2
Leen Dr Hucknall NG15 ...3 A3
  Nottingham NG6..........21 A3
Leen Gate NG7............74 A4
Leen Mills La NG15 ....2 C3
Leen Mills Prim Sch
  NG15......................3 A2
Leen Pl NG7...............106 A3
Leen Valley Way NG15...12 A3
Lee Rd Burton Joyce NG14 .39 B3
  Calverton NG14............4 C3
Lees Barn Rd NG12 ......64 B1
Lees Hill St NG2............60 C2
Lees Rd NG3...............49 B4
Leicester St NG10.......101 A4
Leigh Cl NG2...............85 B4
Leigh Rd NG9..............80 B1
Leighton St NG3...........61 A4
Leiston Gdns NG5.........22 B2
Leivers Ave NG5...........24 A2
Lema Cl NG6................21 B1
Lendrum Ct NG14.........39 A2
Leniscar Ave DE75..........6 A2
Lennox St NG1............108 C3
Lenton Ave
  Nottingham NG7.........107 B1
  Tollerton NG12............97 B3
Lenton Bvd NG7..........107 B2
Lenton Cir NG12...........97 B3
Lenton Ct NG7.............107 B2
Lenton Hall Dr NG7.......73 B3
Lenton Ind Est E NG7...74 B2
Lenton Ind Est W NG7...74 B2
Lenton La NG7.............74 B2
Lenton Manor NG7......107 A1
Lenton Prim Sch NG7 ..107 B1

Lenton Rd NG7...........109 A2
Lenton St NG10...........69 B1
Leonard Ave NG5.........47 C4
Leonard Cheshire Cl
  DE75......................14 C3
Leonard St NG6...........31 C3
Leopold St NG10..........89 C2
Le Page Ct NG8............45 B1
Leroy Wallace Ave
  NG7......................106 B4
Lerwick Cl NG11...........94 C3
Leslie Ave Beeston NG9 .82 B3
  Kimberley NG16...........29 A3
  ◼ Nottingham NG7......47 B2
Leslie Gr NG14..............5 B2
Leslie Rd NG7..............47 B2
Letchworth Cres NG9....81 B2
Letcombe Rd NG11.......84 A1
Levens Cl NG2.............87 B3
Leverton Gn NG7..........94 A4
Leverton Wlk NG5........24 B2
Levick Ct ◼ NG2..........75 B4
Lewindon Ct NG5.........34 C2
Lewis Cl NG3..............108 C4
Lexington Gdns NG5......34 B2
Leybourne Dr NG5........32 C4
Leys Rd NG11.............102 C4
Ley St NG6.................51 B1
Leys The NG11............93 C3
Leyton Cres NG9..........83 A3
Library Rd NG7.............73 B3
Lichfield Cl NG9...........80 A1
Lichfield Rd NG2...........61 B2
Liddell Gr NG8.............57 A2
Liddington St NG7.........47 A3
Lilac Ave NG4..............50 A2
Lilac Cl Keyworth NG12 .105 A2
  ◼ Nottingham NG8......44 C3
Lilac Cres NG9.............83 A3
Lilac Gr Beeston NG9....83 A3
  Heanor DE75.............13 C3
Lilac Mews DE7............26 B1
Lilac Rd NG15..............11 C3
Lilleker Rise NG5...........23 C3
Lillington Rd NG6..........20 C1
Lily Ave NG4................51 B1
Lily Gr NG9.................83 A3
Lime Ave NG16............15 A4
Lime Cl Nuthall NG16.....29 B4
  Radcliffe on T NG12.....65 A2
Lime Gr Long Eaton NG10 .89 C2
  Sandiacre NG10 ....79 A4
  Stapleford NG9...........79 C3
Lime Gr Ave NG9..........82 A3
Limekiln Ct NG6...........20 B2
Lime St Ilkeston DE7......41 A1
  Nottingham NG6..........20 C1
Lime Terr NG10............89 C2
Lime Tree Ave NG8.......32 A1
Limetree Cl NG12........104 C2
Limetree Ct DE7...........52 A4
Lime Tree Cres NG9......72 C3
Lime Tree Rd NG15.......11 C2
Limetree Rise DE7........52 A4
Limmen Gdns NG3........60 C4
Limpenny St NG7.........106 C4
Linby Ave NG15.............3 A1
Linby Cl Carlton NG4.....50 C4
  Nottingham NG5.........34 B3
Linby Dr NG8...............44 B4
Linby Gr NG15..............3 A1
Linby Rd NG15..............3 A2
Linby Wlk NG15.............2 C2
Lincoln Ave NG10.........78 C2
Lincoln Cir NG7...........107 C2
Lincoln Cl NG9.............70 A3
Lincoln Ct NG8.............44 C1
Lincoln Gr NG12...........65 A2
Lincoln St
  Nottingham NG1.........109 B3
  Nottingham, Old Basford
  NG6......................32 C1
Lindale Cl NG2.............87 B4
Lindbridge Rd NG8.......45 A4
Linden Ave NG11..........93 B3
Linden Gr Beeston NG9 ..82 C3
  Carlton NG4..............51 C3
  Sandiacre NG10 ....68 C1
  Stapleford NG9...........80 A4
Linden Pl NG5..............36 A4

Linden St NG3.............48 B1
Lindfield Cl NG8...........45 B4
Lindfield Rd NG8..........45 A4
Lindisfarne Gdns ◻
  NG5......................22 B3
Lindley St NG16............9 C2
Lindley Terr ◼ NG7.......46 C1
Lindrick Cl NG12...........87 B2
Lindum Gr ◼ NG2........61 A1
Lindum Rd NG6............32 B1
Linette Cl NG5.............47 B4
Linford NG9................55 C1
Ling Cres NG11............95 B2
Lingfield Ct NG8...........56 B1
Lingford NG9...............98 C3
Lingford St NG15..........11 C4
Lings Bar Hospl NG2.....87 C4
Linkin Rd NG9.............81 B4
Linkmel Cl NG2............74 C3
Linkmel Cl NG2............87 B4
Linkmel Rd NG16...........8 A1
Linksfield Ct NG11.........95 B4
Linnell St NG3.............61 A4
Linsdale Cl NG8...........55 C3
Linsdale Gdns NG4.......36 B2
Linton Rise NG3...........61 B4
Linwood Cres NG16......16 B3
Lion Cl NG8.................46 A4
Lismore Cl NG7...........106 A3
Lissett Ave DE7............40 C1
Lister Ct ◼ NG7...........74 A4
Lister Gate NG1..........109 B2
Lister Rd NG7..............74 A4
Listowel Cres NG11......94 A2
Litchen Cl DE7.............41 A4
Litchfield Cl NG10.........90 C1
Litchfield Rise NG5........23 C4
Littlegreen Rd NG5........35 A3
LITTLE HALLAM 52 C3
Little Hallam Hill DE7.....52 C4
Little Hallam La DE7......52 C4
Little Hayes NG2..........85 B2
Little Holland Gd NG16...19 C4
Little John Wlk ◼ NG3...48 B1
Little La Calverton NG14 ...4 C4
  Kimberley NG16...........29 A3
Little Mdw NG12...........98 C2
Littlemoor La NG11......103 B1
Little Oakwood Dr NG5 ..21 B4
Little Ox NG4...............50 C4
Little Tennis St S NG2...76 C4
Little Tennis St NG2......61 B1
Littlewell La DE7...........68 B4
Littlewood Gdns NG8....56 A3
Litton Cl Arnold NG5.....34 C2
  Ilkeston DE7..............26 C2
Liverpool St NG3..........60 C3
Llanberis Gr NG8..........46 A4
LLKESTON 52 A4
Lloyd St NG5...............48 A4
Loach Cl NG8...............58 A3
Lobelia Cl NG3.............48 B1
Lock Cl DE7................52 A4
Lockerbie St NG4..........63 A4
Lock La Long Eaton NG10 .100 B2
  Sandiacre NG10 ....79 B2
Locksley La NG11.........84 A2
Lockton Ave DE75.........13 C2
Lockwood Cl
  Beeston NG9.............83 B2
  ◻ Nottingham NG5......22 B3
Lodge Cl Arnold NG5.....23 C4
  Nottingham NG8.........46 B2
Lodge Farm La NG5......23 C3
Lodge La NG16..............6 C4
Lodge Rd Eastwood NG16 .16 B2
  Long Eaton NG10.......100 C3
Lodgewood Cl NG6.......31 B4
Lodore Cl NG2.............87 B4
Logan St NG6..............32 B4
Lois Ave NG7..............107 B1
Lombard Cl NG7..........107 B2
London Rd NG2............75 C4
Longacre NG5..............35 A2
Longbeck Ave NG3........49 B3
Longbridge La DE75.......6 B1
Longdale Rd NG5.........34 B4
Longden Ct NG9...........70 B4
Longden St ◼ NG3.......60 C3
LONG EATON 89 B1

Long Eaton Sch The
  NG10......................89 C1
Long Eaton Sta NG10..100 B3
Longfellows CI NG5.......22 C2
Longfield Cres DE7........53 A3
Longfield La Ilkeston DE7 .53 A3
  Ilkeston DE7.............53 B3
Longford Cres NG6.......21 A4
Long Hill Rise NG15.......11 A4
Long La Beeston NG9....82 A1
  Shipley DE75.............26 B4
  Watnall NG16.............18 B3
Longlands Cl NG9.........83 A2
Longlands Dr NG2........87 C3
Longlands Rd NG9........83 A2
Longleat Cres NG9........81 B3
Longmead Cl NG5.........34 A4
Longmead Dr NG5........34 A4
Longmoor Gdns NG10 ...89 A4
Longmoor La
  Breaston DE72...........88 A3
  Long Eaton NG10........88 C2
Longmoor Prim Sch
  NG10......................79 B1
Longmoor Rd NG10.......89 A4
Longore Sq NG8..........58 B2
Longridge Rd NG5........35 A2
Long Row NG1.............109 B2
Long Row W NG1.........109 B2
Longue Dr NG14............4 C2
Longwall Ave NG2.........74 C3
Longwest Croft NG14.....4 A2
Longwood Ct NG5.........22 A2
Lonscale Cl NG2...........87 B3
Lonsdale Dr NG9...........90 A3
Lonsdale Rd NG7.........106 A4
Lord Haddon Rd DE7.....40 C3
Lord Nelson St NG2.......61 A2
Lord St NG2................60 C2
Lorimer Ave NG4..........51 A4
Lorne Cl ◼ NG3...........48 A1
Lorne Gr NG12.............65 A2
Lorne Wlk ◻ NG3.........48 A1
Lortas Rd NG5.............47 A4
LOSCOE 6 A1
Loscoe Gdns ◼ NG5.....47 C3
Loscoe Grange DE75......6 A1
Loscoe Mount Rd NG5...48 A4
Loscoe Rd Heanor DE75 ...13 B4
  Nottingham NG5.........48 A3
Lothian Rd NG12..........97 B3
Lothmore Ct ◼ NG2.....75 A4
Lotus Cl NG3..............48 C1
Loughborough Ave NG2 ..61 A2
Loughborough Rd
  Bradmore NG11.........103 B3
  West Bridgford NG12...86 A3
Loughrigg Cl ◼ NG2....75 A3
Louis Ave NG9.............72 A1
Louise Ave NG4............51 B2
Lovell Cl NG6...............31 A3
Lowater St NG4............49 C1
Lowcroft NG5...............35 A2
Lowdham Rd NG4.........36 A1
Lowdham St ◼ NG3......60 C3
Lower Beauvale NG16 .....9 B1
Lower Bloomsgrove Rd
  DE7......................41 A4
Lower Brook St NG10.....90 A1
Lower Canaan NG11......95 C2
Lower Chapel St ◻ DE7 .41 A3
Lower Clara Mount Rd
  DE75......................14 B3
Lower Ct NG9..............83 C4
Lower Dunstead Rd NG16 .7 B1
Lower Eldon St ◼ NG2 ..60 C2
Lower Gladstone St
  DE75......................14 B3
Lower Granby St DE7.....41 A4
Lower Maples DE75.......14 B1
Lower Middleton St ◼ DE7 .41 B3
Lower Nelson St ◼
  DE75......................13 B4
Lower Orch St NG9.......69 C1
Lower Parliament St
  NG1......................109 C2
Lower Pk St NG9..........79 B3
Lower Rd NG9..............73 A1
Lower Regent St NG9....82 C4
Lower Stanton Rd DE7...53 A4

Lower Whitworth Rd
  DE7......................53 A4
Loweswater Ct NG2......77 B1
Lowlands Dr NG12.......104 C4
Lowlands Lea DE75.......14 A4
Low Pavement NG1.....109 B2
Low's La DE7...............69 A4
Low Wood Rd NG6.......31 A4
Lucerne Cl NG11..........85 A4
Lucknow Ave NG3.........48 B3
Lucknow Cl NG3...........48 B2
Lucknow Dr NG3..........48 B3
Lucknow Rd NG3.........48 B2
Ludford Rd NG6...........21 A2
Ludgate Cl NG5............20 C2
Ludham Ave NG16........16 B1
Ludlam Ave NG16.........16 B1
Ludlow Cl NG9.............71 C3
Ludlow Hill Rd NG2.......86 B3
Lulworth Cl NG2...........85 B3
Lulworth Ct NG16.........18 A1
Lune Cl NG9................82 A1
Lupin Cl NG3...............48 B1
Luther Cl NG3..............48 B1
Luton Cl NG8...............46 B3
Lutterell Ct NG2...........85 C3
Lutterell Way NG2.........87 B3
Lybster Mews ◼ NG2...75 A4
Lydia Gdns NG16..........15 C3
Lydney Pk NG2............85 B3
Lyle Cl NG16................17 C1
Lyme Pk NG2..............85 A3
Lymington Gdns NG3....61 B4
Lymn Ave NG4.............51 A4
Lyncombe Gdns NG12 ..104 C3
Lyndale Rd NG9...........70 C2
Lynden Ave NG10........100 C4
Lyndhurst Gdns NG2.....85 C2
Lyndhurst Rd NG2........61 A2
Lynmouth Cres NG7......46 C1
Lynmouth Dr DE7..........26 B1
Lynncroft NG16.............9 B1
Lynncroft Prim Sch NG16. 9 B1
Lynstead Dr NG15.........10 A3
Lynton Gdns NG5.........24 B2
Lynton Rd NG9............81 B4
Lyons Cl NG11.............95 A2
Lytham Dr NG12...........87 B1
Lytham Gdns NG5.........22 B3
Lythe Cl NG11..............84 C3
Lytton Cl NG3..............60 C3

M

Mabel Gr NG2..............76 C2
Mabel St NG2..............75 C4
MacAulay Gr NG16........29 C4
MacDonald Sq DE7.......52 B3
Machins La NG12..........86 C1
McIntosh Rd NG4.........36 B1
Mackinley Ave NG9.......70 A3
MacLaren Gdns NG11...103 A3
Maclean Rd NG4...........50 A1
Macmillan Cl NG3.........49 A4
Madford Ret Pk NG5.....34 B4
Madryn Wlk ◼ NG5......22 B1
Mafeking St NG2..........61 B2
Magdala Rd NG3..........48 A2
Magdalene Way NG15 ....2 C1
Magnolia Cl ◼ NG8.......44 C3
Magnolia Ct NG9..........71 C3
Magnolia Gr NG15........11 C2
Magnus Rd NG5...........34 A1
Magson St NG3............60 C3
Maiden La NG1...........109 C2
Maidens Dale NG5.........23 B2
Maid Marian Way NG1 ..109 B2
Maidstone Dr NG8........71 C4
Main Rd Beeston NG9....83 B3
  Carlton NG4..............51 B3
  Cotgrave NG12...........98 A4
  Nottingham NG11.......75 A1
  Radcliffe on T NG12.....64 C2
  Underwood NG16.........18 B1
Main St Awsworth NG16 ..28 A3
  Bradmore NG11.........103 B1
  Burton Joyce NG14......39 A2
  Calverton NG14...........5 B2

Main St continued
Eastwood, Beauvale
NG16 . . . . .17 A4
Eastwood NG16 . . . . .16 A3
Keyworth NG12 . . . . .104 B2
Kimberley NG16 . . . . .29 A4
Long Eaton NG10 . . . . . . .90 A1
Nottingham NG6 . . . . .21 A1
Stanton-by-D DE7 . . . . . . .68 B2
Strelley NG16 . . . . .43 B3
West Bridgford NG2 . . . . . .77 B1
Maitland Ave NG5 . . . . . .35 A2
Maitland Rd NG5 . . . . . . .35 A2
Major St NG1 . . . . .108 B3
Malbon Cl NG3 . . . . .49 A2
Malcolm Cl NG3 . . . . .48 A1
Maldon Cl NG9 . . . . .81 A2
Malin Cl NG5 . . . . .24 C2
Malin Hill NG1 . . . . .109 C2
Malkin Ave NG12 . . . . . . .65 B3
Mallard Cl Bingham NG13 . .67 C1
Nottingham NG6 . . . . .33 A2
Mallard Ct NG9 . . . . .82 C3
Mallard Rd NG4 . . . . .63 C4
Mallow Way NG13 . . . . . .66 B2
Malmesbury Rd NG3 . . . . .35 B2
Maltby Cl NG8 . . . . .45 C4
Maltby Rd NG3 . . . . .35 B2
Malt Cotts NG7 . . . . .47 A3
Malthouse Cl NG16 . . . . . .16 A3
Malthouse Rd
Ilkeston DE7 . . . . .53 A2
Ilkeston DE7 . . . . .53 B2
Malting Cl NG11 . . . . . . .102 C4
Maltmill La NG1 . . . . . . .109 B2
Malton Rd NG5 . . . . .47 A4
Malvern Cl NG3 . . . . .48 C3
Malvern Cres NG2 . . . . . .86 B3
Malvern Gdns ☑ NG10 . . .88 C2
Malvern Rd
Nottingham NG3 . . . . .48 C3
West Bridgford NG2 . . . . . .86 A3
Manchester St NG10 . . . .100 C4
Mandalay St NG6 . . . . . . .32 B2
Manesty Cres NG11 . . . . .94 A1
Manifold Gdns NG2 . . . . . .75 B4
Manly Cl NG5 . . . . .21 C2
Manners Ave DE7 . . . . . . .40 B3
Manners Ind Est DE7 . . . .41 A4
Manners Rd DE7 . . . . .40 C3
Manners St DE7 . . . . .53 B4
Manning Comp Sch
NG8 . . . . .45 C2
Manning St NG3 . . . . .48 B1
Manning View DE7 . . . . . .41 A4
Mannion Cres NG10 . . . . .100 A3
Manns Leys NG12 . . . . . . .98 A2
Mann St ☑ NG7 . . . . .47 A4
Manor Ave Beeston NG9 . . .82 B3
17 Nottingham NG2 . . . . .60 C2
Stapleford NG9 . . . . .69 C2
Manor Cl NG12 . . . . .87 A1
Manor Cres NG4 . . . . .51 A2
Manor Croft NG6 . . . . . . .32 C1
Manor Ct Beeston NG9 . . . .71 A1
Breaston DE72 . . . . .88 A2
Carlton NG4 . . . . .51 A1
Manor Farm Cl NG11 . . . .103 B1
Manor Farm La NG4 . . . . .51 C4
Manor Fields Dr DE7 . . . . .40 B1
Manor Gn Wlk NG2 . . . . . .74 A2
Manor House Rd NG10 . . .101 B4
Manorleigh DE72 . . . . . . .88 A2
Manor Leigh DE72 . . . . . .88 A2
Manor Pk NG11 . . . . .95 B1
Manor Pk Inf Sch NG14 . . .5 A3
Calverton NG14 . . . . .3 B2
Carlton NG4 . . . . .51 A2
Eastwood NG16 . . . . .16 A3
Ilkeston DE7 . . . . .40 C3
Keyworth NG12 . . . . .104 B3
Manor St NG2 . . . . .60 C2
Manorwood Rd NG12 . . . .98 B2
Mansell Cl NG16 . . . . .16 C3
Mansfield Ct ☑ NG5 . . . . .47 C2
Mansfield Gr NG1 . . . . . .108 A4
Mansfield La NG14 . . . . . . .5 B2

Mansfield Rd
Brinsley NG16 . . . . .9 A2
Heanor DE75 . . . . .14 B4
Nottingham NG5 . . . . .34 B2
Mansfield St NG5 . . . . . . .48 A4
Manthorpe Cres NG5 . . . . .35 A1
Manton Cres NG9 . . . . . . .72 C2
Manvers Ct ☑ NG2 . . . . . .60 C2
Manvers Gr NG12 . . . . . . .65 A2
Manvers Rd NG2 . . . . .86 A4
Manvers St Carlton NG4 . . .63 B4
Nottingham NG2 . . . . .60 C2
Manville Cl Beeston NG9 . . .55 C1
Nottingham NG8 . . . . .58 A4
Maori Ave NG15 . . . . .10 B3
Maple Ave Beeston NG9 . . .83 A3
Sandiacre NG10 . . . . .69 A1
Maplebeck Rd NG5 . . . . . .24 B1
Maple Cl Keyworth NG12 . .105 A2
Radcliffe on T NG12 . . . . . .75 C3
Mapledene Cres NG8 . . . . .56 A1
Maple Dr Carlton NG4 . . . . .51 C4
Hucknall NG15 . . . . .10 C3
Nuthall NG16 . . . . .30 A4
Maple Gdns ▌ DE75 . . . . .13 B3
Maple Gr DE72 . . . . .88 B2
Maples St ▐ NG7 . . . . . . .47 C4
Maplestead Ave NG11 . . . .85 A4
Mapletree Cl NG5 . . . . . . .22 C1
MAPPERLEY 34 C1
Mapperley Cres NG3 . . . . .48 C4
Mapperley Hall Dr NG3 . . .48 B4
Mapperley Orch NG5 . . . . .25 A1
MAPPERLEY PARK 34 C1
Mapperley Pk Dr ▌
NG3 . . . . .48 A2
Mapperley Plains NG3 . . . .36 A4
Mapperley Plains Prim Sch
NG3 . . . . .35 C1
Mapperley Rd NG3 . . . . . .48 A3
Mapperley Rise NG3 . . . . .48 C4
Mapperley St NG5 . . . . . . .48 A4
March Cl NG5 . . . . .21 C1
Marches Cl NG15 . . . . .10 C2
Marchwood Cl NG8 . . . . . .58 B3
Mardale Cl NG2 . . . . .87 B4
Mardling Av NG5 . . . . .33 B3
Margaret Ave
Ilkeston DE7 . . . . .41 A2
Long Eaton NG10 . . . . . . .90 B3
Sandiacre NG10 . . . . .79 A2
Margaret Cres NG4 . . . . . .50 C4
Margaret Pl NG13 . . . . . . .66 C3
Margaret's Ct NG9 . . . . . .70 C2
Marham Cl NG2 . . . . .60 C1
Marhill Rd NG4 . . . . .51 A1
Marie Gdns NG15 . . . . . . .11 B3
Marina Ave NG9 . . . . .82 B3
Mariner Cl NG6 . . . . .31 B4
Marion Ave NG15 . . . . .3 B3
Marion Murdoch Ct NG4 . .50 C4
Maris Cl NG11 . . . . .93 B4
Maris Dr NG14 . . . . .38 C1
Market Pl Bingham NG13 . .67 A2
▌ Heanor DE5 . . . . .13 C3
Hucknall NG15 . . . . .2 C1
Ilkeston DE7 . . . . .40 C2
Long Eaton NG10 . . . . . . .90 A2
Nottingham NG1 . . . . . . .109 B2
Market Pl The NG5 . . . . . .24 A1
Market Side ▌ NG6 . . . . . .20 C1
Market St Bingham NG13 . .67 A2
Heanor DE75 . . . . .13 C3
Ilkeston DE7 . . . . .41 A2
Nottingham NG1 . . . . . . .109 B2
Markham Cres NG5 . . . . . .34 A2
Markham Rd NG9 . . . . .71 C3
Mark St NG10 . . . . .79 B3
Marlborough Rd
Arnold NG5 . . . . .34 C2
Beeston NG9 . . . . .72 B1
Long Eaton NG10 . . . . . . .90 B3
Marlborough St ▌ NG7 . . . .74 A3
Marldon Cl NG8 . . . . .56 A3
Marlow Ave NG6 . . . . .46 C4
MARLPOOL 14 A2
Marl Rd NG12 . . . . .65 C2
Marlwood NG12 . . . . .98 C2
Marmion Rd NG3 . . . . .61 B4
Marnham Dr NG3 . . . . .48 C3
Marple Sq NG3 . . . . .48 A1

Marriott Ave NG9 . . . . . . .80 C3
Marriott Cl NG9 . . . . .80 C3
Marsant Cl ▌ NG8 . . . . . . .58 A3
Marshall Dr NG9 . . . . .70 C2
Marshall Hill Dr NG3 . . . . .49 C4
Marshall Rd NG3 . . . . .49 B3
Marshall St Heanor DE75 . .14 A4
Nottingham NG5 . . . . .48 A4
Marshall Way DE7 . . . . . . .52 A4
Marston Rd NG3 . . . . .49 C1
Martin Cl NG6 . . . . .20 B2
Martin Ct NG6 . . . . .20 B2
Martindale Cl NG2 . . . . . . .77 B1
Martinmass Cl NG7 . . . . .107 A1
Martins Hill NG4 . . . . .50 C4
Martin's Pond Nature
Reserve ▶ NG8 . . . . .56 C3
Marton Rd Beeston NG9 . . .81 B1
Nottingham NG6 . . . . .21 A3
Marvin Rd NG9 . . . . .82 B4
Marwood Cres NG4 . . . . . .50 A4
Marwood Rd NG4 . . . . .50 A4
Mary Howitt Inf Com Sch
DE75 . . . . .13 B4
Maryland Ct NG9 . . . . .70 A3
Mary Rd NG16 . . . . .16 C3
Masonic Pl NG1 . . . . .108 A3
Mason Rd DE7 . . . . .40 B4
Massey Cl NG14 . . . . .38 C1
Massey Gdns ▌ NG3 . . . . .60 C4
Masson Ct ▌ NG7 . . . . . . .22 B3
Matlock Ct
Long Eaton NG10 . . . . . . .99 B3
Nottingham NG1 . . . . . . .108 B3
Matlock St NG4 . . . . .51 A1
Matthews Ct NG9 . . . . . . .70 B4
Mattingly Rd NG6 . . . . . . .31 B3
Maud St NG7 . . . . .47 B3
Maun Ave NG7 . . . . .58 B4
Maurice Dr NG3 . . . . .48 C4
Maws La NG16 . . . . .17 C1
Maxtoke Rd NG7 . . . . . . .107 C1
Maxwell Cl NG7 . . . . .107 B1
Maxwell St DE72 . . . . .88 B2
May Ave NG8 . . . . .56 C2
Maycroft Gdns NG3 . . . . . .49 A4
May Ct ▌ NG5 . . . . .47 C3
Maydene Cl NG11 . . . . . . .93 C3
Mayes Rise NG6 . . . . .12 C2
Mayfair Cl NG7 . . . . .47 A3
Mayfair Gdns NG5 . . . . . . .33 A3
Mayfield Ave
Burton Joyce NG14 . . . . . .39 A3
Heanor DE75 . . . . .13 C3
Mayfield Ct NG2 . . . . .75 B4
Mayfield Dr NG9 . . . . .70 B4
Mayfield Gr NG10 . . . . . . .90 A3
Mayfield Rd NG4 . . . . .49 C1
Mayflower Cl NG2 . . . . . . .76 C1
Mayflower Rd NG16 . . . . . .16 C2
Mayland Cl NG8 . . . . .56 A4
Maylands Ave DE72 . . . . . .88 A2
Mayo Rd NG5 . . . . .47 C3
Maypole NG15 . . . . .84 A1
Maypole Yd NG1 . . . . .108 B3
May S DE7 . . . . .26 B1
Mays Ave NG4 . . . . .62 B4
Mays Cl NG4 . . . . .62 A4
May St DE7 . . . . .26 C2
Maythorn Cl NG11 . . . . . . .85 B1
Maythorne Wlk NG5 . . . . .23 A1
Meadowbank Day Hospl
NG2 . . . . .75 A3
Meadowbank Way NG16 . . .8 B1
Meadow Cl Eastwood NG16 . .9 A2
Hucknall NG15 . . . . .10 B3
Nottingham NG2 . . . . .74 A2
Meadow Cotts NG4 . . . . . .51 A1
Meadow Ct NG2 . . . . .76 B4
Meadow Dr NG12 . . . . . . .105 A3
Meadow Gdns
Beeston NG9 . . . . .82 A2
Heanor DE75 . . . . .14 C3
Meadow Gr NG2 . . . . .74 A3
Meadow La Beeston NG9 . . .82 A2
Burton Joyce NG14 . . . . . .39 A2
Long Eaton NG10 . . . . . . .90 B1
▌ Nottingham NG2 . . . . . .61 A1
Meadow Lane Inf Sch
NG9 . . . . .82 A2

Meadow La (Notts Cty FC)
NG2 . . . . .76 A2
Meadow Rd
Awsworth NG16 . . . . .28 A3
Beeston NG9 . . . . .83 A2
Carlton NG4 . . . . .51 A1
Meadow Rise NG6 . . . . . . .31 A4
MEADOWS 75 B4
Meadows Ed Ctr NG2 . . . . .75 C3
Meadow St DE7 . . . . .41 A3
Meadows The ▌ DE75 . . . .13 C3
Meadows Way NG2 . . . . . .75 B4
Meadowsweet Hill NG13 . .66 B2
Meadowvale Cres NG7 . . . .94 A3
Meadow View Ct DE72 . . . .78 A2
Medawar Cl NG11 . . . . . . .93 B3
Meden Cl NG11 . . . . .84 A1
Meden Gdns NG7 . . . . .46 B1
Medway Cl NG9 . . . . .81 B3
Meeks Rd NG5 . . . . .24 C2
Meerbrook Pl DE7 . . . . . . .52 A3
Meer Rd NG9 . . . . .80 C3
Melbourne Ct
Long Eaton NG10 . . . . . . .99 B2
Nottingham NG8 . . . . .46 A3
Melbourne Rd
Nottingham NG8 . . . . .46 A3
Stapleford NG9 . . . . .70 A3
West Bridgford NG2 . . . . . .76 C3
Melbury Rd
Nottingham, Bilborough
NG8 . . . . .44 B2
Nottingham, Woodthorpe
NG5 . . . . .35 B2
Meldreth Rd NG8 . . . . .56 C4
Melford Hall Dr NG2 . . . . .85 B2
Melford Rd NG8 . . . . .44 B2
Melksham Rd NG5 . . . . . . .23 A2
Mellbreak Cl NG2 . . . . . . .87 B4
Mellers Prim Sch NG7 . . .106 B3
Mellors Rd Arnold NG5 . . . .24 A3
West Bridgford NG2 . . . . . .86 B4
Melrose Ave
Beeston NG9 . . . . .82 C3
▌ Nottingham NG5 . . . . . .34 A1
Melrose Gdns NG2 . . . . . . .85 B2
Melrose St NG5 . . . . .48 A4
Melton Cl NG10 . . . . .78 C3
Melton Gdns NG12 . . . . . .87 A2
Melton Gr NG2 . . . . .86 A1
Melton Rd NG12 . . . . .86 C1
Melville Ct ▌ NG3 . . . . . . .60 C4
Melville Gdns NG3 . . . . . . .60 C4
Melville St NG1 . . . . .109 B1
Melvyn Dr NG13 . . . . .67 A3
Mendip Cl NG10 . . . . .88 C3
Mendip Ct NG5 . . . . .22 A2
Mensing Ave NG12 . . . . . .98 A3
Merchant St NG6 . . . . .20 C2
Mercury Cl NG6 . . . . .32 C3
Mere Ave NG14 . . . . .5 B2
Mere Cl NG14 . . . . .5 B2
Meredith Cl NG2 . . . . .75 A3
Meredith Ct NG9 . . . . .70 A4
Meregill Cl NG5 . . . . .22 A3
Merevale Ave NG11 . . . . . .84 B2
Mere Way NG11 . . . . .103 A3
Meriac Cl NG5 . . . . .22 A2
Meriden Ave NG9 . . . . .72 C2
Meridian Cl DE7 . . . . .26 C2
Meridian Ct NG5 . . . . .47 B4
Merlin Cl NG7 . . . . .94 A4
Merlin Dr NG15 . . . . .10 C2
Merlin Way Ilkeston DE7 . . .53 A2
Ilkeston DE7 . . . . .53 B1
Merrivale Cl NG3 . . . . .48 A2
Mersey St NG6 . . . . .20 C1
Merton Cl Arnold NG5 . . . . .24 C3
▌ Heanor DE75 . . . . .14 A3
Merton Ct NG9 . . . . .70 A3
Metcalf Rd NG16 . . . . .9 C1
Mettham St NG7 . . . . .107 B1
Mews La NG14 . . . . .5 A3
Meynell Gr ▌ NG7 . . . . . . .47 B3
Meynell Rd NG10 . . . . .100 C3
Miall Ct NG7 . . . . .94 A3
Mickleborough Ave NG3 . . .49 B2
Mickleborough Way
NG2 . . . . .85 B1
Mickleden Cl ▌ NG2 . . . . .75 A4

Mickledon Cl ▌ NG10 . . .89 A2
Middle Ave NG4 . . . . .50 A2
Middlebeck Ave NG5 . . . . .25 A2
Middlebeck Dr NG5 . . . . . .25 A2
Middledale Rd NG4 . . . . . .62 A4
Middlefell Way NG11 . . . . .93 C3
Middle Furlong Gdns ▌
NG2 . . . . .75 A4
Middle Furlong Mews ▐
NG2 . . . . .75 A4
Middle Hill NG1 . . . . .109 B2
Middle La NG9 . . . . .82 A3
Middle Pavement NG1 . . .109 B2
Middle St NG9 . . . . .82 C4
Middleton Bvd NG8 . . . . . .58 A1
Middleton Cl NG16 . . . . . . .30 A4
Middleton Cres NG9 . . . . . .72 A3
Middleton Prim Sch
NG8 . . . . .58 A2
Middleton Rd DE7 . . . . . . .53 B3
Middleton St
Awsworth NG16 . . . . .28 A2
Beeston NG9 . . . . .72 B1
Cossall DE7 . . . . .41 B3
Nottingham NG7 . . . . . . .106 A3
Midhurst Cl NG9 . . . . .81 B2
Midhurst Way NG7 . . . . . . .94 A4
Midlame Gdns NG6 . . . . . .20 A1
Midland Ave Carlton NG4 . .51 B1
Nottingham NG7 . . . . . . .107 A1
Stapleford NG9 . . . . .79 B3
Midland Cres NG4 . . . . . . .51 A1
Midland Ct NG7 . . . . .58 B3
Midland Gr NG4 . . . . .51 B2
Midland Rd Carlton NG4 . . .51 A1
Eastwood NG16 . . . . .16 A4
Heanor DE75 . . . . .13 C4
Midland St NG10 . . . . .90 A2
Midway The NG7 . . . . .74 A1
Mikado Rd NG10 . . . . . . .100 B3
Mike Powers Pottery ▶
NG11 . . . . .95 B1
Milburn Gr NG13 . . . . .66 B2
Mildenhall Cres NG5 . . . . .23 A2
Mile End Rd NG4 . . . . .62 C3
Milford Ave NG10 . . . . . . .79 A1
Milford Cl NG6 . . . . .20 B2
Milford Ct NG5 . . . . .34 B4
Milford Dr Ilkeston DE7 . . . .26 B1
Nottingham NG3 . . . . .50 A1
Milford Prim Sch NG11 . . .94 A2
Millbank DE75 . . . . .14 B2
Millbank Cl DE7 . . . . .26 B1
Millbeck Ave NG8 . . . . . . .56 A1
Millbeck Cl NG2 . . . . .87 B4
Millbrook Dr NG4 . . . . .50 A3
Mill Cl The NG8 . . . . .32 C1
Mill Cres NG5 . . . . .23 C2
Milldale Cl NG11 . . . . .93 B4
Milldale Rd NG10 . . . . . . .100 A4
Millennium Way E NG6 . . .31 B2
Millennium Way W NG6 . . .31 B2
Miller Hives Cl NG12 . . . . .98 A3
Millers Bridge NG12 . . . . .98 A2
Millers Ct NG7 . . . . .106 A4
Millersdale Ave DE7 . . . . . .26 C3
Millers Gn ▌ NG2 . . . . . . .61 B2
Millfield Cl DE7 . . . . .26 A1
Mill Field Cl NG14 . . . . . . .38 C1
Millfield Rd Ilkeston DE7 . . .41 B2
Kimberley NG16 . . . . .17 C1
Mill Hill La DE72 . . . . .88 A3
Mill Hill Rd NG13 . . . . .66 C1
Millicent Gr NG2 . . . . .76 B2
Millicent Rd NG2 . . . . .76 A2
Millidge Cl NG5 . . . . .33 A3
Millingdon Ave NG16 . . . . .30 B1
Mill La Arnold NG5 . . . . . . .23 C2
Cossall NG16 . . . . .42 A3
Cotgrave NG12 . . . . .98 A4
Sandiacre NG10 . . . . .79 B4
Mill Lakes ▶ NG6 . . . . . . .20 C4
Mill Rd Eastwood NG16 . . . . .9 C1
Heanor DE75 . . . . .14 B2
Stapleford NG9 . . . . .69 C2
Mill St Ilkeston DE7 . . . . . .40 C4
Nottingham NG6 . . . . .32 B1
Millview Cl ▌ NG2 . . . . . . .61 A2
Millview Ct ▐ NG2 . . . . . . .60 C2
Mill Yd Beeston NG9 . . . . . .82 B4
Hucknall NG15 . . . . .2 C1

Milner Rd
Long Eaton NG10 . . . . 89 C2
Nottingham NG5 . . . . 48 A4
Milnhay Rd NG16 . . . . 15 A4
Milton Ave DE7 . . . . 26 C2
Milton Cres NG9 . . . . 91 B4
Milton Ct NG5 . . . . 24 C1
Milton Rd DE7 . . . . 27 A2
Milton Rise NG15 . . . . 10 A3
Milton St Ilkeston DE7 . . . . . 27 A2
Long Eaton NG10 . . . . 89 C1
Nottingham NG1 . . . . 108 B3
Milverton Rd NG5 . . . . 23 A2
Milward Rd DE7 . . . . 13 B4
Mimosa Cl NG11 . . . . 93 B3
Minerva St NG6 . . . . 20 C2
Minster Cl NG15 . . . . 3 A2
Minster Gdns NG16 . . . . . . 16 C3
Minstrel Av NG5 . . . . 47 B4
Minstrel Cl NG15 . . . . 11 B3
Mint Cl NG10 . . . . 88 C1
Minver Cres NG8 . . . . 45 C4
Mirberry Mews NG7 . . . . . 107 A1
Misk Hollows NG15 . . . . . . 2 A2
Misk View NG16 . . . . 16 C4
Mitchell Ave NG16 . . . . 7 B2
Mitchell Cl NG6 . . . . 31 B4
Mitchell St NG10 . . . . 90 A1
Mitchell Terr DE7 . . . . 53 B3
Moffat Cl NG3 . . . . 41 A1
Mollington Sq NG6 . . . . . . 31 C1
Monarch Way DE75 . . . . . . 13 B4
Mona Rd NG2 . . . . 76 C3
Mona St NG9 . . . . 83 A4
Monks Cl DE7 . . . . 41 B2
Monksway NG11 . . . . 84 C2
Monkton Cl DE7 . . . . 26 A1
Monkton Dr NG8 . . . . 44 C1
Monmouth Cl NG8 . . . . 55 C2
Monroe Wlk 11 NG5 . . . . . 22 B1
Monsaldale Cl NG10 . . . . . 100 A4
Monsall Ave DE7 . . . . 26 C3
Monsall St NG7 . . . . 47 A3
Monsell Dr NG5 . . . . 23 C3
Montague Rd NG15 . . . . . . 2 C2
Montague St
Beeston NG9 . . . . 72 A1
Nottingham NG6 . . . . 21 A1
Montfort Cres NG3 . . . . . . 34 B2
Montfort St NG7 . . . . 106 C3
Montgomery Cl 8 NG9 . . . 91 B4
Montgomery St NG7 . . . . . 106 C4
Montpelier Rd NG7 . . . . . . 74 A3
Montrose Ct NG9 . . . . 70 A3
Monyash Cl DE7 . . . . 26 C1
Moor Bridge NG6 . . . . 21 B3
Moorbridge Cotts NG6 . . . . 21 B4
Moorbridge La NG6 . . . . . . 69 C3
Moorbridge Rd NG13 . . . . . 67 A3
Moorbridge Rd E NG13 . . . 67 A3
Moore Cl NG2 . . . . 77 A3
Moore Gate NG9 . . . . 82 C4
Moore Rd NG3 . . . . 49 B4
Moores Ave NG10 . . . . 69 B1
Moore St NG6 . . . . 32 A3
Moor Farm Inn La NG9 . . . 70 C4
Moorfield Cres NG10 . . . . . 79 A4
Moorfield Ct NG9 . . . . 70 A3
Moorfields Ave NG16 . . . . . 9 A1
Moorgate St NG7 . . . . 106 C3
Moorgreen Dr NG8 . . . . . . 44 B4
Moorhouse Rd NG8 . . . . . . 56 C4
Moorings The 3 NG7 . . . . . 74 B4
Moor La Beeston NG9 . . . . . 71 A4
Bingham NG13 . . . . 67 A3
Ruddington NG11 . . . . 102 C4
Moorland Ave NG9 . . . . . . 79 C4
Moorlands Cl NG10 . . . . . . 89 A4
Moor Rd
Bestwood Village NG6 . . . . 12 C4
Calverton NG14 . . . . 5 C2
Nottingham NG8 . . . . 44 B3
Moorsholm Dr NG8 . . . . . . 56 B2
Moor St NG4 . . . . 51 B1
Moray Ct NG16 . . . . 18 A1
Morden Cl NG8 . . . . 44 B2
Morden Rd NG16 . . . . 17 A2
Moreland Ct Carlton NG4 . . 50 A1
10 Nottingham NG2 . . . . . . 61 A1
Moreland Pl 11 NG2 . . . . . 61 A1

Moreland St NG2 . . . . 61 A1
Morello Ave NG4 . . . . 51 A1
Moreton Rd NG11 . . . . . . 94 A1
Morgan Mews NG7 . . . . . . 93 C4
Morkinshire Cres NG12 . . . 98 B4
Morkinshire La NG12 . . . . 98 A4
Morley Ave NG3 . . . . 48 C4
Morley Ct 5 NG2 . . . . 60 C2
Morley Dr DE7 . . . . 26 B1
Morley Rd NG3 . . . . 49 B3
Morley St NG5 . . . . 34 B4
Mornington Cl NG10 . . . . . 79 B4
Mornington Cres NG8 . . . . 30 B1
Mornington Prim Sch
NG16 . . . . 30 B2
Morrell Bank NG5 . . . . 33 A4
Morris Ave NG9 . . . . 91 A3
Morris Rd NG8 . . . . 44 B3
Morris St NG4 . . . . 51 B1
Morval Rd NG8 . . . . 56 C4
Morven Ave NG15 . . . . 11 A4
Mosley St Hucknall NG15 . . 11 B4
Nottingham NG7 . . . . 47 A2
Moss Cl NG5 . . . . 23 A3
Mosscroft Ave NG11 . . . . . 93 C3
Mossdale Rd NG5 . . . . 34 A3
Moss Dr NG9 . . . . 71 A1
Moss Rd Hucknall NG15 . . . 21 B1
Ilkeston DE7 . . . . 40 C1
Moss Rise NG3 . . . . 49 C4
Moss Side NG11 . . . . 84 C2
Mosswood Cres NG5 . . . . . 22 C1
Mottram Rd NG9 . . . . 81 B4
Mountbatten Ct DE7 . . . . . 27 A1
Mountbatten Gr NG4 . . . . . 50 C4
Mountbatten Way NG9 . . . . 55 B4
Mountfield Ave NG10 . . . . . 79 A2
Mountfield Dr NG5 . . . . . . 22 B1
Mountford House Sch
NG5 . . . . 48 A3
Mount Hooton Rd NG7 . . . 106 C4
Mount Hooton St NG7 . . . . 47 B1
Mount Pleasant
Carlton NG4 . . . . 50 C1
Ilkeston DE7 . . . . 26 C2
Keyworth NG12 . . . . 105 A2
Nottingham NG6 . . . . 46 C4
Radcliffe on T NG12 . . . . . . 76 A3
Mountsorrel Dr NG2 . . . . . 87 A4
Mount St Breaston DE72 . . . 88 B1
Heanor DE75 . . . . 13 C3
Nottingham, New Basford
NG7 . . . . 47 A3
Nottingham NG1 . . . . 109 A2
Stapleford NG9 . . . . 70 A1
Mount The Arnold NG5 . . . 23 B3
Bestwood Village NG6 . . . . 12 C2
Nottingham, Broxtowe
NG8 . . . . 44 C3
Nottingham, Portchester
NG3 . . . . 50 A4
Stapleford NG9 . . . . 79 C4
Mowbray St NG3 . . . . 108 C3
Mowbray Gdns NG2 . . . . . 86 B3
Mowbray Rise NG5 . . . . . . 24 A2
Moyra Dr NG5 . . . . 23 A1
Mozart Cl NG7 . . . . 106 A3
Muir Ave NG12 . . . . 97 C2
Muirfield Rd NG5 . . . . 22 B3
Mulberry Cl NG2 . . . . 85 A3
Mulberry Gdns 11 NG6 . . . 20 B2
Mulberry Gr NG15 . . . . 11 C2
Mundella Rd NG2 . . . . 75 C3
Mundy CE Jun Sch DE75 . . 14 A2
Mundy's Dr DE75 . . . . 14 A2
Mundy St Heanor DE75 . . . 13 C3
Ilkeston DE7 . . . . 40 C4
Munford Circ NG6 . . . . 31 C1
Munks Ave NG15 . . . . 2 B1
Murby Cres NG6 . . . . 20 C2
Murden Way NG9 . . . . 83 A4
Muriel Rd NG9 . . . . 72 B1
Muriel St NG6 . . . . 20 C1
Murray Cl NG5 . . . . 33 A3
Muskham Ave DE7 . . . . . . 27 A1
Muskham St NG2 . . . . 75 C3
Musters Cres NG2 . . . . 86 B3
Musters Croft NG4 . . . . . . 63 A2
Musters Rd
Bingham NG13 . . . . 66 C2
Ruddington NG11 . . . . 102 C4

Musters Rd continued
West Bridgford NG2 . . . . . . 86 A3
Musters Wlk 4 NG6 . . . . . 20 B1
Muston Cl NG3 . . . . 49 A3
Myrtle Ave
Long Eaton NG10 . . . . 100 B4
1 Nottingham NG7 . . . . . . 47 C2
Stapleford NG9 . . . . 80 A4
Myrtle Gr NG9 . . . . 72 C1
Myrtle Rd NG4 . . . . 50 A2
Myrtus Cl NG11 . . . . 93 B4
Mytholme Cl NG10 . . . . . . 89 B4

N

Nabbs La NG15 . . . . 10 C3
Naburn Ct 4 NG8 . . . . 46 B2
Nairn Cl NG5 . . . . 24 C2
Nairn Mews NG4 . . . . 50 C1
Nansen St NG6 . . . . 32 A4
Naomi Cres NG6 . . . . 21 A3
Naomi Ct NG6 . . . . 21 A3
Naseby Cl NG5 . . . . 33 A2
Naseby Dr NG10 . . . . 101 A2
Nathaniel Rd NG10 . . . . . . 90 B1
National CE Inf Sch NG15 . 2 C2
National Jun Sch 1
NG15 . . . . 2 C2
National Sch The NG15 . . . 2 B3
National Water Sports Ctr
NG12 . . . . 63 A1
Navenby Wlk NG7 . . . . 94 A4
Naworth Cl NG6 . . . . 32 C3
Neal Ct NG16 . . . . 7 B1
Neale St NG10 . . . . 90 A1
Near Mdw NG10 . . . . 101 A3
Nearsby Dr NG2 . . . . 87 A4
Needham Rd NG3 . . . . 24 B2
Needham St NG13 . . . . 67 A2
Needwood Ave NG9 . . . . . . 69 C4
Negus Ct NG4 . . . . 37 C4
Neighwood Cl NG9 . . . . . . 82 C4
Nell Gwyn Cres NG5 . . . . . 23 A3
Nelper Cres DE7 . . . . 53 B3
Nelson Rd Arnold NG5 . . . . 23 C1
Beeston NG9 . . . . 82 C2
Nottingham NG6 . . . . 21 A1
Nelson St Ilkeston DE7 . . . 27 A1
Long Eaton NG10 . . . . 100 C4
Nottingham NG1 . . . . 109 C2
Nene Cl NG15 . . . . 10 C1
Nesfield Ct DE7 . . . . 40 C3
Nesfield Rd DE7 . . . . 40 C3
Neston Dr NG6 . . . . 32 A2
Nether Cl Eastwood NG16 . 9 A2
Nottingham NG3 . . . . 61 B4
NETHERFIELD 63 C4
Netherfield Prim Sch
NG4 . . . . 51 B1
Netherfield Rd
Long Eaton NG10 . . . . 100 B2
Sandiacre NG10 . . . . 79 A2
Netherfield Sta NG4 . . . . . 63 A4
Nethergate NG11 . . . . 93 B4
Nethergate Specl Sch
NG11 . . . . 94 C3
Nether Pasture NG4 . . . . . 63 C4
Nether St NG9 . . . . 82 C4
Nettlecliff Wlk NG5 . . . . . 21 C2
Neville Rd NG14 . . . . 5 B1
Neville Sadler Ct NG9 . . . . 73 A1
Newall Dr NG9 . . . . 91 B4
Newark Ave 16 NG2 . . . . . 60 C2
Newark Cres NG2 . . . . 60 C2
Newark Ct NG5 . . . . 33 A3
Newark St NG2 . . . . 60 C2
Newbery Ave NG10 . . . . . . 101 B4
Newbury Cl NG3 . . . . 35 A3
Newbury Ct 3 NG5 . . . . . . 47 C2
Newbury Dr NG16 . . . . 30 B1
Newcastle Ave
Beeston NG9 . . . . 82 B4
Carlton NG4 . . . . 50 C4
Newcastle Cir NG7 . . . . . . 107 C2
Newcastle Dr NG7 . . . . . . 106 C3
Newcastle Farm Dr NG8 . . 44 A1
Newcastle St
Nottingham, Bulwell
NG6 . . . . 21 A4
Nottingham NG1 . . . . 108 B3

New Coll Nottingham
Hucknall NG15 . . . . 3 A1
Nottingham NG1 . . . . 108 B4
Nottingham NG5 . . . . 47 C2
Newcombe Dr NG5 . . . . . . 25 A1
New Derby Rd NG16 . . . . . 8 A1
Newdigate Rd NG16 . . . . . 18 B1
Newdigate St
Ilkeston DE7 . . . . 53 B4
Kimberley NG16 . . . . 29 B4
Nottingham NG7 . . . . 106 C3
Newdigate Villas NG7 . . . 106 C3
New Eaton Rd NG9 . . . . . . 80 A3
New Farm La NG16 . . . . . . 30 A4
Newfield Rd NG5 . . . . 33 B1
Newgate Cl NG4 . . . . 50 C1
Newgate St NG13 . . . . 67 A3
Newhall Gr NG2 . . . . 76 B3
Newham Cl DE75 . . . . 14 B3
Newholm Dr NG11 . . . . . . 84 C2
Newland Cl Beeston NG9 . . 90 C4
Nottingham NG8 . . . . 58 A3
NEWLANDS 14 A4
Newlands Cl NG2 . . . . 87 B2
Newlands Dr Carlton NG4 . 51 A3
Heanor DE75 . . . . 6 C1
New Lawn Rd DE7 . . . . . . 40 C2
New Line Rd NG8 . . . . 46 B2
Newlyn Gdns NG8 . . . . . . 46 B2
Newmanleys Rd NG16 . . . . 15 C2
Newmanleys Rd S NG16 . . 15 C2
Newman Rd NG14 . . . . 5 A3
Newmarket Rd NG6 . . . . . 31 C4
Newmarket Way NG9 . . . . 90 B3
Newport Dr NG8 . . . . 46 B3
Newquay Ave 1 NG7 . . . . 46 C1
New Rd Nottingham NG7 . . 58 B4
Radcliffe on T NG12 . . . . . . 65 A2
Stapleford NG9 . . . . 69 C3
New Row NG4 . . . . 50 B1
New St Long Eaton NG10 . . 90 A4
15 Nottingham NG5 . . . . . 47 C3
Newstead Ave
Nottingham NG3 . . . . 50 A4
Radcliffe on T NG12 . . . . . . 65 B3
Newstead Dr NG2 . . . . 77 A1
Newstead Gr
Bingham NG13 . . . . 66 B2
Nottingham NG1 . . . . 108 A4
Newstead Rd NG10 . . . . . . 79 B1
Newstead Rd S DE7 . . . . . 26 B1
Newstead St NG5 . . . . 34 A1
Newstead Terr NG15 . . . . . 2 C2
Newstead Way NG8 . . . . . . 44 A4
New Terr NG10 . . . . 79 A4
Newthorpe Comm NG16 . . 18 B3
Newthorpe St NG2 . . . . . . 75 C4
Newton Ave
Bingham NG13 . . . . 66 C2
Radcliffe on T NG12 . . . . . . 65 B3
Newton Cl NG5 . . . . 35 C4
Newton Rd NG4 . . . . 36 C1
Newton's La NG16 . . . . 27 C2
Newton St Beeston NG9 . . 82 A4
Nottingham NG7 . . . . 74 A3
New Tythe St NG10 . . . . . . 90 B1
New Vale Rd NG4 . . . . 62 C3
Nicholas Rd NG9 . . . . 71 C3
Nicker Hill NG12 . . . . 105 A3
Nicklaus Ct 5 NG5 . . . . . . 22 B2
Nidderdale NG8 . . . . 56 A2
Nidderdale Cl NG8 . . . . . . 56 A1
Nightingale Cl NG16 . . . . . 30 B4
Nightingale Way NG13 . . . 67 C1
Nile St NG1 . . . . 108 C3
Nilsson Rd NG9 . . . . 91 A1
Nimbus Way NG16 . . . . . . 18 B1
Nine Acre Gdns NG6 . . . . . 20 A2
Nixon Rise NG15 . . . . 10 B3
Noburn Cres NG6 . . . . 33 A1
Noel St Kimberley NG16 . . . 29 B4
Nottingham NG7 . . . . 47 A2
Nook End Rd DE75 . . . . . . 13 B3

Nook The
Beeston, Chilwell NG9 . . . . 82 A2
Beeston NG9 . . . . 72 C1
Calverton NG14 . . . . 5 B2
Heanor DE75 . . . . 6 A2
Nottingham NG8 . . . . 56 C2
Norbett Cl NG9 . . . . 81 B1
Norbett Ct NG5 . . . . 24 B3
Norbett Rd NG5 . . . . 24 B3
Norbreck Cl NG8 . . . . 31 C1
Norbury Way NG10 . . . . . . 78 C4
Nordean Rd NG5 . . . . 35 B3
Norfolk Ave NG9 . . . . 90 C3
Norfolk Cl NG15 . . . . 10 B3
Norfolk Pl Arnold NG5 . . . 35 C3
Nottingham NG1 . . . . 108 B3
Norfolk Rd NG10 . . . . 90 B3
Norfolk Wlk NG10 . . . . 79 A3
Norland Cl NG3 . . . . 48 C1
Normanby Rd NG8 . . . . . . 56 A1
Norman Cl Beeston NG9 . . 81 B4
Nottingham NG3 . . . . 108 B4
Norman Cres DE7 . . . . 26 C1
Norman Dr
Eastwood NG16 . . . . 16 C4
Hucknall NG15 . . . . 10 C2
Norman Rd NG3 . . . . 49 B2
Norman St Carlton NG4 . . . 63 B4
Ilkeston DE7 . . . . 26 C1
Kimberley NG16 . . . . 18 A1
Normanton La NG12 . . . . . 104 C3
Northall Ave NG6 . . . . 31 C4
Northampton St 2 NG3 . . 60 C4
North Ave NG10 . . . . 79 A4
North Church St NG1 . . . . 108 B3
North Cir St NG1 . . . . 109 A2
Northcliffe Ave NG3 . . . . . 49 C4
Northcote St NG10 . . . . . . 90 A1
Northcote Way NG6 . . . . . 32 A3
Northdale Rd NG3 . . . . . . 49 C1
Northdown Dr NG9 . . . . . . 81 B2
Northdown Rd NG8 . . . . . . 58 B4
North Dr NG9 . . . . 82 A4
Northern Ct NG6 . . . . 32 B2
Northern Dr NG9 . . . . 54 B1
Northern Rd DE75 . . . . . . 13 B4
Northfield Ave
Ilkeston DE7 . . . . 40 C4
Long Eaton NG10 . . . . 99 C2
Northfield Cres NG9 . . . . . 80 C2
Northfield Rd NG9 . . . . . . 80 C2
Northfields NG10 . . . . 100 A2
North Gate NG7 . . . . 47 A3
North Gate Pl NG7 . . . . . . 47 A3
Northgate Prim Sch
NG7 . . . . 47 A3
Northgate St 4 DE7 . . . . . 41 A3
North Gn NG14 . . . . 4 C4
North Hill Ave NG15 . . . . . 2 B1
North Hill Cres NG15 . . . . . 2 B1
Northolme Ave NG6 . . . . . 21 A1
Northolt Dr NG8 . . . . 30 B1
North Rd
Long Eaton NG10 . . . . 100 B4
Nottingham NG7 . . . . 107 C2
Ruddington NG11 . . . . 95 A2
West Bridgford NG2 . . . . . 76 A1
North Sherwood St
NG1 . . . . 108 B4
Northside Wlk NG5 . . . . . . 24 A4
North St Beeston NG9 . . . . 82 A4
Eastwood NG16 . . . . 17 A4
7 Ilkeston DE7 . . . . 41 A3
Kimberley NG16 . . . . 29 B3
Langley Mill NG16 . . . . 7 C1
4 Nottingham NG2 . . . . . . 60 C2
Northumberland Cl
NG3 . . . . 108 C4
Northwold Ave NG2 . . . . . 85 C4
Northwood Cres NG5 . . . . 34 A4
Northwood Rd NG5 . . . . . . 34 A4
Northwood St NG9 . . . . . . 69 C2
Norton Cl NG5 . . . . 106 B3
Norwich Gdns NG6 . . . . . . 20 C3
Norwood Rd NG7 . . . . 106 A3
Notintone St NG2 . . . . 60 C2
Nottingham Arts Theatre *
NG1 . . . . 109 C2

Nottingham Bluecoat Sch
The NG8 . . . . **46** A2
Nottingham Canal Nature
Reserve★ NG9 . . . . **42** A1
Nottingham Castle (site
of)★ NG7 . . . . **109** A2
Nottingham Cath★
NG1 . . . . **109** A2
Nottingham City Hospl
NG5 . . . . **33** B2
Nottingham Com Coll
NG3 . . . . **60** C3
Nottingham Emmanuel Sch
The NG11 . . . . **75** B2
Nottingham High Jun Sch
NG7 . . . . **108** A4
Nottingham High Sch
NG7 . . . . **108** A4
Nottingham High Sch for
Girls NG1 . . . . **108** A4
Nottingham Ice Ctr &
Arena NG1 . . . . **109** C2
Nottingham Nuffield Hospl
The NG5 . . . . **34** B2
Nottingham Playhouse★
NG1 . . . . **109** A2
Nottingham Racecourse★
NG2 . . . . **61** C1
Nottingham Rd
Arnold NG5 . . . . **34** C4
Beeston NG9 . . . . **91** A3
Bingham NG13 . . . . **66** C2
Burton Joyce NG14 . . . . . **38** B1
Eastwood, Giltbrook
NG16 . . . . **17** A2
Eastwood NG16 . . . . **16** B4
Gunthorpe NG14 . . . . **39** C4
Hucknall NG15 . . . . **12** A2
Ilkeston DE7 . . . . **53** B4
Keyworth NG12 . . . . **104** B3
Kimberley NG16 . . . . **29** B3
Long Eaton NG10 . . . . **90** A2
Nottingham, New Basford
NG7 . . . . **47** A3
Nuthall NG16 . . . . **31** A2
Radcliffe on T NG12 . . . . **64** B1
Stapleford NG9 . . . . **70** A1
Trowell NG9 . . . . **54** C3
Woodborough NG14 . . . . **25** C4
Nottingham Rd E NG16 . . **16** C3
Nottingham Science &
Tech Pk NG2 . . . . **73** C3
Nottingham Sta NG2 . . . **109** C1
Nottingham S & Wilford
Ind Est NG2 . . . . **85** A2
Nottingham Transport Her
Ctr★ NG11 . . . . **102** C3
Nottingham Trent Univ
The
Clifton NG11 . . . . **83** C1
Nottingham NG1 . . . . **108** A3
Nuart Rd NG9 . . . . **72** B1
Nugent Gdn NG3 . . . . **60** C4
Nugent Gdns 4 NG3 . . . . **60** C4
Nurseries The NG16 . . . . . **16** B4
Nursery Ave Beeston NG9 . **81** B3
Sandiacre NG10 . . . . **78** B3
Nursery Cl Hucknall NG15 . **11** B2
Radcliffe on T NG12 . . . . **65** C2
Nursery Dr NG4 . . . . **50** B2
Nursery Hollow DE7 . . . . . **52** C4
Nursery La NG6 . . . . **32** C2
Nursery Rd Arnold NG5 . . **24** B2
Radcliffe on T NG12 . . . . **65** C2
Nutbrook Cres DE7 . . . . . . **52** B2
NUTHALL **30** B3
Nuthall Circ DE7 . . . . **52** A2
Nuthall Gdns NG8 . . . . **46** B2
Nuthall Rd NG8 . . . . **46** A4

O

Oak Acres NG9 . . . . **80** C3
Oak Apple Cres DE7 . . . . **52** C4
Oak Ave Aldercar NG16 . . . . **7** C3
Bingham NG13 . . . . **67** C2
Radcliffe on T NG12 . . . . **64** C3
Sandiacre NG10 . . . . **68** C1

Oakdale Dr NG9 . . . . **81** B2
Oakdale Rd Arnold NG5 . . **24** C2
Carlton NG3 . . . . **62** A4
Oak Dr Eastwood NG16 . . **15** C4
Nuthall NG16 . . . . **29** C4
Oakenhall Ave NG15 . . . . . **3** B1
Oakfield Cl NG8 . . . . **56** A1
Oakfield Dr NG10 . . . . **79** A1
Oakfield Rd
Hucknall NG15 . . . . **11** C4
Nottingham NG8 . . . . **56** A1
Stapleford NG9 . . . . **69** C1
Oakfields Rd NG2 . . . . **76** C3
Oak Flatt NG9 . . . . **80** C3
Oakford Cl NG8 . . . . **45** B4
Oak Gr NG15 . . . . **11** B2
Oakham Cl NG5 . . . . **22** A1
Oakhampton Cres NG3 . . **36** A4
Oakham Rd NG11 . . . . **95** C4
Oakington Cl NG5 . . . . **33** C3
Oakland Ave NG10 . . . . . **100** B3
Oakland Cl NG9 . . . . **70** C3
Oakland Gr NG14 . . . . **5** B2
Oaklands Ave DE75 . . . . . **14** B4
Oakland St 6 NG7 . . . . . **46** C1
Oakland Terr NG10 . . . . **100** B3
Oakleigh Ave NG3 . . . . . . **50** A4
Oakleigh St NG6 . . . . **32** B2
Oakley Mews NG6 . . . . . . **31** A4
Oakley's Rd NG10 . . . . **90** A1
Oakley's Rd W NG10 . . . **100** C4
Oak Lodge Dr NG16 . . . . . **18** A1
Oakmead Ave NG8 . . . . . . **45** A2
Oakmere Cl NG2 . . . . **87** B2
Oak St NG5 . . . . **47** C3
Oak Tree Ave NG4 . . . . . . **65** A3
Oak Tree Cl
Hucknall NG15 . . . . **10** B2
West Bridgford NG2 . . . . . **76** C2
Oak Tree Dr NG4 . . . . **51** B4
Oakwell Cres DE7 . . . . . . **40** C2
Oakwell Dr DE7 . . . . **40** C2
Oakwood Dr NG8 . . . . **46** A1
Oban Rd NG9 . . . . **81** B4
Occupation Rd
Hucknall NG15 . . . . **11** B3
Nottingham NG6 . . . . **31** C3
Ochbrook Ct DE7 . . . . **27** A1
Ockerby St NG6 . . . . **32** A4
Odesa Dr NG6 . . . . **31** C2
Ogdon Ct NG3 . . . . **61** A4
Ogle Dr NG7 . . . . **109** A1
Ogle St NG15 . . . . **2** C1
Old Basford Prim Sch
NG6 . . . . **32** B1
Old Brickyard NG3 . . . . . . **49** B1
Oldbury Cl NG11 . . . . **93** C1
Old Church St 9 NG7 . . . **74** A4
Old Coach Rd
Nottingham NG8 . . . . **57** A3
Nottingham NG8 . . . . **57** A4
Old Coppice Side DE75 . . **13** C1
Old Derby Rd NG16 . . . . . . **8** B1
Old Dr NG9 . . . . **72** A2
Old Farm Rd NG5 . . . . **22** A2
Old Hall Cl NG14 . . . . **5** A2
Old Hall Dr NG3 . . . . **48** B4
Oldknow St NG7 . . . . **47** A1
Old La NG12 . . . . **95** C3
OLD LENTON **58** B1
Old Lenton St NG1 . . . . **109** C2
Old Main Rd NG14 . . . . . . **39** C3
Old Mill Cl Beeston NG9 . . **71** B4
Bestwood Village NG6 . . **12** B1
Nottingham NG7 . . . . . . **106** B3
Old Mill Ct NG13 . . . . **67** B3
Old Mkt Sq NG1 . . . . **109** B2
Oldoak Rd NG11 . . . . **94** C4
Old Pk The NG12 . . . . **98** B4
Old Sch Cl NG11 . . . . **94** A2
Old St NG1 . . . . **108** B3
Old Tollerton Rd NG2 . . . . **77** B1
Olga Ct NG3 . . . . **61** A4
Olga Rd NG3 . . . . **61** A4
Olive Ave NG10 . . . . **90** A3
Olive Gr NG14 . . . . **39** A3
Oliver Cl Heanor DE75 . . . . **14** C4
Nottingham NG7 . . . . . . **106** C4
Oliver Rd DE7 . . . . **52** A4
Oliver St NG7 . . . . **106** C3

Olton Ave NG9 . . . . **72** B3
Olympus Ct NG15 . . . . **10** B1
Onchan Ave NG4 . . . . **62** C4
Orange Gdns NG2 . . . . . . **75** C4
Orby Cl NG3 . . . . **61** A4
Orby Wlk NG3 . . . . **61** A4
Orchard Ave
Bingham NG13 . . . . **66** C2
Carlton NG4 . . . . **50** C1
Orchard Bsns Pk
Ilkeston DE7 . . . . **40** B3
Sandiacre NG10 . . . . **79** B4
Orchard Cl Breaston DE72 **88** B2
Burton Joyce NG14 . . . . . **39** A3
Radcliffe on T NG12 . . . . **64** C2
Tollerton NG12 . . . . **97** C3
Orchard Cres NG9 . . . . **81** B3
Orchard Ct Carlton NG4 . . **50** C1
Gedling NG4 . . . . **50** B4
Hucknall NG15 . . . . **11** B4
Langley Mill NG16 . . . . **7** C1
Nottingham NG8 . . . . **46** C2
Orchard Dr NG14 . . . . **5** C2
Orchard Gr NG5 . . . . **34** A4
Orchard Rise DE75 . . . . . . **14** A4
Orchard St
Eastwood NG16 . . . . **16** B3
Hucknall NG15 . . . . **11** B4
Ilkeston DE7 . . . . **41** A1
Kimberley NG16 . . . . **29** A4
Langley Mill NG16 . . . . **7** C1
Long Eaton NG10 . . . . **90** A1
Stapleford NG9 . . . . **69** C1
Orchards The NG4 . . . . . . **51** B3
Orchard The DE7 . . . . **68** B2
Orchard Way NG10 . . . . . **78** C1
Orchid Cl NG11 . . . . **85** B2
Orford Ave
Nottingham NG11 . . . . . . **84** B2
Radcliffe on T NG12 . . . . **65** A1
Orion Cl NG8 . . . . **44** C1
Orion Dr NG8 . . . . **44** C1
Orlando Dr NG4 . . . . **51** A2
Orlock Wlk NG5 . . . . **33** C3
Ormonde St NG16 . . . . **7** C2
Ormonde Terr
Aldercar NG16 . . . . **7** C2
Nottingham NG5 . . . . **48** A4
Ornsay Cl NG5 . . . . **21** C3
Orpean Way NG9 . . . . **90** A4
Orston Ave NG5 . . . . **24** B1
Orston Dr NG8 . . . . **58** B2
Orston Gn NG8 . . . . **58** B1
Orston Rd E NG2 . . . . **76** B3
Orston Rd W NG2 . . . . . . **76** A3
Orton Ave NG9 . . . . **81** B4
Ortzen St NG7 . . . . **106** B4
Orville Rd NG5 . . . . **32** C3
Osborne Ave 2 NG5 . . . . **34** A1
Osborne Cl NG10 . . . . **79** A2
Osborne Gr NG5 . . . . **34** A1
Osborne St NG7 . . . . **106** A4
Osgood Rd NG5 . . . . **36** A3
Osier Rd NG2 . . . . **75** B4
Osman Cl NG2 . . . . **75** A4
Osmaston Cl NG10 . . . . . . **99** B3
Osmaston St
Nottingham NG7 . . . . . . **107** B1
Sandiacre NG10 . . . . **79** B3
Osprey Cl NG11 . . . . **93** B3
Ossington Cl NG1 . . . . . . **108** B4
Ossington St NG7 . . . . . **106** B4
Osterley Gr NG8 . . . . **44** B4
Oulton Cl NG5 . . . . **35** A4
Owen Ave NG10 . . . . **101** C4
Owers Ave DE75 . . . . **14** A1
Owlston Cl NG16 . . . . **9** A1
Owsthorpe Cl NG5 . . . . . . **22** B2
Owthorpe Gr NG5 . . . . . . **47** C4

Owthorpe Rd NG12 . . . . . **98** B2
Oxborough Rd NG5 . . . . . **23** A1
Oxbow Cl NG2 . . . . **75** B3
Oxbury Rd NG16 . . . . **18** A2
Oxclose La NG5 . . . . **34** A4
Oxendale Cl NG2 . . . . **87** B4
Oxengate NG5 . . . . **34** A4
Oxford Rd NG2 . . . . **76** C1
Oxford St Carlton NG4 . . . **50** C2
Eastwood NG16 . . . . **16** A4
4 Ilkeston DE7 . . . . **41** A1
Long Eaton NG10 . . . . **89** C2
Nottingham NG1 . . . . **109** A2
Oxton Ave NG5 . . . . **34** A2
Oxton Rd NG14 . . . . **4** C4
Ozier Holt Carlton NG4 . . **62** C2
Long Eaton NG10 . . . . . . **100** B4

P

Packman Dr NG11 . . . . **95** C2
Paddington Ms NG3 . . . . . **49** B1
Paddock Cl Calverton NG14 . **5** B2
Nottingham NG6 . . . . **31** C3
Radcliffe on T NG12 . . . . **64** C1
Paddocks The
Sandiacre NG10 . . . . **78** C3
West Bridgford NG12 . . . . **87** A1
Paddocks View NG10 . . . . **88** C2
Paddock The
Beeston NG9 . . . . **91** C4
Nottingham NG3 . . . . **67** A2
Padge Rd NG9 . . . . **83** A4
Padgham Ct 11 NG5 . . . . **22** B2
Padleys La NG14 . . . . **38** C3
Padstow Rd NG5 . . . . **33** A4
Paget Cres NG11 . . . . **95** B2
Paignton Cl NG8 . . . . **45** C4
Paisley Gr NG9 . . . . **91** B3
Palatine St NG7 . . . . **109** A1
Palin Gdns NG12 . . . . **65** B2
Palin St NG7 . . . . **106** B4
Palm Ct Ind Ctr NG7 . . . . **47** A3
Palmer Ave NG15 . . . . **2** C2
Palmer Cres NG4 . . . . **50** B1
Palmer Dr NG9 . . . . **79** C3
Palmerston Gdns NG3 . . **108** B4
Palmerston Rd 4 DE7 . . . **41** A2
Palm St NG7 . . . . **47** A3
Palmwood Ct NG6 . . . . . . **32** A3
Palm Wood Ct NG6 . . . . . **32** A4
Papplewick Grange NG15 . **3** C3
Papplewick La NG15 . . . . . **3** B2
Park Ave Arnold NG5 . . . . **34** C3
Awsworth NG16 . . . . **27** C3
Burton Joyce NG14 . . . . . **38** C2
Carlton NG4 . . . . **51** A2
Eastwood NG16 . . . . **8** C1
Hucknall NG15 . . . . **2** B1
Ilkeston DE7 . . . . **41** A2
Keyworth NG12 . . . . **104** C4
Kimberley NG16 . . . . **29** B2
Nottingham NG3 . . . . **48** A1
West Bridgford NG2 . . . . . **76** B2
Park Ave E NG12 . . . . **104** A3
Park Ave W NG12 . . . . . . **104** A3
Park Chase NG6 . . . . **31** C3
Park Cl Nottingham NG3 . . **48** C4
Stanton-by-D DE7 . . . . **68** B2
Park Cres Eastwood NG16 . . **9** A2
Ilkeston DE7 . . . . **41** B2
Nottingham NG8 . . . . **56** A2
Parkcroft Rd NG2 . . . . **86** B4
Park Ct DE75 . . . . **14** A3
Parkdale Prim Sch NG4 . . **62** B4
Parkdale Rd NG3 . . . . **62** A4
Park Dr Hucknall NG15 . . . **11** C4
Ilkeston DE7 . . . . **41** A1
Nottingham NG7 . . . . **107** C2
Sandiacre NG10 . . . . **78** C1
Park Gate NG15 . . . . **3** A3
Parkham Rd NG16 . . . . **18** A1
Park Hill NG16 . . . . **27** C3
Park House Gates NG3 . . **48** B3
Park Hts NG7 . . . . **107** C1
Park La NG6 . . . . **32** C2
Parkland Cl NG11 . . . . **83** C1
Parklands Adult Ctr
NG10 . . . . **89** C2

Parklands Cl 1 NG5 . . . . **22** C3
Parklands Inf Sch NG10 . . **89** A3
Park Mews NG3 . . . . **48** A2
Park Ravine NG7 . . . . . . **107** C1
Park Rd Arnold NG5 . . . . . **34** C3
Beeston, Bramcote NG9 . . **70** C2
Beeston, Chilwell NG9 . . . **82** A4
Bestwood Village NG6 . . **12** C2
Calverton NG14 . . . . **5** A2
Carlton NG4 . . . . **51** A1
Hucknall NG15 . . . . **2** B1
Ilkeston DE7 . . . . **41** A1
Ilkeston DE7 . . . . **41** B1
Nottingham NG7 . . . . **107** B1
Radcliffe on T NG12 . . . . **65** A3
Park Rd E NG14 . . . . **5** C2
Park Rd N NG9 . . . . **82** A4
Park Row NG1 . . . . **109** A2
Parkside Keyworth NG12 . **104** C4
Nottingham NG8 . . . . **72** A4
Parkside Ave NG10 . . . . . . **89** A2
Parkside Dr NG10 . . . . **89** A2
Parkside Gdns NG8 . . . . . **72** A4
Parkside Rise NG8 . . . . . . **72** A4
Park St Beeston NG9 . . . . . **82** A4
Breaston DE72 . . . . **88** B2
Heanor DE75 . . . . **13** B4
Long Eaton NG10 . . . . **89** B3
Nottingham NG7 . . . . **107** B2
Stapleford NG9 . . . . **79** B3
Parkstone Cl NG2 . . . . **85** B3
Park Terr NG1 . . . . **109** A2
Park The NG12 . . . . **98** B4
Park Valley NG7 . . . . **109** A2
Park View Beeston NG9 . . **81** C4
Heanor DE75 . . . . **13** B3
Nottingham NG3 . . . . **48** C4
Parkview Rd NG5 . . . . **22** B1
Parkway Ct NG8 . . . . **56** B3
Parkwood Cres NG5 . . . . **34** C1
Parkwood Ct NG6 . . . . . . **32** C3
Parkyn Rd NG5 . . . . **34** B4
Parkyns St NG11 . . . . **102** C4
Parliament Terr NG1 . . . . **108** A3
Parr Gate NG9 . . . . **80** C3
Parrs The NG9 . . . . **83** A4
Parry Ct 5 NG3 . . . . **61** B4
Parry Way NG5 . . . . **24** C2
Parsons Mdw NG4 . . . . . . **63** A2
Pasteur Ct 5 NG7 . . . . . . **74** A4
Pasture Cl NG2 . . . . **62** C2
Pasture La
Long Eaton NG10 . . . . . . **101** C3
Ruddington NG11 . . . . **94** C1
Pasture Rd NG9 . . . . **69** C3
Pastures Ave NG11 . . . . . . **93** C1
Pastures The
Calverton NG14 . . . . **4** C2
Eastwood NG16 . . . . **16** C2
Pateley Rd NG3 . . . . **35** B2
Paton Rd NG5 . . . . **32** C3
Patricia Dr NG5 . . . . **24** B3
Patrick Rd NG2 . . . . **76** A2
Patriot Cl NG16 . . . . **18** B1
Patterdale Cl NG2 . . . . **87** B4
Patterdale Rd NG5 . . . . . . **35** A3
Patterson Rd 13 NG7 . . . . **47** A1
Pavilion Cl 2 NG2 . . . . . . **75** B1
Pavilion Rd Ilkeston DE7 . . **27** A4
Nottingham NG5 . . . . **22** C3
West Bridgford NG2 . . . . . **76** A3
Paviour Rd NG5 . . . . **33** A3
Paxton Gdns NG3 . . . . **60** C3
Payne Rd NG9 . . . . **81** A1
Peache Way NG9 . . . . **71** B1
Peachey St NG1 . . . . **108** B3
Peach St DE75 . . . . **13** B3
Peacock Cl NG11 . . . . **102** B4
Peacock Cres NG7 . . . . . . **94** A4
Peacock Pl DE7 . . . . **26** B2
Peakdale Cl NG10 . . . . **99** C4
Pearce Dr NG8 . . . . **45** C1
Pearmain Dr NG3 . . . . **49** A1
Pearson Ave NG9 . . . . **81** A3
Pearson Cl NG9 . . . . **81** A3
Pearson St Carlton NG4 . . **63** B4
Nottingham NG7 . . . . **47** A4
Pear Tree Ct NG6 . . . . **32** C2
Peartree Orch NG11 . . . . . **95** B1
Peary Cl NG5 . . . . **33** A4
Peas Hill Rd NG3 . . . . **108** C4

eatburn Ave DE75 . . . . . . **13** A3
Peveril Rd NG9 . . . . . . **69** C3
eck La NG1 . . . . **109** B2
edley St DE7 . . . . **41** A1
edmore Valley NG5 . . . . **22** B1
eel St Langley Mill NG16 . . **7** C1
Long Eaton NG10 . . . . **90** A2
elgrave St NG1 . . . . . . **108** A4
elham Ave Ilkeston DE7 . . **40** A3
Nottingham NG5 . . . . . . **47** C2
elham Cres
Beeston NG9 . . . . **73** A1
Nottingham NG7 . . . . . . **107** B3
elham Ct **4** NG5 . . . . . . **47** C2
elham Rd NG5 . . . . **47** C2
elham St NG1 . . . . **109** B2
emberton St NG1 . . . . **109** C2
embrey Cl NG9 . . . . **69** C4
embridge Cl NG6 . . . . . . **46** B4
embroke Dr NG3 . . . . . . **48** A3
embury Rd NG3 . . . . **56** C3
enarth Gdns NG5 . . . . . . **34** C1
enarth Rise NG5 . . . . . . **34** C1
endennis Cl NG4 . . . . . . **51** C3
endine Cl NG5 . . . . **23** B3
endle Cres NG3 . . . . **49** A3
enhale Dr NG15 . . . . **10** A3
enhurst Cl NG11 . . . . . . **84** C2
enllech Cl NG5 . . . . **22** B1
enllech Wlk **4** NG5 . . . . **22** B1
ennant Rd NG6 . . . . **46** B4
ennard Wlk NG11 . . . . . . **93** C2
enn Ave NG7 . . . . **107** C1
ennhome Ave **8** NG5 . . **48** A4
Pennine Cl
Long Eaton, Breaston
NG10 . . . . **88** C3
Long Eaton, New Sawley
NG10 . . . . **100** C2
Nottingham NG5 . . . . **22** C3
enn Moor Cl NG10 . . . . . **99** C4
ennyfields Bvd NG10 . . **88** C1
ennyfoot St NG1 . . . . . . **60** C2
enrhyn Cl NG3 . . . . **108** C4
enrhyn Cres NG9 . . . . . . **81** A2
enrith Ave NG12 . . . . . . **65** B3
enrith Cres NG6 . . . . **46** A4
enshore Cl NG11 . . . . . . **93** C3
entland Dr NG5 . . . . **22** C4
entland Gdns NG10 . . . . **88** C3
entwood Ave NG5 . . . . . **24** A4
Peoples Coll The
Nottingham NG1 . . . . . . **109** B1
Peppercorn Gdns NG8 . . **58** A3
Pepper La DE7 . . . . **68** A3
Pepper Rd NG14 . . . . **5** A3
Pepper St NG1 . . . . **109** B2
Percival Rd NG5 . . . . **48** A4
Percy St Eastwood NG16 . . **16** B4
Ilkeston DE7 . . . . **41** A1
Nottingham NG6 . . . . **32** B1
Peregrine Cl NG7 . . . . . . **107** A2
Perivale Cl NG16 . . . . **30** B1
Perlethorpe Ave
Carlton NG4 . . . . **50** C4
18 Nottingham NG1 . . . . **60** C2
Perlethorpe Cl NG4 . . . . **50** C4
Perlethorpe Cres NG4 . . **50** C4
Perlethorpe Dr
Carlton NG4 . . . . **50** C4
Hucknall NG15 . . . . **3** A1
Perry Gdns NG15 . . . . . . **33** C1
Perry Gr NG13 . . . . **67** B2
Perry Rd NG5 . . . . **33** C1
Perth Dr NG9 . . . . **70** B3
Perth St NG1 . . . . **108** B3
Peters Cl Arnold NG5 . . . . **36** A4
Eastwood NG16 . . . . **17** A4
Petersfield Cl NG5 . . . . . . **22** A1
Petersgate Cl NG10 . . . . **88** C3
Petersgate NG10 . . . . . . **88** C3
Petersham Mews NG7 . . **107** B1
Petersham Rd NG10 . . . . **88** C3
Petworth Ave NG9 . . . . . **80** B1
Petworth Dr NG5 . . . . . . **33** A2
Peveril Cres
Long Eaton NG10 . . . . **99** B3
Long Eaton NG10 . . . . **99** C3
Peveril Dr Ilkeston DE7 . . . **40** B4
Nottingham NG7 . . . . . . **109** A1
West Bridgford NG2 . . . . . **86** A1

Peveril Mews NG7 . . . . **107** C2
Peveril Rd NG9 . . . . **72** C1
Peveril St Hucknall NG15 . . **2** C1
Nottingham NG7 . . . . . . **106** B4
Pharaoh Ct NG8 . . . . **44** B4
Philip Ave Eastwood NG16 . **16** B3
Nuthall NG16 . . . . **30** A4
Philip Gr NG4 . . . . **50** C4
Phoenix Ave NG4 . . . . . . **50** C4
Phoenix Cl NG2 . . . . **75** A4
Phoenix Ct
Eastwood NG16 . . . . **16** B3
Nottingham NG7 . . . . . . **74** B2
Phoenix Ctr NG6 . . . . **31** B2
Phoenix Inf Sch **1** NG4 . . **50** C3
Phyllis Cl NG15 . . . . **2** B1
Phyllis Gr NG10 . . . . **90** B1
Piccadilly NG6 . . . . **32** B4
Pickering Ave NG16 . . . . **16** A4
Pieris Dr NG11 . . . . **93** B3
Pierrepont Ave NG4 . . . . **50** C3
Pierrepont Gamston Prim
Sch NG2 . . . . **87** A4
Pierrepont Rd NG2 . . . . . **76** C3
Pilcher Gate NG1 . . . . . . **109** B2
Pilkington Rd NG3 . . . . . **49** B3
Pilkington St **8** NG6 . . . **20** C1
Pimlico DE7 . . . . **40** C2
Pimlico Ave NG9 . . . . **55** C1
Pinder St NG1 . . . . **109** C2
Pine Ave NG16 . . . . **7** B1
Pine Hill Cl NG5 . . . . **22** A3
Pinehurst Ave NG15 . . . . **10** A3
Pine Tree Wlk NG16 . . . . **15** C4
Pinewood Ave NG15 . . . . **24** C3
Pinewood Gdns NG11 . . . **93** C2
Pinewood Inf Sch NG15 . . **24** C3
Pinfold NG13 . . . . **67** B2
Pinfold Cl NG12 . . . . **98** B4
Pinfold La
Nottingham NG11 . . . . . . **85** A4
Stapleford NG9 . . . . **70** A1
Pinfold Rd NG16 . . . . **17** A3
Pingle Cres NG5 . . . . **22** A2
Pingle The NG10 . . . . **89** C2
Pintail Cl NG4 . . . . **63** C3
Piper Cl NG15 . . . . **3** A3
Pippin Cl NG3 . . . . **49** A1
Pitcairn Cl NG2 . . . . **75** B3
Pitch Cl NG4 . . . . **50** A2
Plains Farm Cl NG3 . . . . . **36** A3
Plains Gr NG3 . . . . **35** B2
Plains Rd NG3 . . . . **35** C2
Plane Cl NG6 . . . . **20** A1
Plantagenet St **3** NG3 . . **108** C3
Plantagenet St NG3 . . . . **108** C3
Plantation Cl NG5 . . . . . . **22** B3
Plantation Rd
Keyworth NG12 . . . . **104** A3
Nottingham NG8 . . . . **56** A2
Plantation Side NG7 . . . . **46** C1
Plantations The **7**
NG10 . . . . **88** C2
Plant La NG10 . . . . **99** C2
Platts Ave DE75 . . . . **13** A3
Player St NG7 . . . . **106** B4
Plaza Gdns NG6 . . . . **32** C2
Pleasant Row NG7 . . . . . **47** A1
Plough La NG2 . . . . **60** C2
Plover Wharf **3** NG2 . . . **74** C4
Plowman Ct NG9 . . . . **79** C4
Plowright Cl **5** NG3 . . . . **48** B1
Plowright St **4** NG3 . . . . **48** B1
Plumb Rd NG15 . . . . **2** B1
Plumptre NG16 . . . . **7** C3
Plumptre Almshouses
NG1 . . . . **109** C1
Plumptre Cl NG16 . . . . . . **16** A3
Plumptre Pl NG1 . . . . . . **109** C2
Plumptre Sq NG1 . . . . . . **109** C2
Plumptre St NG1 . . . . . . **109** C2
Plumptre Way NG16 . . . . **16** A3
Plumtree Gdns NG14 . . . . **5** B2
Plumtree Rd NG12 . . . . . . **98** A3
Plungar Cl NG8 . . . . **57** C4
Podder La NG3 . . . . **36** A4
Point The NG3 . . . . **48** B2
Polperro Way NG15 . . . . . **10** B3
Pond Hills La NG5 . . . . . . **24** A3
Poole Mdw NG12 . . . . **63** A2
Popham St NG1 . . . . . . **109** C1

Popham St NG1 . . . . . . **109** C1
Poplar Ave
Nottingham NG5 . . . . **47** B3
Sandiacre NG10 . . . . **68** C1
Poplar Cl Bingham NG13 . . **67** C2
Carlton NG3 . . . . **62** B4
Poplar Cres NG16 . . . . . . **29** C4
Poplar Rd DE72 . . . . **88** B2
Poplars Ave NG14 . . . . . . **39** B3
Poplars Cl NG12 . . . . . . **104** C4
Poplar St NG1 . . . . **60** C2
Poplars The Beeston NG9 . **72** B1
Nottingham NG1 . . . . **46** C2
West Bridgford NG2 . . . . . **76** B1
Poplar Way DE7 . . . . **52** B3
PORCHESTER **49** C4
Porchester Cl NG15 . . . . . **3** B1
Porchester Jun Sch
NG4 . . . . **49** B3
Porchester Rd
Bingham NG13 . . . . **66** C2
Nottingham NG3 . . . . **49** B3
Porlock Cl **2** NG10 . . . . **88** C2
Portage Cl NG12 . . . . **64** C1
Port Arthur Rd NG2 . . . . . **61** B2
Porter Cl NG11 . . . . **93** B2
Porters Wk NG3 . . . . **49** B1
Portinscale Cl NG2 . . . . . **87** B3
Portland Cres NG9 . . . . . **80** A4
Portland Cl NG5 . . . . **33** C3
Portland Gdns NG15 . . . . . **2** B1
Portland Grange NG15 . . . . **2** A1
Portland Hill NG7 . . . . **73** B3
Portland L Ctr NG2 . . . . . **75** C3
Portland Pk Cl NG15 . . . . . **2** B1
Portland Prim Sch NG8 . . **56** A3
Portland Rd Beeston NG9 . **90** B3
Carlton NG4 . . . . **50** A4
Eastwood NG16 . . . . **16** C2
Hucknall NG15 . . . . **11** C4
Ilkeston DE7 . . . . **27** A1
Long Eaton NG10 . . . . . . **100** A2
Nottingham NG7 . . . . . . **106** C3
West Bridgford NG2 . . . . . **86** B4
Portland St Arnold NG5 . . **34** C4
Beeston NG9 . . . . **72** C1
Portree Dr NG5 . . . . **22** A3
Postern St NG1 . . . . **109** A2
Potters Cl NG5 . . . . **22** B1
Potters Ct NG9 . . . . **71** C3
Potters Way DE7 . . . . **41** B2
Poulter Cl NG7 . . . . **46** B1
Poulton Dr NG2 . . . . **76** A4
Poultry NG1 . . . . **109** B2
Powtrell Pl DE7 . . . . **53** C4
Poynter Cl DE75 . . . . **13** A3
Poynton St NG1 . . . . . . **109** A2
Poyser Cl **2** NG7 . . . . . . **47** B3
Precinct The NG12 . . . . . **98** B3
Premier Rd NG7 . . . . **47** B2
Prendwick Gdns NG5 . . . **22** C2
Prestwick Cl NG8 . . . . . . **44** B4
Prestwood Dr NG8 . . . . . **45** C1
Previn Gdns NG3 . . . . **61** A4
Primrose Bank NG13 . . . . **66** C2
Primrose Cl NG3 . . . . **48** B1
Primrose Cres NG4 . . . . . **51** A1
Primrose Rise Carlton NG4 . **51** A1
Ilkeston DE7 . . . . **26** C1
Primula Cl NG11 . . . . **93** B4
Prince Edward Cres
NG12 . . . . **64** C1
Princess Ave NG9 . . . . . . **82** C4
Princess Cl Carlton NG4 . . **50** C4
Heanor DE75 . . . . **13** B4
Princess Dr NG10 . . . . . . **79** A2
Princess St Eastwood NG16 . **9** A1
Long Eaton NG10 . . . . **89** C2
Prince St Ilkeston DE7 . . . **26** C2
Long Eaton NG10 . . . . **89** C2
Prioridge NG12 . . . . **98** C2
Prior Rd NG5 . . . . **34** B4
Priors Cl NG13 . . . . **67** C3
Priory Ave NG12 . . . . **97** B3
Priory Cir NG12 . . . . **97** B3
Priory Cl DE7 . . . . **52** A4
Priory Cres NG4 . . . . **51** A3
Priory Ct NG4 . . . . **51** A3
Priory Jun Sch **1** NG4 . . **51** A3
Priory Mews **7** NG7 . . . . **74** A4

Priory RC Prim Sch The
NG16 . . . . **16** C3
Priory Rd Carlton NG4 . . . **51** A3
Eastwood NG16 . . . . **16** A3
Hucknall NG15 . . . . **2** A1
West Bridgford NG2 . . . . . **76** C2
Priory St NG7 . . . . **74** A4
Pritchard Dr NG9 . . . . . . **80** A4
Private Rd Hucknall NG15 . . **2** A1
Nottingham NG5, NG3 . . . **48** B4
Prize Cl NG11 . . . . **93** B3
Promenade NG3 . . . . . . **108** C3
Prospect Pl NG7 . . . . . . **107** B1
Prospect Rd Carlton NG4 . . **49** C3
Heanor DE75 . . . . **14** B2
Prospect St NG7 . . . . . . **106** A4
Prospect Terr NG7 . . . . . **106** A4
Providence Pl **5** DE7 . . . **40** C3
Prudhoe Ct **3** NG2 . . . . **75** C3
Pulborough Cl NG5 . . . . . **33** A2
Pullman Rd **4** NG2 . . . . . **61** A2
Purbeck Cl NG10 . . . . . . **88** C2
Purbeck Dr NG2 . . . . **85** B3
Purchase Ave DE75 . . . . . **13** A4
Purdy Mdw
Long Eaton NG10 . . . . **99** B3
Long Eaton NG10 . . . . **99** C3
Pyatt St NG2 . . . . **75** C3
Pym Leys NG10 . . . . **99** B3
Pym St NG3 . . . . **61** A4
Pym Wlk NG3 . . . . **60** C2

Q

Quantock Cl NG5 . . . . **22** C4
Quantock Gr NG13 . . . . . **66** B2
Quantock Rd NG10 . . . . . **88** C3
Quarry Ave NG6 . . . . **31** C4
Quarry Hill NG10 . . . . **68** C2
Quarry Hill Ind Est DE7 . . **53** A3
Quarry Hill Rd DE7 . . . . . **53** A3
Quayside NG7 . . . . **76** A3
Queen Elizabeth Rd
NG9 . . . . **83** A4
Queen Elizabeth Way
DE7 . . . . **52** A3
Queens Ave Heanor DE75 . **13** B4
Ilkeston DE7 . . . . **53** B3
Queen's Ave NG4 . . . . . . **50** C4
Queensberry St NG6 . . . . **32** C2
Queens Bower Rd NG5 . . **23** A2
Queen's Bridge Rd
NG2 . . . . **109** B1
Queensbury Ave NG2 . . . **85** B1
Queen's Ct NG13 . . . . . . **66** C3
Queens Dr Beeston NG9 . . **82** C4
Nottingham NG5 . . . . **74** C2
Sandiacre NG10 . . . . **79** A2
Queen's Dr Ilkeston DE7 . . **40** C2
Nuthall NG16 . . . . **30** A4
Queens Dr Ind Est NG2 . . **74** C3
Queens Gr NG2 . . . . . . **109** B1
Queen's Medical Ctr (Univ
Hospl) NG7 . . . . **73** C4
Queens Rd NG9 . . . . **82** C4
Queen's Rd
Nottingham NG2 . . . . . . **109** C1
Radcliffe on T NG12 . . . . . **65** B3
Queens Rd E NG9 . . . . . . **73** A1
Queens Rd N NG16 . . . . . **16** A4
Queens Rd S NG16 . . . . . **16** A3
Queens Rd W NG9 . . . . . **82** A2
Queen's Sq NG16 . . . . . . **16** A4
Queen St Arnold NG5 . . . . **24** B3
Hucknall NG15 . . . . **2** B1
Ilkeston DE7 . . . . **40** C2
Langley Mill NG16 . . . . **8** A1
Long Eaton NG10 . . . . **90** A1
Nottingham NG1 . . . . . . **108** B3
Queen's Wlk NG2 . . . . . . **75** A3
Quernby Ave NG3 . . . . . . **48** C4
Querneby Rd NG3 . . . . . . **48** C4
Quinton Cl NG11 . . . . **84** C3
Quorn Gr NG9 . . . . **82** A1
Quorndon Cres NG10 . . . **100** C3
Quorn Gr NG5 . . . . **33** B1
Quorn Rd NG5 . . . . **47** B4

R

Racecourse Rd NG2 . . . . . **61** B2
Radbourne Rd **9** NG2 . . . **61** A1
Radburn Ct NG9 . . . . **70** A3
Radcliffe Gdns NG4 . . . . . **50** B2
Radcliffe Mount NG2 . . . . **76** B3
RADCLIFFE ON TRENT . . . **64** C2
Radcliffe on Trent Inf Sch
NG12 . . . . **65** B2
Radcliffe on Trent Jun Sch
NG12 . . . . **65** A1
Radcliffe Rd NG2 . . . . **77** C2
Radcliffe St NG2 . . . . **75** C3
Radcliffe Sta NG12 . . . . . **65** A2
RADFORD **106** A3
Radford Bridge Rd NG8 . . **58** A3
Radford Bvd NG7 . . . . . . **106** A4
Radford Cres NG4 . . . . . . **50** C4
Radford Ct NG7 . . . . **106** B3
Radford Gr La NG7 . . . . . **106** A4
Radford Prim Sch NG7 . . **106** A4
Radford Rd NG7 . . . . **47** A1
Radley Sq NG6 . . . . **32** B3
Radmarsh Rd NG7 . . . . . **107** A1
Rad Mdws NG10 . . . . . . **100** B4
Radnor Gr NG13 . . . . **66** B2
Radstock Rd NG3 . . . . . . **49** B1
Radway Dr NG11 . . . . **84** C3
Raeburn Dr NG9 . . . . **90** A4
Ragdale Rd NG6 . . . . **20** C2
Raglan Cl NG3 . . . . **48** B1
Raglan Ct NG9 . . . . **72** C3
Raglan Dr NG4 . . . . **51** C3
Raglan St NG16 . . . . **16** B3
Raibank Gdns NG5 . . . . . **34** C3
Railway Cotts NG16 . . . . . **29** A4
Rainham Gdns NG11 . . . . **102** C4
Raithby Cl NG5 . . . . **33** B4
Raleigh Cl Ilkeston DE7 . . . **27** A1
Nottingham NG11 . . . . . . **93** B3
Raleigh St NG7 . . . . **106** C3
Ralf Cl NG2 . . . . **86** A2
Ramblers Cl NG4 . . . . **62** C3
Ramsdale Ave NG14 . . . . . **4** C3
Ramsdale Cres NG5 . . . . **48** B4
Ramsdale Rd NG4 . . . . . . **50** C3
Ramsey Cl NG9 . . . . **70** A4
Ramsey Ct **5** NG5 . . . . . **47** C3
Ramsey Dr NG5 . . . . **36** A4
Ranby Wlk NG3 . . . . **61** A4
Rancliffe Ave NG12 . . . . **104** A3
Rancliffe Farm Mews
NG11 . . . . **103** B1
Randal Gdns **4** NG7 . . . . **47** A1
Randal St **3** NG7 . . . . . . **47** A1
Ranelagh Gr NG8 . . . . . . **57** C3
Ranmere Rd NG8 . . . . . . **45** B1
Ranmoor Rd NG4 . . . . . . **51** A3
Ranmore Cl NG9 . . . . **71** A4
Rannerdale Cl NG2 . . . . . **87** B4
Rannoch Rise NG5 . . . . . **24** A3
Rannock Gdns NG12 . . . **104** C3
Ranskill Gdns NG5 . . . . . **22** B2
Ransom Dr NG3 . . . . **48** C3
Ransom Rd NG3 . . . . **48** C2
Ranson Rd NG9 . . . . **91** B4
Ratcliffe St NG16 . . . . **16** A4
Rathgar Cl NG8 . . . . **56** B2
Rathmines Cl NG7 . . . . . **107** A1
Rathvale Ct NG9 . . . . **80** C2
Raven Ave NG5 . . . . **33** C2
Ravenhill Cl NG9 . . . . **81** A2
Ravens Ct NG5 . . . . **33** C4
Ravensdale Ave NG10 . . . **89** A4
Ravensdale Dr NG8 . . . . . **56** A1
Ravensdene Ct **2** NG3 . . **48** B2
Ravensmore Rd NG5 . . . . **47** C4
Ravenswood Rd NG5 . . . . **24** B2
Ravensworth Rd NG6 . . . **20** C2
Rawson St NG7 . . . . **47** A3
Raymede Cl NG5 . . . . **33** A4
Raymede Dr NG5 . . . . . . **32** C4
Raymond Dr NG13 . . . . . **67** C2
Raynham Rd DE7 . . . . . . **26** A2
Rayner Ct NG7 . . . . **106** B3
Raynford Ave NG9 . . . . . . **81** B2

Ray's Ave DE75 . . . . 13 C3
Ray St DE75 . . . . 13 C3
Read Ave NG9 . . . . .82 C4
Readman Rd NG9 . . . . .80 C1
Rearsby Cl NG8 . . . . .56 B3
Recreation Rd NG10 . . . . .79 A4
Recreation St NG10 . . . . .90 B2
Recreation Terr NG9 . . . . .79 C4
Rectory Ave NG8 . . . . .56 C2
Rectory Dr NG11 . . . . .75 A2
Rectory Dr The NG4 . . . . .51 A4
Rectory Gdns NG8 . . . . .57 A2
Rectory Rd
 Breaston DE72 . . . . .88 A2
 Carlton NG4 . . . . .62 C3
 Cotgrave NG12 . . . . .98 A3
 West Bridgford NG2 . . . . .76 B1
Redbourne Dr NG8 . . . . .58 A4
Redbridge Dr NG16 . . . . .30 B1
Redcar Cl NG4 . . . . .50 C4
Redcliffe Gdns NG3 . . . . .48 A2
Redcliffe Rd NG3 . . . . .48 A2
Redfield Rd NG7 . . . . .74 A2
Redfield Way NG7 . . . . .74 A2
Redgates Ct NG14 . . . . 4 C2
Redhill L Ctr NG5 . . . . .23 C3
Redhill Lodge Dr NG5 . . . . . . .23 B3
Redhill Rd NG5 . . . . .23 C3
Redhill Sch NG5 . . . . .23 C3
Redland Ave NG4 . . . . .51 A2
Redland Cl Beeston NG9 . . . .81 B2
 Ilkeston DE7 . . . . .41 A4
Redland Dr NG9 . . . . .81 B2
Redland Gr NG4 . . . . .50 C2
Red Lion Sq DE75 . . . . .13 C3
Redmays Dr NG14 . . . . .39 C4
Redmile Rd NG8 . . . . .46 A4
Redoubt St NG7 . . . . .106 A3
Redruth Cl NG8 . . . . .56 A4
Redwood NG2 . . . . .85 B4
Redwood Ave NG8 . . . . .56 B1
Redwood Cres NG9 . . . . .82 C3
Redwood Ct NG15 . . . . 2 B2
Reedham Wlk 2 NG5 . . . . . . .22 C2
Reedman Rd NG10 . . . . .100 A2
Rees Gdns NG5 . . . . .22 B4
Regatta Way NG2 . . . . .77 B2
Regency Ct NG9 . . . . .72 C1
Regents Pk Cl NG2 . . . . .85 B3
Regent St Beeston NG9 . . .72 C1
 Ilkeston DE7 . . . . .41 A1
 Kimberley NG16 . . . . .29 A4
 Langley Mill NG16 . . . . 7 C1
 Long Eaton NG10 . . . . .89 C2
 Nottingham, New Basford
 NG7. .47 B3
 Nottingham, Standard Hill
 NG1. . . . . .109 A2
 Stapleford NG10 . . . . .79 B3
Regina Cl NG12 . . . . .64 C1
Reid Gdns NG16 . . . . .18 C1
Reigate Cl NG9 . . . . .92 A4
Reigate Dr NG9 . . . . .92 A4
Reigate Rd NG7 . . . . .47 A4
Rempstone Dr NG6 . . . . .32 B3
Renals Way NG14 . . . . 5 B2
Renfrew Dr NG8 . . . . .56 C2
Repton Dr DE7 . . . . .41 C1
Repton Rd
 Long Eaton NG10 . . . . .99 B2
 Nottingham NG6. . . . . .32 B4
 West Bridgford NG2 . . . . .86 A3
Retford Rd NG5 . . . . .33 B1
Revelstoke Ave NG5 . . . . .21 B3
Revelstoke Way NG5 . . . . .21 C3
Revesby Gdns NG8 . . . . .46 A1
Revesby Rd NG5 . . . . .35 A3
Revill Cl DE7 . . . . .40 A4
Revill Cres NG9 . . . . .70 B2
Reydon Dr NG8 . . . . .46 B3
Reynolds Dr NG8 . . . . .57 A3
Rhyl Cres NG4 . . . . .50 C4
Ribblesdale DE7 . . . . .52 A3
Ribblesdale Ct NG9 . . . . .80 C2
Ribblesdale Rd
 Long Eaton NG10 . . . . .99 C3
 Nottingham NG5. . . . . .34 A3
Riber Cl NG10 . . . . .100 C3

Riber Cres NG5 . . . . .33 A3
Richard Bonington Prim
 Sch NG5 . . . . .24 A3
Richard Herrod Ctr NG4 . . .50 B2
Richardson Cl NG11 . . . . . .93 B3
Richborough Pl NG8 . . . . .71 C4
Richey Cl NG5 . . . . .24 C1
Richmond Ave
 Breaston DE72 . . . . .88 C2
 Calverton NG14 . . . . 5 C3
 Eastwood NG16 . . . . .16 C4
 Ilkeston DE7 . . . . .27 A2
 Nottingham NG3. . . . . .49 A1
 Sandiacre NG10 . . . . .78 C2
Richmond Dr
 Beeston NG9 . . . . .82 A3
 Nottingham NG3. . . . . .48 B4
 Radcliffe on T NG12 . . . . .65 A3
Richmond Gdns NG5 . . . . .23 C3
Richmond Rd NG2 . . . . .76 B3
Richmond Terr NG12 . . . . .65 A2
Ricklow Ct 1 NG5 . . . . .22 B2
Rick St NG1 . . . . .108 C3
Ridding Terr NG3 . . . . .108 B4
Ridge La NG12 . . . . .65 B4
Ridgeway Heanor DE75 . . . .14 A2
 Nottingham NG5. . . . . .22 B2
Ridgeway St NG3 . . . . .60 C4
Ridgeway Wlk 17 NG5 . . . . .22 B2
Ridgewood Dr NG9 . . . . .81 B2
Ridgmont Wlk NG11 . . . . .93 C2
Ridgway Cl NG2 . . . . .87 B3
Ridings The Bulcote NG14 . .39 C3
 Keyworth NG12 . . . . .105 A3
Ridsdale Rd NG5 . . . . .34 A3
Rifle St NG7 . . . . .106 A3
Rigley Ave 16 DE7 . . . . .41 A3
Rigley Dr NG5 . . . . .21 C1
Ring Leas NG12 . . . . .98 C2
Ringstead Cl NG2 . . . . .85 B3
Ringstead Wlk NG5 . . . . .22 C2
Ringwood Cres NG8 . . . . .58 A3
Ringwood Rd NG13 . . . . .66 B2
Ripon Rd NG3 . . . . .61 C3
Riseborough Wlk NG6 . . . . . . .21 A3
Risegate NG12 . . . . .98 B3
Riseholme Ave NG8 . . . . .56 A1
Rise Park Prim Sch NG5 . . .22 A3
Rise Pk Rd NG5 . . . . .21 C3
Rise The NG5 . . . . .34 B1
RISLEY 78 A1
Risley Ct DE7 . . . . .27 A1
Risley Dr NG2 . . . . .85 B3
Risley Lower Gram CE Prim
 Sch DE72 . . . . .78 A2
Riste's Pl NG2 . . . . .109 C2
Ritchie Cl NG2 . . . . .98 C2
Ritson Cl NG3 . . . . .108 C4
Riverdale Rd NG9 . . . . .91 B4
Rivergreen NG11 . . . . .84 A1
Rivergreen Cl NG9 . . . . .71 B4
Rivergreen Cres NG9 . . . . .71 B4
Riverleen Sch NG6 . . . . .21 A2
Rivermead NG12 . . . . .98 C3
River Rd NG4 . . . . .62 C2
Riverside Prim Sch NG2 .75 A3
Riverside Rd NG9 . . . . .82 C1
Riverside Ret Pk NG11 . . .74 C2
Riverside Way NG2 . . . . .75 A3
River View NG2 . . . . .75 C3
Riverway Gdns NG2 . . . . .75 C4
Rivington Rd NG9 . . . . .90 A4
Road No 1 NG4 . . . . .63 A4
Road No 2 NG4 . . . . .63 A3
Road No 3 NG4 . . . . .63 B3
Road No 4 NG4 . . . . .64 A4
Road No 5 NG4 . . . . .63 A3
Road No 7 NG4 . . . . .63 A4
Road No 8 NG4 . . . . .63 A3
Robbie Burns Rd NG5 . . . . . .23 A2
Robert Mellors Prim Sch
 NG5. .24 A2
Robert Miles Jun Sch
 NG13. . . . . .67 B2
Robert Shaw Prim Sch
 NG8. .58 B4
Robert's La NG15 . . . . 2 A1
Roberts St Ilkeston DE7 . . .53 B4
 Nottingham NG3. . . . . .60 C2
Roberts Yd NG9 . . . . .72 C1
Robey Cl NG15 . . . . 2 C3

Robey Dr NG16 . . . . 9 A1
Robina Dr NG16 . . . . .17 A2
Robinet Rd NG9 . . . . .82 B3
Robinettes La NG16 . . . . .42 B3
Robin Hood Cl NG16 . . . . .16 A3
Robin Hood Dr NG15 . . . . .10 C3
Robin Hood Ind Est 2
 NG3. .73 A3
Robin Hood Jun & Inf Sch
 NG5. .33 B4
Robin Hood Rd NG5 . . . . .22 C3
Robin Hood St NG3 . . . . .60 C3
Robin Hood Terr NG3 . . . . . .108 C3
Robin Hood Way NG2 . . . . . . .75 B4
Robinia Ct NG2 . . . . .86 C3
Robinson Gdns NG11 . . . . . . .93 B3
Robinson Rd NG3 . . . . .49 B4
Robin's Wood Rd NG8 . . . . . .45 C1
Rob Roy Ave NG7 . . . . .107 B1
Roche Cl NG5 . . . . .25 A1
Rochester Ave NG4 . . . . .51 B1
Rochester Ct NG10. . . . . .88 C1
Rochester Ct NG6 . . . . .31 A4
Rochford Ct NG12 . . . . .87 B1
Rock Ct NG6 . . . . .32 B1
Rock Dr NG7 . . . . .107 C1
Rocket Cl NG16. . . . . .18 B1
Rockford Ct NG9 . . . . .70 A3
Rockford Rd NG5 . . . . .33 A1
Rockingham Gr NG13 . . . . . . .66 B2
Rockley Ave
 Eastwood NG16 . . . . .16 B3
 Radcliffe on T NG12 . . . . .65 A3
Rockley Cl NG15 . . . . .10 A4
Rock St NG6 . . . . .20 C2
Rockwood Wlk NG15 . . . . .10 C4
Rodel Ct NG3 . . . . .108 C4
Roden St NG3 . . . . .60 C3
Roderick St NG6 . . . . .32 B2
Rodney Rd NG2 . . . . .86 C4
Rodney Way DE7 . . . . .27 A1
Rodwell Cl NG8 . . . . .58 A4
Roebuck Cl NG5 . . . . .22 C2
Roecliffe NG2 . . . . .86 A2
Roehampton Dr NG9 . . . . .69 C4
Roes La NG14 . . . . 5 C2
Roker Cl NG8 . . . . .45 B3
Roland Ave
 Nottingham NG11. . . . . .75 A1
 Nuthall NG16 . . . . .30 C2
Rolleston Cl NG15 . . . . .10 B3
Rolleston Cres NG16 . . . . .18 A3
Rolleston Dr Arnold NG5 . .24 B1
 Eastwood NG16 . . . . .16 C2
 Nottingham NG7. . . . . .107 B1
Roman Dr NG6 . . . . .32 C2
Romans Ct NG6 . . . . .46 C4
Romilay Cl NG9 . . . . .72 C3
Romney Ave NG8 . . . . .71 C4
Rona Ct NG6 . . . . .32 C3
Ronald St NG7 . . . . .106 B3
Rookery Gdns NG5 . . . . .24 A2
Rookwood Cl NG9 . . . . .82 A4
Rookwood Cres NG15 . . . . . . .10 B4
Roosa Cl NG6 . . . . .31 A3
Roosevelt Ave NG10 . . . . . . .100 B3
Roper Ave DE75 . . . . .14 A1
Ropewalk Ind Ctr DE7 . .41 B3
Ropewalk The
 Heanor DE75 . . . . .14 A2
 Ilkeston DE7 . . . . .41 B3
 Nottingham NG1. . . . . .109 A2
Ropsley Cres NG2 . . . . .76 C2
Roscoe Ave NG5 . . . . .23 C4
Roseacre NG2 . . . . .82 C3
Rose Ash La NG5 . . . . .22 C2
Rose Ave DE7 . . . . .40 C4
Rosebank Dr NG5 . . . . .24 C3
Rosebay Av NG7 . . . . .46 B2
Roseberry Ave NG2 . . . . .76 A3
Roseberry Gdns NG15 . . . . . .12 A4
Roseberry St NG6 . . . . .32 C1
Rose Cl NG3 . . . . .48 B1
Rose Cotts NG14 . . . . .38 C3
Rosecroft Dr NG5 . . . . .34 A4
Rose Ct NG10. . . . . .89 A3
Rosedale Cl NG10 . . . . .100 A4
Rosedale Dr NG8 . . . . .55 C2
Rosedale Rd NG3 . . . . .62 A4
Rosegarth Wlk NG6 . . . . .32 B2

Rose Gr Beeston NG9 . . . . .83 A3
 Keyworth NG12 . . . . .104 C4
Rosegrove Ave NG5 . . . . .24 A3
Rose Hill NG12 . . . . .104 B3
Rosehill Specl Sch NG3. .60 C4
Roseleigh Ave NG5 . . . . .49 C4
Rosemary Cl 1 NG8 . . . . . . .44 C3
Rosenauth Ave NG5. . . . . .21 C3
Rosetta Rd NG7 . . . . .47 A3
Rosewall Ct NG5 . . . . .21 C3
Rosewood Cres DE75 . . . . . . .14 C4
Rosewood Gdns
 Nottingham NG6. . . . . .20 A1
 West Bridgford NG2. . . . . .85 B1
Roslyn Ave NG4 . . . . .50 C4
Rossell Dr NG9 . . . . .80 A3
Rossendale DE7 . . . . .26 C2
Rossett Cl NG2 . . . . .87 C4
Rossington Rd NG2 . . . . .61 A3
 Nottingham NG6. . . . . .45 B4
Rosslyn Dr Hucknall NG15 . . 3 B2
 Nottingham NG8. . . . . .45 C3
Rosslyn Pk Prim Sch
 NG8. .45 C3
Rosthwaite Cl NG2. . . . . .87 B3
Rothbury Ave NG9 . . . . .69 C4
Rothbury Gr NG13 . . . . .66 B3
Rothesay Ave NG7. . . . . .107 B2
Rothley Ave NG3 . . . . .61 A3
Rothwell Cl NG11 . . . . .84 C2
Roughs Wood La NG15. . . . . .10 B2
Round Hill Prim Sch
 NG9. .72 B1
Roundwood Rd NG5 . . . . .23 A1
Rowan Ave NG9 . . . . .70 A4
Rowan Cl Calverton NG14. . . 4 C2
 Ilkeston DE7 . . . . .53 A3
Rowan Ct NG16. . . . . .29 C4
Rowan Dr
 Keyworth NG12 . . . . .105 A2
 Nottingham NG11. . . . . .84 C2
Rowan Gdns NG6 . . . . .20 A1
Rowan Wlk NG3 . . . . .49 B2
Rowe Gdns NG6 . . . . .32 B4
Rowland Ave NG3 . . . . .49 B4
Rowland Mews NG3 . . . . .48 C1
Rowsley Ave NG10 . . . . .99 C3
Roxton Ct NG16. . . . . .18 A1
Royal Ave NG10. . . . . .89 C3
Royal Ctr (Theatre Royal &
 Royal Concert Hall)*
 NG1. . . . . .108 B3
Royal Mews NG9 . . . . .81 B1
Roy Ave NG9 . . . . .83 A2
Royce Ave NG15 . . . . .10 C2
Royston Cl NG2 . . . . .85 B4
Ruby Paddocks NG16 . . . . . . .29 A3
RUDDINGTON 103 A4
Ruddington Framework
 Knitters Mus* NG11 . .102 C4
Ruddington La NG11. . . . . .85 A3
Ruddington Village Mus*
 NG11. . . . . .95 B1
Rudge Cl NG8 . . . . .57 A3
Ruffles Ave NG5 . . . . .35 C3
Rufford Ave Beeston NG9. .70 C2
 Carlton NG4 . . . . .50 B4
Rufford Cl NG15 . . . . .12 A3
Rufford Gr NG13 . . . . .66 B2
Rufford Jun & Inf Sch
 NG6. .20 B1
Rufford Rd
 Long Eaton NG10 . . . . .100 A2
 Nottingham NG5. . . . . .34 A1
 Ruddington NG11. . . . . .95 C1
Rufford Way NG2 . . . . .87 A4
Rufford Wlk 1 NG6. . . . . .20 C1
Ruffs Dr NG15 . . . . .10 C3
Rugby Cl NG5 . . . . .21 C1
Rugby Rd NG2 . . . . .85 B3
Rugby Terr 17 NG7 . . . . .47 A1
Rugeley Ave NG10 . . . . .90 C1
Ruislip Cl NG16 . . . . .17 C1
Runcie Cl NG12 . . . . .98 B2
Runnymede Ct NG7. . . . . . . .106 C3
Runswick Dr Arnold NG5 . .24 A2
 Nottingham NG8. . . . . .57 C3
Runton Dr NG6 . . . . .33 A2
Rupert Rd NG13 . . . . .66 C2
Rupert St DE7 . . . . .41 B3
Rushcliffe Arena* NG2. .85 C4

Rushcliffe Ave
 Carlton NG4 . . . . .50 B1
 Radcliffe on T NG12 . . . . .65 A2
Rushcliffe Cts NG6 . . . . .32 B1
Rushcliffe Ctry Pk*
 NG11. . . . . .102 C1
Rushcliffe L Ctr NG2. . . . . . . .86 B1
Rushcliffe Rd NG15 . . . . .10 C1
Rushcliffe Rise NG5 . . . . .34 B1
Rushcliffe Sch NG2. . . . . .86 B1
Rushford Dr NG8 . . . . .56 B1
Rush Leys NG10 . . . . .100 C3
Rushmere Wlk NG5 . . . . .35 A1
Rushton Gdns NG3 . . . . .49 A1
Rushworth Ave NG2 . . . . .76 A1
Rushworth Cl NG3 . . . . .48 C1
Rushy Cl NG8 . . . . .56 B1
Rushy La NG10, DE72 . . . . . . .78 A2
Ruskin Ave NG10 . . . . .100 A2
Ruskin Cl NG5 . . . . .23 B1
Russell Ave 5 NG8 . . . . .57 B1
Russell Cres 6 NG8 . . . . . . .57 B1
Russell Dr NG8 . . . . .57 C1
Russell Gdns 5 NG9. . . . . . .91 B4
Russell Pl NG1 . . . . .108 A2
Russell Rd NG7 . . . . .47 A3
Russell St
 Long Eaton NG10 . . . . .89 C2
 Nottingham NG7. . . . . .106 C2
Russet Ave NG4 . . . . .51 A2
Russley Rd NG9 . . . . .70 C2
Ruth Dr NG5. . . . . .24 B1
Ruthwell Gdns NG5 . . . . .22 B2
Rutland Ave NG9 . . . . .90 C2
Rutland Cl DE7 . . . . .40 B4
Rutland Gr NG10. . . . . .79 B1
Rutland House Sch NG3 .48 A4
Rutland Rd
 Bingham NG13 . . . . .67 B4
 Carlton NG4 . . . . .36 B1
 West Bridgford NG2. . . . . .76 C1
Rutland St Ilkeston DE7 . . .41 A4
 Nottingham NG1. . . . . .109 A1
Rutland Terr DE7 . . . . .41 A1
Rydal Ave NG10. . . . . .89 A4
Rydal Dr Beeston NG9. . . . . .71 C2
 Hucknall NG15 . . . . 2 A2
Rydale Rd NG5 . . . . .34 A1
Rydal Gdns NG2 . . . . .86 C2
Rydal Gr NG6. . . . . .32 C2
Ryder St NG6 . . . . .32 B1
Ryecroft St NG9 . . . . .70 B1
Ryehill Cl NG2 . . . . .75 C4
Ryehill St NG2 . . . . .75 C4
Ryeland Gdns NG2 . . . . .75 B4
Ryemere Cl NG16 . . . . .15 C4
Rye St NG7 . . . . .47 A3
Rylands Cl NG9 . . . . .83 A3
Rylands Jun Sch NG9. . . . . . .82 C2
Ryton Ct 7 NG2 . . . . .75 C1
Ryton Sq NG8 . . . . .45 C2

S

Sacred Heart RC Prim Sch
 NG4. .50 B1
Saddleworth Ct NG3 . . . . . . .108 B4
Saffron Gdns NG2 . . . . .75 A4
St Agnes Cl NG8 . . . . .44 B2
St Aidan's Ct NG6. . . . . .32 C2
St Albans Cl NG10 . . . . .101 A3
St Albans Ct NG5 . . . . .22 C4
St Albans Mews NG6 . . . . . . .32 B4
St Albans Rd Arnold NG5 . .23 C4
 Bestwood Village NG6. . . . . . .13 C1
 Nottingham NG6. . . . . .21 B3
St Albans St NG5 . . . . .34 A3
St Andrews Cl NG6 . . . . .21 A3
St Andrew's Cl NG15 . . . . 2 C2
St Andrews Ct NG6 . . . . .21 B3
St Andrew's Dr NG3 . . . . .47 C1
St Andrew's Rd NG3 . . . . .47 C1
St Ann's Gdns NG3. . . . . .48 C1
St Ann's Hill Rd NG3 . . . . . . .48 A1
St Ann's Hill Rd NG3 . . . . . . .48 A3
St Ann's St NG1 . . . . .108 B3
St Ann's Valley NG3 . . . . .48 C1
St Ann's Way NG3. . . . . .108 B4
St Anns Well Inf Sch
 NG3. .48 B1

St Anns Well Jun Sch NG3 .... 49 A2
St Ann's Well Rd NG3 .... 60 C4
St Anthony Ct NG7 .... 74 A4
St Augustines Ct 8 NG7 .... 47 B3
St Augustines RC Prim Sch NG3 .... 48 A2
St Austell Dr NG11 .... 85 A4
St Austins Ct NG4 .... 51 A2
St Austins Dr NG4 .... 51 A2
St Bartholomew's Rd NG3 .... 49 A1
St Catherines St NG12 .... 64 C1
St Cecilia Gdns NG3 .... 108 C4
St Chad's Rd NG3 .... 60 C3
St Christopher St 9 NG2 .... 61 A2
St Cuthbert's Rd 11 NG3 .... 60 C3
St Edmund Campion Prim Sch NG2 .... 86 C4
St Edwards RC Prim Sch NG3 .... 49 A1
St Ervan Rd NG11 .... 85 A4
St Francis Hospl NG5 .... 33 C3
St George's Ct NG15 .... 2 C2
St George's Dr NG2 .... 75 A4
St Georges Priory NG2 .... 75 B4
St Helen's Cres
  Burton Joyce NG14 .... 39 A2
  Trowell NG9 .... 54 A2
St Helen's Gr NG14 .... 38 C1
St Helen's Rd NG2 .... 86 B4
St Helen's St NG7 .... 106 C3
St James Ave DE7 .... 41 B1
St James Ct NG10 .... 79 A1
St James's Ct NG15 .... 2 C2
St James's St
  Nottingham NG1 .... 109 A2
  Stapleford NG9 .... 79 B4
St James's Terr NG9 .... 79 C4
St Jame's Terr NG1 .... 109 A2
St John Baptist CE Prim Sch NG4 .... 62 C4
Saint John Houghton RC Sch DE7 .... 52 A4
St Johns CE Prim Sch NG9 .... 70 A1
St John's Cres NG15 .... 12 A3
St Johns Ct NG4 .... 50 B1
St John's Rd Ilkeston DE7 .... 41 B1
  Ruddington NG11 .... 95 B1
St John's St NG10 .... 89 C1
St Josephs Sch NG1 .... 108 A3
St Jude's Ave NG3 .... 48 C4
St Laurence CE Prim Sch NG10 .... 101 A4
St Laurence Ct NG10 .... 101 A4
St Lawrence Bvd NG12 .... 64 C1
St Lawrence Cl DE75 .... 14 A4
St Leonard's Dr NG8 .... 57 A2
St Leven Cl NG8 .... 44 B2
St Luke's Cl NG2 .... 87 A3
St Luke's St 6 NG3 .... 60 C3
St Margaret Clitherow Cath Prim Sch NG5 .... 23 A2
St Margarets Ave NG8 .... 46 A2
St Marks St NG3 .... 108 C3
St Martin's Ct NG8 .... 44 C2
St Martin's Rd NG8 .... 44 C2
St Mary's Ave NG4 .... 50 C4
St Marys Cath Prim Sch NG7 .... 47 A2
St Mary's CE Prim Sch NG6 .... 21 A2
St Mary's Church★ NG1 .... 109 C2
St Marys Cl NG9 .... 91 C3
St Mary's Cl NG5 .... 24 A3
St Mary's Cres NG11 .... 95 B1
St Mary's Gate NG1 .... 109 C2
St Mary's Pl NG1 .... 109 C2
St Marys Rd NG13 .... 67 B3
St Mary St DE7 .... 40 C2
St Matthias Rd NG3 .... 60 C4
St Mawes Ave NG11 .... 85 A4
St Michaels Ave NG4 .... 44 B2
St Michael's Ave NG8 .... 50 C4
St Michael's Sq NG7 .... 71 A2
St Michael's View NG15 .... 3 A3
St Nicholas Cl NG5 .... 23 C1

St Nicholas St NG1 .... 109 B2
St Norbert Dr DE7 .... 52 B2
St Patricks Cath Prim Sch NG11 .... 75 A2
St Patrick's Rd
  Hucknall NG15 .... 2 B1
  Nuthall NG16 .... 30 A4
St Paul's Ave NG7 .... 47 A1
St Paul's St 1 NG8 .... 58 B3
St Paul's Terr NG7 .... 47 A1
St Peters CE Jun Sch NG11 .... 95 C2
St Peter's Church Wlk NG1 .... 109 B2
St Peter's Cres NG11 .... 95 B1
St Peter's Gate NG1 .... 109 B2
St Peter's Sq NG1 .... 109 B2
St Peter's St NG7 .... 106 A3
St Saviour's Gdns NG2 .... 75 C4
St Stephen's Ave 7 NG2 .... 61 A2
St Stephen's Rd NG2 .... 61 A2
St Teresas RC Prim Sch NG8 .... 45 B2
St Thomas RC Prim Sch DE7 .... 52 C4
St Vincent Cl NG10 .... 101 A4
St Wilfrids Prim Sch NG14 .... 5 A2
St Wilfrid's Sq NG14 .... 5 B2
Salamander Cl NG4 .... 50 B4
Salcey Dr NG5 .... 69 C4
Salcombe Cir NG5 .... 23 B3
Salcombe Cl NG16 .... 17 A3
Salcombe Cres NG11 .... 95 C2
Salcombe Dr NG5 .... 23 B3
Salcombe Rd NG5 .... 33 A1
Salford Gdns NG3 .... 108 C3
Salisbury Sq NG7 .... 107 A2
Salisbury St Beeston NG9 .... 73 A1
  Long Eaton NG10 .... 90 A1
  Nottingham NG7 .... 107 A2
Salmon Cl NG6 .... 20 A1
Salop St NG5 .... 23 B1
Saltburn Rd NG8 .... 57 B4
Salterford Ave NG14 .... 5 B3
Salterford Rd NG15 .... 10 C3
Saltford Cl NG4 .... 51 A4
Salthouse Cl NG9 .... 72 C1
Salthouse La NG9 .... 72 C2
Saltney Way NG11 .... 84 C1
Samson Ct NG11 .... 95 A2
Sandale Cl NG2 .... 87 B4
Sandays Cl NG9 .... 81 B3
Sanderson Dr NG3 .... 36 B4
Sandfield Ctr NG7 .... 107 B2
Sandfield Rd Arnold NG5 .... 35 A3
  Beeston NG9 .... 90 A4
  Nottingham NG7 .... 107 B2
Sandford Ave NG10 .... 90 A1
Sandford Rd NG3 .... 35 B1
Sandgate NG9 .... 71 C3
Sandhurst Dr
  Beeston NG9 .... 91 B4
  Ruddington NG11 .... 102 B4
Sandhurst Rd NG6 .... 21 A3
SANDIACRE 78 C4
Sandiacre Rd NG9 .... 79 B4
Sandon St NG7 .... 47 B3
Sandown Rd NG9 .... 90 B4
Sandpiper Cl NG13 .... 67 B1
Sandpiper Way NG7 .... 107 A2
Sandringham Ave NG2 .... 76 A2
Sandringham Cl NG8 .... 56 A3
Sandringham Dr
  Beeston NG9 .... 71 B3
  Heanor DE75 .... 13 A4
Sandringham Pl
  Hucknall NG15 .... 3 A2
  Ilkeston DE7 .... 52 B3
Sandringham Rd
  2 Nottingham NG2 .... 61 A2
  Sandiacre NG10 .... 79 A1
Sands Cl NG4 .... 62 C3
Sandside NG12 .... 98 B2
Sandwell Cl NG10 .... 99 C4
Sandyford Cl NG6 .... 32 A1
Sandy La Beeston NG9 .... 71 C3
  Hucknall NG15 .... 2 C1
Sanger Cl NG11 .... 93 B2
Sanger Gdns NG11 .... 93 B2

Sankey Dr NG6 .... 20 B1
Sapele Cl NG4 .... 51 B4
Sargent Gdns 1 NG3 .... 61 A4
Saskatoon Cl NG12 .... 64 C1
Saunby Cl NG5 .... 24 C1
Savage's Rd NG11 .... 95 B2
Savages Row NG11 .... 95 B2
Saville Cl NG9 .... 70 A2
Saville Rd NG5 .... 35 A3
SAWLEY 99 C2
Sawley Jun & Inf Sch NG10 .... 99 C3
Sawley Rd DE72 .... 99 A4
Sawmills Ind Pk DE75 .... 6 B1
Saxelby Gdns NG6 .... 20 C2
Saxondale Dr NG6 .... 32 C3
Saxon Gn NG7 .... 107 A1
Saxon Way NG12 .... 98 C1
Saxton Ave DE75 .... 14 A4
Saxton Cl NG9 .... 83 A4
Scafell Way NG11 .... 93 C1
Scalby Cl NG16 .... 15 B4
Scalford Dr NG8 .... 58 A2
Scarborough Ave DE7 .... 40 C2
Scarborough St NG3 .... 108 C3
Scarfell Cl NG2 .... 87 B3
Scarf Wlk NG2 .... 75 A1
Scargill Ave NG16 .... 16 C3
Scargill Cl NG16 .... 16 C3
Scargill Wlk NG16 .... 9 A1
Scarrington Rd NG2 .... 76 B3
Sceptre St NG5 .... 48 A4
School Ave NG15 .... 10 B2
School Cl NG2 .... 75 C3
School La Beeston NG9 .... 81 B2
  Bingham NG13 .... 67 A3
  Stanton-by-D DE7, NG10 .... 68 B2
School Wlk NG6 .... 12 C2
Science Rd NG7 .... 73 C3
Scotholme Ave 7 NG7 .... 47 A2
Scotholme Prim Sch NG7 .... 47 A2
Scotland Bank NG12 .... 98 B3
Scotland Rd NG5 .... 33 A1
Scott Ave NG9 .... 82 C3
Scott Cl NG6 .... 31 A3
Scrimshire La NG12 .... 98 A3
Script Dr NG6 .... 20 A1
Scrivelsby Gdns NG9 .... 81 C2
Seaburn Rd NG9 .... 90 A4
Seaford Ave NG8 .... 57 C3
Seaford Way DE7 .... 27 A3
Seagrave Prim Sch NG8 .... 44 B4
Seagrave Rd NG8 .... 44 B3
Seamer Rd NG16 .... 18 A1
Seatallen Cl NG2 .... 87 B4
Seathwaite Cl NG2 .... 87 C2
Seatoller Cl NG2 .... 87 B3
Seaton Cres NG8 .... 44 B3
Second Ave Beeston NG9 .... 83 B4
  Carlton, Gedling NG4 .... 51 A3
  Carlton, Thorneywood NG4 .... 50 A2
  Nottingham NG6 .... 20 C1
  Risley DE7 .... 78 B3
Sedgebrook Cl NG6 .... 32 A1
Sedgeley Rd NG12 .... 97 C3
Sedgewood Gr NG11 .... 84 A1
Sedgley Ave NG2 .... 61 A3
Sedgwick St NG16 .... 71 C1
Sedley Ave NG16 .... 30 A4
Seely Ave NG14 .... 5 A3
Seely Jun Sch NG5 .... 34 A1
Seely Rd NG7 .... 106 C3
Sefton Ave NG9 .... 70 A2
Sefton Dr NG3 .... 48 B4
Selassie Ct NG8 .... 44 B4
Selby Cl NG9 .... 80 A1
Selby La NG12 .... 104 C2
Selby Rd NG2 .... 86 B3
Selhurst Ct NG7 .... 47 A1
Selhurst St 8 NG7 .... 47 A1
Selkirk Way 13 NG5 .... 47 C3
Sellars Ave NG11 .... 102 C4
Seller's Wood Dr NG6 .... 20 B1
Seller's Wood Dr W NG6 .... 20 A2
Sellers Wood Nature Reserve★ NG6 .... 19 C1
Selside Ct NG9 .... 80 C2
Selston Dr NG8 .... 58 A1
Selwyn Cl NG6 .... 32 C3

Serif Cl NG5 .... 47 C3
Serlby Rd NG16 .... 9 B1
Serlby Rise NG3 .... 48 B3
Seven Oaks Cres NG9 .... 71 B3
Seven Oaks Rd DE7 .... 68 C3
Seventh Ave NG9 .... 83 B3
Severals NG9 .... 70 B1
Severn St NG6 .... 20 C1
Seymour Rd
  Eastwood NG16 .... 16 A3
  Hucknall NG15 .... 10 C3
  West Bridgford NG2 .... 77 A2
Seymour St NG3 .... 60 C3
SGCS Bsns Pk NG11 .... 82 C3
Shackleton Cl NG8 .... 44 B4
Shacklock Cl NG5 .... 22 B4
Shadwell Gr NG12 .... 64 C2
Shady La NG9 .... 91 C4
Shaftesbury Ave
  Burton Joyce NG14 .... 39 B3
  Long Eaton NG10 .... 100 A2
  Sandiacre NG10 .... 78 C3
Shaftesbury St 4 NG7 .... 47 B3
Shakespeare Cl NG4 .... 62 C3
Shakespeare Rd NG16 .... 28 A3
Shakespeare St
  Long Eaton NG10 .... 89 C3
  Nottingham NG1 .... 108 B3
Shakespeare Villas NG1 .... 108 B3
Shaldon Cl NG5 .... 22 A3
Shandwick Cl NG5 .... 24 C3
Shanklin Dr NG9 .... 69 C1
Shanwell Cl NG8 .... 44 B4
Sharnford Way NG9 .... 55 C1
Sharp Cl Ilkeston DE7 .... 52 A4
  Long Eaton NG10 .... 100 B4
Sharphill Rd NG12 .... 87 A2
Shaw Cres NG15 .... 10 C2
Shaw St E DE7 .... 53 B4
Shaw St W DE7 .... 53 B4
Shaw St NG11 .... 102 C4
Shearing Cl NG4 .... 51 B3
Shearing Hill NG4 .... 51 B3
Sheepfold La NG11 .... 102 C4
Sheet Stores Ind Est NG10 .... 100 C3
Shelby Cl NG7 .... 107 A2
Sheldon Cl NG10 .... 79 A1
Sheldon Rd DE75 .... 6 B3
Shelford Ct Beeston NG9 .... 81 C2
  Radcliffe on T NG12 .... 65 B3
Shelford Cres NG14 .... 39 B3
Shelford Dr NG13 .... 66 C2
Shelford Rd Carlton NG4 .... 36 B1
  Radcliffe on T NG12 .... 65 B4
Shelford Rise NG3 .... 61 B3
Shellbourne Cl NG5 .... 21 C2
Shelley Ave NG11 .... 84 A1
Shelley Cl Hucknall NG15 .... 10 B4
  Nuthall NG16 .... 29 C4
Shelley Rd NG5 .... 23 B1
Shelton Ave NG15 .... 12 B2
Shelton Gdns NG11 .... 95 A1
Shelton St NG3 .... 108 C4
Shenfield Gdns NG11 .... 21 B3
Shepard Cl NG6 .... 31 A4
Shepherds Cl NG8 .... 45 B1
Shepherd Specl Sch NG8 .... 45 A2
Shepherds Wood Dr NG8 .... 46 A1
Shepton Cl DE7 .... 26 B1
Shepton Cres NG8 .... 45 C3
Sheraton Dr NG8 .... 56 C1
Sherborne Rd
  Nottingham NG8 .... 45 B3
  West Bridgford NG2 .... 86 B3
Sherbrook Ave NG5 .... 34 B4
Sherbrook Cl NG14 .... 5 A3
Sherbrooke Rd NG5 .... 47 C3
Sherbrook Rd NG5 .... 34 B4
Sherbrook Terr NG5 .... 34 B4
Sheridan Ct NG9 .... 70 B3
Sheridan Wy
  Hucknall NG15 .... 11 B3
  Nottingham NG5 .... 33 B1
Sheriff's Lodge The★ NG1 .... 109 C1
Sheriffs Way NG2 .... 75 B4
Sheringham Cl NG5 .... 35 A4

Sherman Dr NG9 .... 91 B4
Sherriff's Lea NG9 .... 90 A4
Sherrington Cl NG11 .... 93 B2
Sherwin Cl NG3 .... 108 B4
Sherwin Gr NG7 .... 107 A1
Sherwin Rd
  Nottingham NG7 .... 107 A1
  Stapleford NG9 .... 70 B3
Sherwin Wlk NG3 .... 108 B4
SHERWOOD 33 C1
Sherwood Ave
  Calverton NG14 .... 4 C3
  5 Nottingham NG5 .... 34 B1
Sherwood Day Hospl NG5 .... 33 C2
Sherwood Gr
  Bingham NG13 .... 66 C2
  Calverton NG14 .... 5 B3
Sherwood Rise
  Eastwood NG16 .... 16 A3
  Nottingham NG7 .... 47 C2
Sherwood St NG15 .... 12 A4
Sherwood Vale NG5 .... 34 C1
Sherwood Wlk NG15 .... 2 C4
Shilling Way NG10 .... 88 C1
Shilo Way NG16 .... 27 C4
Shipley Country Park Visitor Ctr★ DE75 .... 13 C1
Shipley Cl NG8 .... 40 B3
Shipley Rd NG8 .... 45 A4
Shipley Rise NG4 .... 50 C1
Shipstone St
  Ilkeston DE7 .... 53 C4
  3 Nottingham NG7 .... 47 A2
Shipstones Yd NG6 .... 21 A2
Shirebrooke Cl NG6 .... 32 A1
Shirley Dr NG5 .... 24 C1
Shirley Rd NG3 .... 48 A2
Shirley St NG10 .... 99 C2
Shoreswood Cl 1 NG5 .... 22 C2
Shortcross Ave NG3 .... 35 A2
Short Hill NG1 .... 109 C2
Shortwood Ave NG15 .... 11 A3
Shortwood Cl NG1 .... 109 C1
Shorwell Rd NG3 .... 50 A1
Shotton Dr NG5 .... 24 B4
Shrewsbury Rd NG2 .... 61 B2
Shrimpton Cl NG11 .... 103 A4
Sibson Wlk NG5 .... 24 A4
Sidings The NG16 .... 29 B4
Sidlaw Rise NG5 .... 22 C4
Sidmouth Cl NG12 .... 104 B4
Sidney Rd NG9 .... 72 A1
Sidney St Kimberley NG16 .... 29 A4
  Long Eaton NG10 .... 100 C3
Silbury Cl NG11 .... 93 C1
Silver Birch Cl NG6 .... 31 C2
Silverdale NG9 .... 80 A3
Silverdale Rd NG7 .... 47 A4
Silver Hill Cl NG8 .... 44 B4
Silverhow Cl NG2 .... 57 B4
Silverwood Rd NG9 .... 82 A4
Simkin Ave NG3 .... 49 B3
Simone Gdns NG7 .... 94 A3
Simons Ct NG9 .... 71 C3
Sinclair Cl DE75 .... 13 B2
Sir John Sherbrooke Jun Sch NG14 .... 5 A3
Sisley Ave NG9 .... 80 A4
Sixth Ave NG9 .... 83 C4
Skeavington's La DE7 .... 26 C3
Skelwith Cl NG2 .... 87 B3
Sketchley Ct 2 NG6 .... 20 B1
Sketchley St NG3 .... 61 A4
Skiddaw Cl NG2 .... 87 C3
Skipton Cir NG3 .... 61 B3
Skipton Cl DE7 .... 26 B1
Skylark Cl NG13 .... 67 B1
Skylark Dr NG6 .... 32 A4
Skylarks Nature Reserve★ NG12 .... 63 B1
Slack La DE75 .... 13 C2
Slade Rd NG9 .... 81 A3
Slaidburn Ave NG11 .... 84 A1
Sloan Dr NG9 .... 55 C1
Sloane Ct NG11 .... 85 B1
Slowthorne Gdns 2 NG5 .... 23 B2

Smedley Ave DE7 . . . . 41 B1
Smedley Cl NG8 . . . . 45 C4
Smedley's Ave NG10 . . . . . 79 A3
Smeeton St DE75 . . . . 14 C3
Smith Dr NG16 . . . . 7 B1
Smithfield Ave NG9 . . . . . . 54 B2
Smithson Dr NG8 . . . . 56 C2
Smithurst Rd NG16 . . . . . . 16 C1
Smithy Cl NG11 . . . . 93 C4
Smithy Cres NG5 . . . . 24 A2
Smithy Row NG1 . . . . 109 B2
Smithy View NG14 . . . . 9 C2
Snape Nook Ct NG6 . . . . . 20 A1
Snape Wood Prim Sch
  NG6 . . . . 20 A1
Snape Wood Rd NG6 . . . . . 20 A1
Snead Ct NG5 . . . . 22 B3
SNEINTON 60 C2
Sneinton Bvd NG2 . . . . . . 61 B2
Sneinton CE Prim Sch
  NG2 . . . . 61 A3
Sneinton Dale NG2 . . . . . . 61 B3
Sneinton Hermitage
  NG2 . . . . 60 C1
Sneinton Hollows NG2 . . . 61 A2
Sneinton Rd NG2 . . . . 60 C2
Snowdon Cl ☑ NG5 . . . . . 22 C3
Soarbank Cl NG16 . . . . . . 17 C1
Sobers Gdns NG5 . . . . . . 35 C4
Softwood Cl NG6 . . . . 20 A1
Soloman Pk NG16 . . . . . . 41 C4
Soloman Rd NG16 . . . . . . 41 C4
Solway Cl NG9 . . . . 82 A3
Somerby Cl NG5 . . . . 55 C1
Somerleyton Dr DE7 . . . . . 53 B2
Somersby Rd NG5 . . . . . . 35 B3
Somerset Cl NG10 . . . . . . 90 C2
Somerton Ave NG11 . . . . . 84 C2
Songthrush Ave NG6 . . . . 32 B2
Sophie Rd NG7 . . . . 106 B4
Sorrel Dr NG13 . . . . 66 B2
Soudan Dr NG2 . . . . 75 A3
Southampton St NG3 . . . . 60 C4
South Ave NG12 . . . . 65 C2
Southchurch Dr NG7 . . . . . 94 B4
Southcliffe Rd NG4 . . . . . . 50 B1
Southdale Dr NG4 . . . . . . 50 B1
Southdale Rd NG4 . . . . . . 50 B1
South Devon Ave NG3 . . . 49 C4
South East Derbyshire
  Coll
    Heanor DE75 . . . . 14 A3
    Ilkeston DE7 . . . . 41 A1
Southey St NG7 . . . . 106 C4
Southfield Rd NG8 . . . . . . 58 B4
Southfields NG10 . . . . 90 A1
Southglade Food Pk
  NG5 . . . . 32 C4
Southglade Jun & Inf Sch
  NG5 . . . . 22 B1
Southglade L Ctr NG5 . . . 22 A1
Southglade Rd NG5 . . . . . 33 A4
Southlea Rd NG4 . . . . 50 B1
South Nottingham Coll
  NG11 . . . . 94 C3
South Par NG1 . . . . 109 B2
Southport Terr ☑ NG7 . . . 46 C1
South Rd Beeston NG9 . . . 83 A2
  Nottingham, Dunkirk NG7 . . 73 C4
  Nottingham, The Park
    NG7 . . . . 107 C1
  West Bridgford NG2 . . . . 86 A4
South Sherwood St
  NG1 . . . . 108 B3
Southside NG5 . . . . 25 A1
South Snape Cl NG6 . . . . 20 A1
South St
  Eastwood, Bailey Grove
    NG16 . . . . 15 C4
  Eastwood, Giltbrook
    NG16 . . . . 17 A2
  Hucknall NG15 . . . . 2 C1
  Ilkeston DE7 . . . . 41 A2
  Long Eaton NG10 . . . . . 90 A1
South View Rd NG4 . . . . . 50 B3
Southwark Prim Sch
  NG6 . . . . 32 C1
Southwark St NG6 . . . . . . 32 C1

Southwell Rd NG1 . . . . . 109 C2
Southwell Rise NG16 . . . . 16 C1
South Wilford Endowed
  Prim Sch NG11 . . . . 75 A1
Southwold Dr NG8 . . . . . . 58 A3
Southwold Prim Sch
  NG8 . . . . 58 B3
Sovereigh Gr NG10 . . . . . 89 A1
Sovereign Way DE75 . . . . 13 B3
Sowbrook Brook DE7 . . . . 52 B2
Sowbrook La DE7 . . . . . . 52 C1
Spalding Rd NG3 . . . . 61 A3
Spaniel Row NG1 . . . . . . 109 B2
Sparrow Cl DE7 . . . . 53 B2
Spean Ct ☑ NG8 . . . . 57 B3
Spean Dr NG8 . . . . 45 C1
Speedwell La NG16 . . . . . 28 C4
Spencer Ave Arnold NG3 . 36 A3
  Sandiacre NG10 . . . . . . 79 A4
Spencer Cl NG11 . . . . 95 A1
Spencer Cres NG9 . . . . . . 70 B2
Spencer Dr NG16 . . . . . . 30 A4
Spey Cl NG15 . . . . 10 B1
Spicer Cl NG9 . . . . 91 B4
Spindle Gdns NG6 . . . . . . 20 B1
Spindle View NG14 . . . . . . 5 B1
Spinney Cl Cotgrave NG12 . 98 B2
  West Bridgford NG2 . . . . 87 B2
Spinney Cres NG9 . . . . . . 80 B1
Spinney Dr NG10 . . . . 89 B4
Spinney Rd
  Bingham NG13 . . . . 66 C2
  Ilkeston DE7 . . . . 52 C4
  Keyworth NG12 . . . . . . 104 B3
  Long Eaton NG10 . . . . . 89 B4
Spinney Rise NG9 . . . . . . 80 A1
Spinney The Arnold NG5 . . 34 C2
  Bestwood Village NG6 . . 12 C3
  Bulcote NG14 . . . . 39 C3
  Ilkeston DE7 . . . . 52 C4
  Stanton-by-D NG10 . . . . 68 B2
Spinney Way NG11 . . . . . . 84 C2
Spinningdale NG5 . . . . . . 24 C2
Spondon St NG5 . . . . 48 A4
Spray Cl NG4 . . . . 62 C3
Spridgeon Cl NG10 . . . . . 89 A4
Spring Cl NG16 . . . . 18 B1
Spring Dale Gdns NG9 . . . 54 B1
Springfield Ave
  Eastwood NG16 . . . . 16 B4
  Long Eaton NG10 . . . . . 90 B2
  Sandiacre NG10 . . . . . . 79 A1
Springfield Ct NG9 . . . . . . 70 A3
Springfield Dr NG6 . . . . . . 31 A4
Springfield Gdn DE7 . . . . 41 A4
Springfield Prim Sch
  NG6 . . . . 21 A3
Springfield Rd
  Arnold NG5 . . . . 23 C3
  Hucknall NG15 . . . . 10 B4
Springfields Ret Pk NG6 . . 21 A2
Springfields NG5 . . . . 85 C4
Springfield St NG7 . . . . . . 47 A3
Spring Gdn Terr DE7 . . . . 41 A4
Spring Gn NG11 . . . . 94 A1
Springhead Ct NG6 . . . . . 31 B4
Spring Hill NG16 . . . . 29 A3
Springhill Cl NG6 . . . . 20 C3
Spring La Arnold NG3 . . . . 36 C4
  Heanor DE75 . . . . 13 C3
  Lambley NG4 . . . . 37 C4
Springland Farm Cotts
  NG16 . . . . 30 B4
Spring Mdw NG12 . . . . . . 98 C3
Spring Moor NG2 . . . . 62 B3
Spring Rd NG6 . . . . 21 A1
Spring St NG15 . . . . 2 C1
Spring Street Prim Sch
  NG15 . . . . 2 C1
Spring Terr NG16 . . . . 30 B3
Spring The NG10 . . . . . . 100 C3
Springwood Gdns NG5 . . . 35 A1
Spruce Gdns NG6 . . . . . . 20 B1
Spruce Gr NG15 . . . . 11 C2
Sprydon Wlk NG11 . . . . . . 94 B1
Square The Beeston NG9 . 82 B4
  Bestwood Village NG6 . . 12 C2
  Keyworth NG12 . . . . . . 104 B3
  Nottingham NG8 . . . . . . 56 C2

Squires Ave NG6 . . . . 20 A3
Squires Way NG2 . . . . . . 85 C4
Stacey Ave NG5 . . . . 22 A2
Stadium Ind Pk NG10 . . . . 90 B2
Stafford Ave NG6 . . . . 31 C4
Stafford Ct NG6 . . . . 31 A3
Stafford St NG10 . . . . 90 B2
Stagsden Cres NG8 . . . . . 56 A3
Staindale Dr NG8 . . . . 46 B3
Stainmore Gr NG13 . . . . . 66 B2
Stainsborough Rd NG15 . . 10 A4
Stainsby Ave DE75 . . . . . 13 C2
Stamford Cl NG10 . . . . . . 101 A2
Stamford Ct ☑ NG5 . . . . . 22 C2
Stamford Rd NG2 . . . . . . 86 C4
Stamford St
  Awsworth NG16 . . . . 28 A2
  Eastwood NG16 . . . . 17 A3
  Heanor DE75 . . . . 13 C4
  ☑ Ilkeston DE7 . . . . 40 C3
Stancliffe Ave NG6 . . . . . . 21 A1
Standard Hill NG1 . . . . . . 109 A2
Standhill Ave NG4 . . . . . . 49 C2
Standhill Inf Sch NG4 . . . . 49 C1
Standhill Rd NG4 . . . . 49 C2
Stanesby Rise NG7 . . . . . 94 A3
Stanford Gdns NG12 . . . . . 65 A3
Stanford St NG1 . . . . 109 B2
Stanhome Dr NG2 . . . . . . 85 C2
Stanhome Sq NG2 . . . . . . 85 C2
Stanhope Ave NG5 . . . . . . 47 C3
Stanhope Cres NG5 . . . . . 23 C2
Stanhope Prim Sch NG4 . . 36 A1
Stanhope Rd Arnold NG5 . 23 C2
  Carlton NG4 . . . . 36 A1
Stanhope St Ilkeston DE7 . 53 B4
  Long Eaton NG10 . . . . . 89 C2
  Nottingham NG1 . . . . . . 109 C2
  Stanton-by-D NG10 . . . . 68 A2
Stanhope Way NG13 . . . . . 67 A2
Staniland Cl ☑ NG9 . . . . . 91 B4
Stanley Ave ☑ NG7 . . . . . 47 B2
Stanley Cl DE7 . . . . 40 C1
Stanley Dr NG9 . . . . 70 C3
Stanley Pl NG1 . . . . 108 A3
Stanley Rd
  Nottingham, Hyson Green
    NG7 . . . . 47 B2
  Nottingham, Portchester
    NG3 . . . . 49 B3
  West Bridgford NG2 . . . . 86 B4
Stanley St Ilkeston DE7 . . 41 A1
  Long Eaton NG10 . . . . . 90 A1
Stanmore Cl NG8 . . . . 30 C1
Stanmore Gdns NG5 . . . . 35 A4
Stannier Wy NG16 . . . . . . 18 B1
Stansfield St NG7 . . . . . . 106 A3
Stanstead Ave
  Nottingham NG5 . . . . 21 B3
  Tollerton NG12 . . . . 97 C3
Stanstead Prim Sch
  NG5 . . . . 21 C2
Stanthorne Cl NG11 . . . . . 84 C2
STANTON-BY-DALE 68 A2
  68 C3
Stanton Gate DE7 . . . . . . 69 B3
Stanton La NG12 . . . . . . 105 B2
STANTON-ON-THE-
  WOLDS 105 C1
Stanton Rd Ilkeston DE7 . . 41 A1
  Sandiacre NG10 . . . . . . 68 C1
Stanton Vale Sch NG10 . . 89 B1
Stanway Cl NG3 . . . . 62 A4
Stanwick Cl NG8 . . . . 44 C2
STAPLEFORD 70 A1
Stapleford La NG9 . . . . . . 80 B1
Stapleford Rd NG9 . . . . . . 54 B1
Staplehurst Dr NG5 . . . . . 33 B2
Staples St NG3 . . . . 48 C4
Stapleton Rd DE7 . . . . . . 26 C2
Starch La NG10 . . . . 69 B1
Starthe Bank DE75 . . . . . 14 A3
Starth Wood Rd NG15 . . . 10 B2
Stathern Wlk NG5 . . . . . . 22 C1
Staton Ave NG4 . . . . 51 B3
Station Cl ☑ DE7 . . . . 40 C3
Station Rd
  Awsworth NG16 . . . . 28 A3
  Beeston NG9 . . . . 82 C3
  Burton Joyce NG14 . . . . 39 A1
  Carlton NG4 . . . . 51 A1

Station Rd continued
  Heanor NG16 . . . . 14 B4
  Hucknall NG15 . . . . 3 A1
  Ilkeston DE7 . . . . 41 A3
  Kimberley NG16 . . . . . . 29 A4
  Langley Mill NG16 . . . . . 14 C4
  Long Eaton NG10 . . . . . 90 B2
  Nottingham NG6 . . . . . . 32 A4
  Sandiacre NG10 . . . . . . 79 B3
Station Dr Bingham NG13 . 66 B3
  Cossall DE7 . . . . 41 B4
  Long Eaton NG10 . . . . . 90 A1
  Nottingham NG2 . . . . . . 109 C1
Station Terr Hucknall NG15 . 3 A1
  Radcliffe on T NG12 . . . . 65 A2
Staunton Dr NG5 . . . . 34 A2
Stavely Wy NG2 . . . . 77 B1
Staverton Rd NG8 . . . . . . 44 C1
Steadfold Cl NG6 . . . . 31 C4
Steads Cl NG4 . . . . 51 A1
Steedman Ave NG3 . . . . . 35 B2
Steinbeck Rd NG4 . . . . . . 50 A1
Stella Ave NG12 . . . . 97 C2
Stella Gr NG12 . . . . 97 C2
Stepney Ct NG8 . . . . 45 A3
Sterndale Rd NG10 . . . . . 100 A4
Steven Cl NG9 . . . . 80 B2
Stevenholme Cres NG5 . . 33 B4
Stevenson Gdns NG11 . . . 103 A4
Stevenson Jun Sch NG9 . 70 B2
Stevens Rd NG10 . . . . . . 78 C3
Stewarton Cl NG5 . . . . . . 24 C3
Stiles Rd NG5 . . . . 36 A4
Stinsford Cl ☑ NG5 . . . . . 23 A2
Stirling Gdns NG9 . . . . . . 91 A4
Stirling Gr
  Kimberley NG16 . . . . . . 17 C1
  Nottingham NG11 . . . . . 94 B2
Stockdale Cl NG5 . . . . 22 B4
Stockgill Cl NG2 . . . . 87 B4
Stockhill Cir NG8 . . . . 46 A4
Stockhill La NG6 . . . . 32 A1
Stocks Rd NG16 . . . . 17 C1
Stockton St ☑ NG6 . . . . . 20 C1
Stock Well NG6 . . . . 31 C4
Stoddard Dr DE75 . . . . . . 14 A4
Stolle Cl NG5 . . . . 25 A1
Stoneacre NG5 . . . . 22 C2
Stonebridge City Farm ★
  NG3 . . . . 60 C3
Stonebridge Ct Ind Est ☑
  NG3 . . . . 60 C3
Stone Bridge Rd NG3 . . . . 60 C3
Stonehaven Cl NG5 . . . . . 24 C3
Stoneleigh Cl NG9 . . . . . . 81 B3
Stoneleigh St NG7 . . . . . 106 C3
Stone Mdws NG10 . . . . . . 101 A3
Stonepit Cl NG3 . . . . 49 A3
Stoneycroft Rd NG6 . . . . . 32 C3
Stoney Houghton Gdns
  NG6 . . . . 20 A2
Stoney La Brinsley NG16 . . 8 B4
  Trowell NG9 . . . . 53 C3
Stoney St Beeston NG9 . . 72 B1
  Nottingham NG1 . . . . . . 109 C2
Stoppard Cl DE7 . . . . 40 B4
Storey Ave NG4 . . . . 50 C4
Stornoway Cl NG9 . . . . . . 83 A3
Storth Ave NG15 . . . . 11 B4
Story Gdns NG15 . . . . 12 A3
Stotfield Rd NG8 . . . . 55 C3
Stourdale Cl NG10 . . . . . . 99 C4
Stowe Ave NG2 . . . . 85 C3
Strand The NG9 . . . . 91 C3
Stratford Cl NG4 . . . . 63 A3
Stratford Rd NG2 . . . . 76 B1
Stratford St DE7 . . . . 27 A2
Strathglen Cl NG16 . . . . . 17 C1
Strathmore Cl NG15 . . . . . 10 C3
Strathmore Rd NG5 . . . . . 24 C3
STRELLEY 43 C2
Strelley La NG8 . . . . 43 C1
Strelley Rd NG8 . . . . 44 C3
Strelley St NG6 . . . . 20 C1
Striding Edge Cl NG10 . . . 89 A4
Stripes View NG14 . . . . . . 5 B1
Strome Cl ☑ NG2 . . . . . . 75 A4
Strome Ct ☑ NG2 . . . . . . 75 B4
Stuart Cl NG5 . . . . 24 C2
Studland Way NG2 . . . . . . 85 B3
Sturgeon Ave NG11 . . . . . 84 B2

Sturton St NG7 . . . . 47 B2
Styring St NG9 . . . . 82 B4
Sudbury Ave Ilkeston DE7 . 41 B1
  Sandiacre NG10 . . . . . . 79 A4
Sudbury Ct NG10 . . . . . . 99 B2
Sudbury Mews NG16 . . . . 15 C3
Suez St NG7 . . . . 47 A3
Suffolk Ave Beeston NG9 . 83 B2
  Hucknall NG15 . . . . 10 A3
Sullivan Cl NG3 . . . . 61 B4
Sumburgh Rd NG11 . . . . . 94 C3
Summerfields Way DE7 . . 26 B1
Summerfields Way S
  DE7 . . . . 26 B1
Summer Leys La NG2 . . . 109 C1
Summer Way NG12 . . . . . 64 C3
Summerwood La NG11 . . . 94 A1
Sunbourne Ct NG7 . . . . . 106 C4
Sunbury Gdns NG5 . . . . . 24 B3
Sunderland Gr NG8 . . . . . 44 B4
Sundridge Pk NG2 . . . . . . 85 B3
Sunlea Cres NG9 . . . . 80 B3
Sunningdale Ave DE75 . . . 14 A2
Sunningdale Rd NG6 . . . . 32 C4
Sunninghill Dr NG11 . . . . . 84 A1
Sunninghill Rise NG5 . . . . 24 B3
Sunnydale Rd NG3 . . . . . . 61 C4
Sunnyside Prim Sch
  NG9 . . . . 81 A4
Sunnyside Rd NG9 . . . . . . 81 B4
Sunridge Ct NG3 . . . . 48 A2
Sunrise Ave NG5 . . . . 33 A3
Sunrise With Nature
  Reserve ★ NG5 . . . . . . 33 B4
Surbiton Sq NG8 . . . . 31 C1
Surfleet Cl NG8 . . . . 56 A1
Surgey's La NG5 . . . . 24 B4
Susan Cl NG15 . . . . 3 A3
Susan Dr NG6 . . . . 32 B2
Sussex Way NG10 . . . . . . 79 A3
Sutherland Dr NG2 . . . . . . 86 C2
Sutherland House Prim
  Sch NG3 . . . . 49 C1
Sutherland House Sec Sch
  NG3 . . . . 48 A3
Sutherland Rd NG3 . . . . . 49 C1
Sutton Ct NG16 . . . . 16 A4
Sutton Gdns NG11 . . . . . 102 C4
Sutton Passeys Cres
  NG8 . . . . 57 C1
Sutton Rd NG5 . . . . 24 A4
Swain's Ave NG3 . . . . 61 B4
Swaledale Cl NG8 . . . . . . 46 A3
Swallow Cl NG6 . . . . 32 B1
Swallow Dr NG13 . . . . 67 B1
Swallow Gdns NG4 . . . . . 49 C3
Swan Mdw NG4 . . . . 63 A2
Swansdowne Dr NG7 . . . . 94 B4
Sweeney Cl ☑ NG5 . . . . . 22 B2
Sweet Leys Rd ☑ NG2 . . . 75 B3
Swenson Ave NG7 . . . . . 107 A1
Swift Ct NG16 . . . . 16 A4
Swigert Cl NG6 . . . . 31 A3
Swildon Wlk NG5 . . . . 22 A2
Swinburne St ☑ NG3 . . . . 61 A4
Swinburne Way NG5 . . . . 23 B1
Swindon Cl NG16 . . . . . . 16 C1
Swiney Way NG9 . . . . 90 C4
Swingate NG16 . . . . 29 B3
Swinscoe Gdns NG5 . . . . 22 A2
Swinstead Cl NG8 . . . . . . 57 A4
Swithland Dr NG2 . . . . . . 86 A2
Sycamore Cl
  Bingham NG13 . . . . 67 C2
  Hucknall NG15 . . . . 10 C3
  Radcliffe on T NG12 . . . . 65 A1
Sycamore Cres NG10 . . . . 68 C1
Sycamore Ct NG9 . . . . . . 72 C1
Sycamore Dr DE7 . . . . . . 41 C1
Sycamore Jun & Inf Sch
  NG3 . . . . 108 C4
Sycamore Millennium Ctr
  NG3 . . . . 48 B2
Sycamore Pl ☑ NG3 . . . . 48 A2
Sycamore Rd
  Awsworth NG16 . . . . 28 A3
  Long Eaton NG10 . . . . . 100 B3
Sycamore Rise NG6 . . . . . 32 A2
Sycamores The NG16 . . . . 15 C3
Sydenham Ct ☑ NG7 . . . . 74 A4
Syderstone Wlk NG5 . . . . 35 A4